Rock Guitar Heroes

ARTISTS, GUITARS & GREAT RIFFS

Playlists | Links
ebooks & more

FlameTreeRock.com

Playlists | Links
ebooks & more

FlameTreeRock.com

Publisher and Creative Director: Nick Wells
Senior Project Editor: Catherine Taylor
Copy Editor: Julia Rolf
Art Director: Mike Spender
Layout Design: Jane Ashley and Mike Spender
Digital Design and Production: Jake Jackson
Digital Manager: Chris Herbert
Proofreader: Dawn Laker
Indexer: Helen Snaith

Special thanks to: Sara Robson, Laura Bulbeck, Esme Chapman, Kamara Williams and Taylor Bentley

This edition first published 2019 by
FLAME TREE PUBLISHING
6 Melbray Mews
Fulham, London SW6 3NS
United Kingdom

www.flametreepublishing.com

First published 2019

19 20 22 23 21

1 3 5 7 9 10 8 6 4 2

The CIP record for this book is available from the British Library.

ISBN 978-1-78755-710-9

Printed in China

Rock Guitar Heroes
ARTISTS, GUITARS & GREAT RIFFS

Foreword by Brian May ● Consultant Editor: Rusty Cutchin

Contributing authors: Rusty Cutchin, Hugh Fielder, Mike Gent, Michael Mueller and Dave Simons

FLAME TREE
PUBLISHING

Contents

Virtuosos 14

The guitar hero is the iconic image of rock'n'roll. Beyond image, the rock-guitar virtuoso is about the playing – the talent, the technique and, above all, the dedication. The dedication involves practising for hours every day, cultivating the talent and the technique, obsessing over sounds and how to create and control them, and then putting it all into the context of a performance as part of a rock band onstage. But while the guitar hero inspires the audience, the guitar virtuoso also inspires and influences other guitarists, who can see beyond the image to the dedication and details in the music and the performance.

From Blues to Rock 46

In 1950s America, rock'n'roll was the subversive product of black music combined with white, the blues mixed with country. The guitarists who pioneered rock'n'roll influenced the next generation, and as the 1960s progressed, styles began to change as pop toughened into rock. For some guitarists in this category, the blues was a jumping-off point from which to develop different approaches like psychedelia, progressive rock and hard rock. Others preferred to stay closer to the original spirit of the blues. Meanwhile, the role of lead guitarist was elevated to even greater heights; the era of the guitar hero had truly arrived.

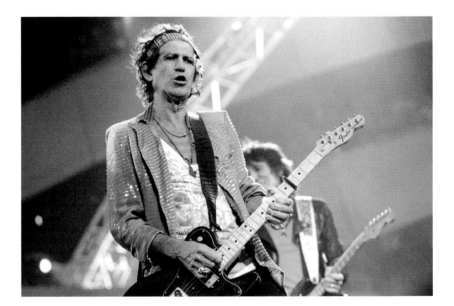

Hard Rock & Metal 90

Jazz has its saxophonists. Blues has its harmonica players. Pop has its synthesizers and dancers. But take the guitar hero out of hard rock and heavy metal, and you've gutted the genre. Nowhere has the guitar had a greater impact than on the sound and style of heavy music, and no other genre of music has produced as many guitar heroes. From Tony Iommi's dark, spine-chilling tritones heralding the birth of heavy metal in 1970 to John 5's twisted, high-tech fretboard fury inspiring this century's guitar hero-in-waiting, the power of the guitar has rarely seen such champions as the 32 iconic players chronicled here.

Soft Rock & Pop

Some guitar heroes blaze trails with fiery histrionics and outrageous behaviour, while others simply revolutionize music with good taste and a unique sound. There can be no doubt that the 12-string shimmer of Roger McGuinn, the inspiring textures of The Edge and the history-making lead lines of George Harrison made these legendary icons burn as brightly as their hard-rock counterparts. They passed the torch to a new generation that would pour fuel on to the rock'n'roll fire, even as direct descendants like Trey Anastasio and Lenny Kravitz continued to create new and tasty licks in both high- and low-intensity musical settings.

Alternative & Indie

Although its roots lie in late-1970s punk, indie and alternative rock have broadened to embrace such a diversity of guitar styles as to render categories irrelevant, particularly when many indie and alternative acts have crossed over into the mainstream and sold millions of records. The unifying factor between the guitarists in this category is perhaps a certain mindset, an attitude likely to regard the term 'guitar hero' with suspicion. For the majority of the musicians here, the guitar is a tool that serves the song; the effect achieved by the music, not the technical skill of the player, is of paramount importance.

Pioneers & Influences

Becoming a virtuoso requires heroic effort, but not all guitar heroes choose the life of the rock star. As befits rock's heritage in the marriage of country and rhythm and blues, many of music's greatest guitarists choose other genres for their life's work. Many rock players have been inspired by the great guitarists of bluegrass, classical, folk, flamenco, jazz, fusion and other disciplines; meanwhile, the blues has always been a driving force – as rock'n'roll matured into rock music, and from there into genres such as heavy metal and punk.

Many Heroes

You only need to discover the hundreds of guitarist websites out there to realize that music fans have strong opinions on who the world's best axe players are. We knew that creating our own guide to the world's greatest rock guitarists would be no easy task, and we were right. Deciding on our final list – including some key blues pioneers and influences from other genres – was a very long and drawn-out process, but we have come up with a book that we hope will satisfy even the most die-hard of music fans.

There are many guitarists who narrowly missed out on a spot in this edition. Apologies must be given to Peter Buck, Bernard Butler, Nels Cline, Tim Farriss, Guthrie Govan, Jeff Loomis, Joey Santiago and Bernard Sumner, each of whom came very close to being included. We also want to give a special mention to Vivian Campbell, Steve Clark, Phil Collen, Jeff Healey, Tony Hicks, Steve Jones, John Mayer, Mick Ralphs, Brian Setzer, Laurie Wisefield and Link Wray, who would also have made it if we had had the space. A final apology must go out to the slightly under-represented girls – Joan Jett and Nancy Wilson didn't make the cut. The list goes on and on.

Our 146 heroes have been grouped into six chapters based on the genre of music they are most closely associated with. Each chapter is then organized alphabetically, some sections starting with two-page entries on the key artists of the genre. Whilst we resisted the temptation to rank our heroes according to their talents, we have hinted at our personal favourites by kicking things off with a special Virtuosos chapter, covering a range of genres.

One thing we can all agree on is that a book like this will never be complete. No doubt we will continue to revise and update it, but to help acknowledge those we have left out, you can find on **FlameTreeRock.com** a full list of all those great guitarists who didn't make the cut.

FlameTreeRock.com offers a very wide range of other resources for your interest and entertainment:

1. **Extensive lists** and **links to artists**, organized by decade: Sixties, Seventies and more.

2. **Free ebooks** with the story of other musical genres, such as soul, R&B, disco, rap and hip hop.

3. **Special features** on the many **styles of rock**: what is the difference between heavy metal and nu metal, grindcore and grunge?

4. **Mixtape selections** from every era, to give you the sounds of each generation of rock music.

5. **YouTube** video selections of the top artists and their great performances.

*I have always felt that the
supreme joy of the guitar is that
it is a voice, a vehicle for
expressing emotion, for every
kid, of any age, who picks it up.*

Brian May

Foreword

There have been many books about guitarists, but none quite like this one. When I was asked to provide a foreword for this project, I was, in the beginning, happy to be included in such auspicious company at all, but then, humbled by the task of introducing such an ambitious work. Following their huge success with *The Definitive Illustrated Encyclopedia of Rock*, Flame Tree decided to take up the challenge of producing a truly extensive work on, not just guitarists, but 'Rock Guitar Heroes'.

I have always felt that the supreme joy of the guitar is that it is a voice, a vehicle for expressing emotion, for every kid, of any age, who picks it up. We are all still kids with a guitar in our hands, and there is little point in debating 'who's best' … we are all outputting our passions in a way which is somehow defined by the passion inside us. So what is it that makes a guitarist into a hero? It has to be simply the passion he elicits in others. Flick through the huge catalogue of guitarists here, covering a wide spectrum of styles within rock … and you will be reminded, on every page, of great moments in guitar music, when the players not only thrilled their audience, but inspired those who followed to reach inside themselves and make new great moments.

Here, you will find the inspiration for almost every known kind of guitar-speak, from pivotal pioneers like Chet Atkins and Les Paul to rock giants like Beck, Van Halen, Page, Townshend and Hendrix. But here also you will find tantalizing tastes of all kinds of greatness, from Santana to Satriani, from Marvin to Malmsteen, from Reinhardt and Burton to Rundgren and Syd Barrett, and beyond. Almost by definition, no catalogue of 'Rock Guitar Heroes' could ever be complete … beauty is in the eye of the beholder, and heroism must surely be in the ears and eyes of those who 'were there'. So there will inevitably be cries of 'shame' from those who witnessed, for instance, a superb player in Nashville breaking five strings in one song and still managing to finish the piece sounding like an orchestra – I'm sorry – you have to be there! Yes, truly there are many great and inspiring players the compilers (not my gig, I'm happy to say!) could not squeeze in. But if you want to have at your bedside, or on your coffee table (or bar) a genuine attempt to collate an across-the-board collection of some of the greatest Rock Guitar Heroes who ever spanked a plank, look no further – this is the encyclopedia for you.

Rock!

Brian May

Introduction

According to legend, a Londoner with a can of paint approached a corrugated metal fence panel near an Islington underground train station sometime in 1967 and proceeded to christen it with a phrase that had circulated in the music scene since a guitarist in John Mayall's Bluesbreakers began to attract rabid attention two years earlier. The painter probably stepped back to admire his work, as in the following years did multiple photographers and any number of dogs, who had an entirely different appreciation of the fence. A couple of the resulting photographs, featuring the painted phrase and the dogs, began to circulate, and the music world began to understand the power imparted to the modern rock guitarist by the phrase 'Clapton is God'...

Eric Clapton

Though Eric Clapton (*see* page 18) may be regarded by many as deserving the title (Clapton himself professed more than once to identify more with the dogs than the deification), even his most loyal worshippers would have to admit that the man known as Slowhand is at best first among equals in a world that in 50 years has seen the guitar, once firmly settled in a niche both Spanish and romantic, explode into an instrument of metaphorical destruction, sweeping emotion and entrancing power wielded by an expanding army of what we now call guitar heroes.

A Wide World of Rock

But just like a real army, the forces armed with axes are made up of players with varied and distinct talents, from different musical worlds and with different musical influences. What unites the ones chosen for this book is their undeniable impact in creating, developing and expanding the role of rock – and rock guitarist – in the worldwide cultural consciousness. Each one has had a heroic effect on either his or her own fans, or on other players who reached new heights as a result of that influence. Heroism, after all, can be appreciated by thousands of fans in a stadium or by a lone student manipulating an audio file, just as his peers – and his heroes – examined a piece of sheet music, a phonograph record or a compact disc.

Or a film. For me, the concept of the modern guitar hero crystallized when Alvin Lee (*see* page 77) took the stage at Woodstock with Ten Years After and ripped through 'Goin' Home' in Michael Wadleigh's classic documentary. Lee's jaw-dropping solos, riffs and runs, wrapped in a

Alvin Lee

container of old-time rock'n'roll, provided a rush that not even the theatrics and emotion of undisputed guitar heroes Pete Townshend (*see* page 54) and Jimi Hendrix (*see* page 26) in the same film could eclipse.

The Creation of the Hero

Those three legends, representing rock, blues and intense performance creativity at the same festival, can be seen clearly not only as forerunners of heroes to come in new genres, from heavy metal to glam to grunge, but also as acolytes to their own heroes in jazz, R&B and early rock. Woodstock and other seminal moments, like the Beatles' performances on 'The Ed Sullivan Show' in February 1964, Cream's live version of 'Crossroads' at the Winterland Ballroom in San Francisco in March 1968 and the Allman Brothers Band's shows at Fillmore East in March 1971, along with countless others in the UK and US, literally set the stage for the combination of virtuosity and performance charisma that would be

essential elements of the guitar-hero persona, from laid-back heroes like the Grateful Dead's Jerry Garcia (*see* page 69) to more flamboyant ones like Prince (*see* page 180).

But whether a guitar hero is a jumping, windmilling juggernaut like Townshend in his heyday, a thoughtful jam-band virtuoso like Trey Anastasio (*see* page 128), a historical figure like Django Reinhardt (*see* page 181) or a trailblazer smashing through barriers like Joni Mitchell (*see* page 137) or Lita Ford (*see* page 97), each of the ones in this book brought something new to the idea of rock guitar, even if that player didn't work exclusively, or at all, in the world of rock as we know it today. And they reached the heroic plain by commanding not only the allegiance of countless fans but also the respect of musical colleagues. They've brought originality, transformative technique and unforeseen insight to an instrument, the predecessor of which dates to ancient Egypt.

Trey Anastasio (left)

Chuck Berry

Evolution of the Axe

Back then, lute heroes played thin, long-necked instruments in the earliest union of fingering and plucking. The 12-string Islamic oud ('ud) influenced world travellers, so that by the Middle Ages, the medieval lute had evolved into a short-necked, pear-shaped 10-stringer (reminiscent of today's mandolin), with intricately carved soundholes in the Arabian style. The 'queen of instruments' reached its zenith in the sixteenth century, as the lute became the principle instrument for accompanying a solo singer. It was essential to the songs of John Dowland (lutenist to King James I), which brought new expressivity to music for singer-lutenists (the James Taylors of their day).

In the sixteenth century, the lute evolved into several forms as it dominated formal music before the emergence of harpsichord and, later, piano. But in Iberia, the lute lengthened, developed its 'S' shape and became a widely popular instrument. By the seventeenth century, the highly decorated 10-string baroque guitar was being used, and even Stradivarius produced a 39-inch 10-stringer.

Guitar played a minor role, subsisting as a folk instrument as Western operas and symphonic works developed, despite the efforts of great composers of classical guitar music, whose works are still played. But in Spain, the development of flamenco and its later popularity in recordings kept awareness of the instrument alive, even as it was supplanted by its stringed relation, the banjo, in early jazz. It took the invention of microphones and the development of the recording industry to bring the guitar upfront in the ears of a general public used to the sound of bigger and bigger bands and orchestras.

But it was the work of two music-loving electronics heroes, Leo Fender and Les Paul (*see* page 179), working independently and for different companies, that equipped the guitar with the power to create music of extraordinary sonic range and a vehicle for a new kind of artistry. Without the efforts of these two visionaries and some contemporaries with their own flair, there would be no arena in which mere virtuosos could transform themselves into guitar heroes.

Who's Your Hero?

There is no way to know who deserves the title of 'first' or 'most important' guitar hero, though this book offers plenty of candidates. Check the entries on Paul, Reinhardt or Robert Johnson (*see* page 174) in the Pioneers and Influences section, or the pages for Chuck Berry (*see* page 48), Ike Turner (*see* page 87) or Scotty Moore (*see* page 80) in From Blues To Rock. If your brand of heroism begins in the 1960s, of course you'll find Clapton, Hendrix,

Jimi Hendrix

Page (*see* page 32), Jeff Beck (*see* page 16) and Townshend inside, along with Keith Richards (*see* page 50) and George Harrison (*see* page 131); but then you may find that some other player, from Angus (*see* page 122) to Zappa (*see* page 45), is your cup of heroic tea.

The younger legends of the 1980s – Van Halen, (*see* page 36), Malmsteen (*see* page 40), The Edge (*see* page 126) – they're all here, as well as other heroes who have enriched our guitar-centric music – Vai (*see* page 44), Satriani (*see* page 34), Allman (*see* page 56), Rhoads (*see* page 43), Vaughan (*see* page 88), Nugent (*see* page 109), Blackmore (*see* page 94), Schenker (*see* page 114), Sambora (*see* page 113), Hammett (*see* page 100), Rundgren (*see* page 141), Frampton (*see* page 130) – plenty of names you would expect, and plenty that will send you off into raging debate with us, with your friends, with yourself.

Because, ultimately, it's not about who's included or who's not, but who you consider to be your guitar hero and the guitar music you love most. As some of the most important contributors to the pop culture and artistry of the twentieth and twenty-first centuries, the men and women in this book all deserve to be here because of their greatness as musicians and entertainers. As the dog at the fence might say: no gods here, but a mighty fine place to take a much-needed break – and rock to the most exalted heroes of the guitar universe.

Ted Nugent

'I've been imitated so well I've heard people copying my mistakes!'

Jimi Hendrix

Virtuosos

Jeff Beck
YARDBIRDS TO PIONEER

The most mercurial guitarist of his generation, Jeff Beck (b. 1944) has never conformed to the conventional image of a guitar hero. He has repeatedly left or broken up bands before their commercial potential could be realized. He restlessly changes style from one album to the next, refusing to be tied down musically. And his live appearances are intermittent. 'I just can't stand endless nights playing,' he told an interviewer in 1990. 'The pitch that I play at is so intense that I just can't do it every night.' But despite these idiosyncrasies, he is widely acclaimed as a genius.

Essential Recordings

1968 Jeff Beck Group:
Truth

1973 Beck Bogert & Appice:
Beck Bogert & Appice

1989 Solo:
Jeff Beck's Guitar Shop

2010 Solo:
Emotion & Commotion

These virtuoso qualities became apparent soon after he joined the Yardbirds in 1965 as a 20-year-old unknown to replace Eric Clapton. His vibrant, fearless playing – using distortion, bottleneck and Indian influences – was a major element of the band's biggest hits: 'Heart Full Of Soul', 'Evil Hearted You', 'Shapes Of Things' and 'Over Under Sideways Down'. But towards the end of 1966, he abruptly quit the band, which had recently added guitarist Jimmy Page, at the start of an American tour.

Early in 1967, Beck scored a solo hit single with 'Hi Ho Silver Lining', an unabashed pop song that he has disowned ever since. But the instrumental flip side, 'Beck's Bolero', a riotous swirl of feedback, overdubbing and backwards guitar, has become something of a signature tune.

He then formed the Jeff Beck Group with Rod Stewart on vocals and Ron Wood on bass. *Truth* (1968) was arguably a template for Led Zeppelin's first album a year later, with Beck taking the blues to excess. But internal tensions broke apart the group after they recorded their second album, *Beck-Ola* (1969), and Stewart and Wood decamped to form the Faces.

Beck had been planning to form a band with bassist Tim Bogert and drummer Carmine Appice from Vanilla Fudge when he cracked his skull in a car crash in 1969, putting his career on hold for 18 months. He returned with a new group of his own that included Bobby Tench (vocals), Max Middleton (keyboards) and Cozy Powell (drums), blending rock with funk on *Rough And Ready* (1972). When *Beck, Bogert & Appice* was finally recorded in 1973, it was suitably bombastic but lacked a singer to match the instrumental pyrotechnics, and by early 1974 Beck, was on his own again.

After another hiatus, Beck re-emerged with the all-instrumental, funk-infused jazz-rock of *Blow By Blow* (1975), his most successful album. Recorded as a quartet with Max Middleton, Phil Chenn (bass) and Richard Bailey (drums), the album was produced by former Beatles producer George Martin. For the follow-up, *Wired* (1976), Beck brought in Mahavishnu Orchestra keyboard player Jan Hammer and drummer Narada Michael

Playlists | Links ebooks & more
FlameTree**Rock**.com

Walden. Hammer also featured on *There And Back* (1980), which included contributions from UK musicians Tony Hymas (keyboards) and Simon Phillips (drums).

While Beck's solo career was becoming less prolific, he was making guest appearances on Stevie Wonder's *Talking Book* (1972), Stanley Clarke's *Journey To Love* (1975) and *Modern Man* (1978), Rod Stewart's *Camouflage* (1984), Robert Plant's *The Honeydrippers Volume One* (1984), Mick Jagger's *She's The Boss* (1985), Roger Waters' *Amused To Death* (1992) and Kate Bush's *The Red Shoes* (1993). He also took part in the 1993 ARMS benefit shows for multiple sclerosis research with Eric Clapton and Jimmy Page – the only time all three legendary Yardbirds guitarists have appeared on the same stage together.

His own albums have taken bold and diverse directions. *Flash* (1985), produced by Nile Rodgers, confronted the 1980s style of rock guitar as well as disco. *Jeff Beck's Guitar Shop* (1989) won a Grammy for Best Instrumental Rock Album. *Crazy Legs* (1993) was a tribute to Gene

Vincent's guitarist Cliff Gallup. *Who Else!* (1999), *You Had It Coming* (2001) and *Jeff* (2003) all set Beck's guitar against a varying backdrop of techno beats and electronica. *Live Beck!* (2006), recorded in 2003, and *Live Bootleg USA 06* (2006), faithfully captured his concert performances.

In recent years, Beck has opened for B.B. King and appeared at Eric Clapton's Crossroads Guitar Festival (2004) and the Grammy Awards (2010). He has performed with artists as diverse as Kelly Clarkson (for charity) and the young bassist Tal Wilkenfeld. Beck announced a world tour in early 2009 and the critically acclaimed *Emotion & Commotion* was released in 2010. A live album, *Live And Exclusive*, was released the same year. In 2013, Beck toured with another 1960s icon, Brian Wilson – an unlikely pairing, but one that was well received by audiences.

Beck's preferred guitar is a **Fender Telecaster**, although in the Yardbirds, he played a **Fender Esquire**. He gets his distinctive sound by using his fingers rather than a plectrum and using the tremolo arm and a wah-wah pedal.

Eric Clapton
YARDBIRDS TO LEGEND

The most famous living guitarist in the world, Eric Clapton's career has passed through an extraordinary series of highs and lows during his long reign as a guitar hero. He has also experimented with numerous stylistic changes, but has always returned to his first love, the blues.

Essential Recordings

1966 John Mayall & the Bluesbreakers: *Bluesbreakers With Eric Clapton*

1967 Cream: *Disraeli Gears*

1970 Derek & the Dominos: *Layla And Other Assorted Love Songs*

1992 Solo: *MTV Unplugged*

A love child born in 1945, Clapton was brought up by his grandparents, whom he believed were his parents until he was nine. He started playing guitar at the age of 13 and in 1963, after playing in a couple of South-London bands, joined the Yardbirds, establishing his reputation on the rough and ready *Five Live Yardbirds* (1964). He quit the Yardbirds in 1965 after recording their first hit, 'For Your Love', and joined John Mayall's Bluesbreakers. *Bluesbreakers With Eric Clapton* (1966) is still regarded as one of the seminal blues guitar albums, characterized by the fierce, sustained notes that Clapton created using controlled feedback.

Before the album was released, Clapton left to form Cream with fellow virtuoso musicians Jack Bruce (bass) and Ginger Baker (drums). Their jazz background was the perfect foil for Clapton's blues and the band became superstars as a result of three albums – *Fresh Cream* (1966), *Disraeli Gears* (1967) and *Wheels Of Fire* (1968) – and a series of American tours. But within two years, the band was worn out and Clapton subsequently hooked up with another virtuoso, ex-Spencer Davis Group and Traffic keyboard player and singer Steve Winwood, to form Blind Faith, which also included Baker. Unfortunately, *Blind Faith* (1969) could not live up to the hype surrounding the group, and they split after one American tour.

Clapton sought refuge in Blind Faith's support group, Delaney & Bonnie, who helped him record his first solo album, *Eric Clapton* (1970) and then provided him with the musicians for his next group. Derek & the Dominos recorded one incandescent album dealing with pain and unrequited love, *Layla And Other Assorted Love Songs* (1970). Here, Clapton was joined by guitarist Duane Allman, and the band toured Britain and America before imploding in a maelstrom of drug use.

Clapton was left with a heroin dependency, and after appearing – just – at George Harrison's *Concert For Bangladesh* (1971), he retreated from view for the next three years, apart from one shaky show at London's Rainbow Theatre. He returned, clean and rejuvenated, with *461 Ocean Boulevard* (1974), a major worldwide hit album that introduced the then-unknown Bob Marley through Clapton's version of 'I Shot The Sheriff', a No. 1 hit in the US. He also broadened his skills from guitar hero to songwriter, notably on *Slowhand* (1977) with 'Wonderful Tonight' and 'Lay Down Sally'. Extensive worldwide touring helped maintain his popularity, but by the end of the decade, another dependency, alcohol, was hampering his playing.

By 1983, he was sober again, and *Money And Cigarettes* (1983) and *Behind The Sun* (1985) confirmed his return to form. His appearance at Live Aid in 1985 and his duet with Tina Turner on 'Tearing Us Apart' in 1987 raised his profile further. *Crossroads* (1988), a four-CD box set, went triple platinum in America, setting new standards in the reissue market, while *Journeyman* (1989) was his most successful contemporary rock album to date.

But it was the blues that set the seal on Clapton's career. In 1992, he played the first Unplugged show for MTV, performing an acoustic version of 'Layla', 'Tears In Heaven' (written after the death of his son Conor) and a selection of blues songs. *MTV Unplugged* (1992) sold over 12 million copies. *From The Cradle* (1994), an electric blues album, topped the UK and US charts, selling 10 million copies.

Since then, Clapton has balanced contemporary albums, such as *Pilgrim* (1998) and *Reptile* (2001), with the blues albums *Riding With The King* (2001) – recorded with B.B. King – and *Me And Mr Johnson* (2004) – featuring songs by Clapton's hero Robert Johnson. Clapton also revisited his past, joining John Mayall for his seventieth birthday concert in 2003, reuniting with Cream in 2005 and teaming up with Winwood for shows throughout 2008 and 2009.

In March 2009, Clapton performed with the Allman Brothers Band for their 40th anniversary, and in 2010 toured again separately with Jeff Beck and Steve Winwood, as well as releasing the album *Clapton*. In February 2012, he appeared at the Howlin' for Hubert tribute concert at New York's Apollo Theater, in memory of guitarist Hubert Sumlin, and celebrated his own seventieth birthday with another series of concerts at London's Royal Albert Hall.

In his early years, Clapton favoured **Gibson** guitars, starting with a **Les Paul Sunburst**, and followed by a **Gibson Firebird**, a **Gibson ES-335** and a **Gibson SG** (painted in psychedelic colours), before moving

to **Fender Stratocasters** in 1969. His most famous **Stratocaster**, 'Blackie', was sold at auction for $959,500 in 2004 to raise money for his Crossroads Centre for drug and alcohol addictions. In 1988, **Fender** inaugurated their signature range of guitars with an **Eric Clapton Stratocaster** model.

Playlists | Links ebooks & more

FlameTreeRock.com

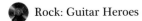
David Gilmour
PINK FLOYD PIONEER

As the guitarist in Pink Floyd, David Gilmour's place in the pantheon of guitar heroes is guaranteed. But it's not simply his playing on albums like *The Dark Side Of The Moon* that has assured his status. His meticulous attention to the sound and tone of his guitar in the studio and in concert has earned the universal admiration of guitarists, as well as millions of Pink Floyd fans.

Gilmour was born in Cambridge in 1946 and as a teenager, he was friends with Syd Barrett, with whom he learned to play guitar, and Roger Waters. When Barrett and Waters moved to London in the early 1960s, where they formed Pink Floyd with Richard Wright and Nick Mason, Gilmour stayed in Cambridge and played with local band Joker's Wild.

Essential Recordings

1973   Pink Floyd:
The Dark Side Of The Moon

1975   Pink Floyd:
Wish You Were Here

1979   Pink Floyd:
The Wall

2006   Solo:
On An Island

At the beginning of 1968, Gilmour was asked by Waters to join Pink Floyd as an additional guitarist to cover for Barrett, whose performances and behaviour were becoming increasingly erratic. Within weeks, Barrett left the group and Gilmour became lead guitarist. The band had already started work on their second album, *A Saucerful Of Secrets* (1968), and Gilmour helped to structure the title track. Gilmour played an important instrumental and vocal role in the band compositions that formed the major part of *Atom Heart Mother* (1970) and *Meddle* (1971), as well as contributing songs of his own. And although Waters was responsible for the underlying concept behind the band's defining album, *The Dark Side Of The Moon* (1973), Gilmour's carefully constructed guitar parts and solos, particularly on 'Time' and 'Money', were a distinctive element of the Pink Floyd sound. While most guitarists created their sound from overdriven distortion, Gilmour focused on getting a strong, clean tone from his guitar that he then blended with a variety of effects pedals.

He developed his sound further on *Wish You Were Here* (1975). His evocative, melancholic playing on 'Shine On You Crazy Diamond'

set the atmosphere for the album's centrepiece. He also cowrote the acoustic 'Wish You Were Here' with Waters. While Waters tightened his grip on the band for *Animals* (1977), Gilmour's guitar continued to characterize lengthy tracks like 'Dogs' and 'Sheep', as Gilmour shared much of the production work with Waters.

By the time of *The Wall* (1979), Waters had assumed complete control over Pink Floyd and Gilmour's expressive scope was becoming limited. Nevertheless, his guitar break on 'Another Brick In The Wall Part 2' is often cited as the best example of his 'clean' tone, and his monumental solo on 'Comfortably Numb' (which he cowrote) was voted the finest guitar solo of all time by listeners to digital radio station Planet Rock in 2006. Gilmour's dissatisfaction with the recording of *The Final Cut* (1983) was such that he had his production credit removed. He had released his first solo album, *David Gilmour*, in 1978 and in 1984, released his second, *About Face*, which was accompanied by a tour of Europe and America.

In 1986, Waters quit Pink Floyd, declaring the band 'a spent force creatively', but Gilmour and the others decided to continue, releasing *A Momentary Lapse Of Reason* in 1987, with Gilmour writing songs with producer Bob Ezrin and guitarist Gary Moore, among others. They embarked on a world tour that eventually ran for three years and yielded the live *Delicate Sound Of Thunder* (1988). *The Division Bell* (1994) and the subsequent world tour produced another live album and video, *Pulse* (1995), reissued on DVD in 2006. Gilmour then resumed his solo

career, playing acoustic shows that were subsequently released on DVD as *David Gilmour In Concert* (2003).

In 2005, Waters rejoined Gilmour, Mason and Wright for a 20-minute set at the climax of the Live 8 concert in London's Hyde Park. The following year, he released his third solo album, *On An Island* (2006), and toured Europe and North America.

A video recording of a show from Gilmour's solo tour, entitled *Remember That Night – Live At The Royal Albert Hall*, was released in 2007. The final show of David Gilmour's 'On an Island' tour was held at the Gdansk Shipyard on 26 August 2006, before a crowd of 50,000. In 2009, he participated in a concert as part of the 'Hidden Gigs' campaign against homelessness. In 2010, Gilmour collaborated with the Orb on

Metallic Spheres and appeared onstage with Roger Waters at a charity event, leading to a joint performance of 'Comfortably Numb' in May 2011 at London's O2 Arena during Waters' The Wall Live tour. Since then Gilmour has focussed on his solo career with an album, *Rattle That Lock* (2015) and a world tour that included in concert in the Roman ruins at Pompeii, Italy where Pink Floyd had played 35 years earlier.

Throughout his career, Gilmour has generally played a **Fender Stratocaster**. He also has an extensive collection of guitars that have been used on various occasions, including a **Gibson Les Paul**, a **Gretsch Duo-Jet** and a **Gibson EH1 50** lap steel guitar. His acoustic guitars include models by **Gibson**, **Ovation** and **Martin**.

Playlists | Links
ebooks & more

FlameTreeRock.com

Jonny Greenwood
RADIOHEAD TO GUITAR HERO

The lead guitarist in Radiohead, Jonny Greenwood, has straddled the line between dissonance and resonance, noise and melody. His arsenal of effects, virtuosity and unconventional phrasing have been key features in this very English band's development. No wonder Pink Floyd's David Gilmour is a fan. 'They've done some very good things. I can see why people make the connection,' he told the *Guardian* in 2003. In fact, Greenwood is a multi-instrumentalist, playing synthesizers, keyboards, xylophone, ondes martenot (an early electronic instrument) and viola (on which he was classically trained) with Radiohead.

Essential Recordings

1995   Radiohead:
         The Bends

1997   Radiohead:
         Ok Computer

2003   Solo:
         Bodysong

2007   Radiohead:
         In Rainbows

Born in Oxford in 1971, Greenwood met the other members of Radiohead in 1986 through his older brother Colin at the nearby Abingdon public school. Singer Thom Yorke, guitarist Ed O'Brien and drummer Phil Selway were all older than Greenwood. Originally called On A Friday, they gigged around Oxford and continued to play after Greenwood's bandmates had left for university and when they returned in 1991. The band changed their name to Radiohead after signing a record deal with EMI.

Pablo Honey (1993) blended guitar-led anthemic rock with atmospheric instrumental passages, veering from thoughtful to angst, often in the same song, such as 'Creep', a slow-burning hit around the world with Yorke's self-loathing lyrics contrasting with Greenwood's scratchy, grunge guitar. **The Bends** (1995) refused to conform to the expected follow-up and was instead a low-key album of melancholic grandeur with Yorke's vocals set against dense guitar arrangements. But they had built up a loyal following; 'High And Dry', 'Fake Plastic Trees', 'Just' and

'Street Spirit' were not pop songs, but they were all UK hit singles. MTV and American radio were less keen on the singles, however, and **The Bends** barely made the US charts, even though Radiohead supported REM on their Monster world tour and built up a broader audience.

OK Computer (1997) was a minimalist art-rock album with structured guitar riffs, mechanical rhythms, pop melodies and the band's trademark production with its cold, emotional feel that changed the face of 1990s rock. Greenwood used a wide range of sounds and effects to enhance the songs: an evocative solo on 'Airbag'; smooth, sliding tones and a squealing solo on 'Paranoid Android'; complex, spacey sounds on 'Subterranean Homesick Alien'; eerie, Pink Floyd-style playing on 'Exit Music'; wailing jangly riffs on 'Electioneering'; droning sounds on 'Climbing Up The Walls'; and melodic textures on 'Lucky'. **OK Computer** topped the UK charts, reached No. 21 in the US, and was a major worldwide success.

Kid A (2000) was a reaction to the success of **OK Computer**, deliberately moving away from conventional melodies or commercial sounds. Guitars were less in evidence although

Playlists | Links ebooks & more

FlameTreeRock.com

Greenwood's guitar was prominent on 'Optimistic', and was sparsely but effectively used on 'Motion Picture Soundtrack'. Greenwood also played the Theremin-like ondes martenot on two tracks and arranged the string orchestra on 'How To Disappear Completely'. Despite its radical nature, *Kid A* topped the US and UK charts.

Recorded at the same time as *Kid A*, *Amnesiac* (2001) had a lighter feel, but the guitars were mostly used for ambient textures, apart from Greenwood's catchy hook on 'I Might Be Wrong'. While the songs on *Hail To The Thief* (2003) remained complex, some of Radiohead's earlier energy returned. After a lengthy hiatus, *In Rainbows* (2007) restored the passion in the studio that Radiohead had never lost onstage, with guitars coming back into favour and making a telling contribution. Meanwhile, Greenwood had become the first member of Radiohead to release a solo album, *Bodysong* (2003), a film soundtrack that featured guitars on just two tracks, as he focused on his multi-instrument and arranging skills. In 2004, he was appointed composer in residence at the BBC and composed several pieces for orchestra, piano and ondes martenot. Some of this work later appeared in his *There Will Be Blood* (2007) soundtrack album, which received critical acclaim and was named Best Film Score at the Evening Standard British Film Awards for 2007. Greenwood and Radiohead worked on various projects in 2008/09, releasing singles from sessions on their website in anticipation of *The King Of Limbs* (2011).

Greenwood's more recent film work includes writing the scores for 2011's *We Need To Talk About Kevin* and 2012's *The Master*. A 2012 album release from Nonesuch Records saw Greenwood collaborating with Polish composer Krzysztof Penderecki in an unusual rock/classical partnership that far exceeded all expectations.

Greenwood has generally favoured **Fender Telecaster** guitars that have been customized and rewired, although he also has a number of **Gibson** electric and acoustic guitars as well as a **Gretsch**. He uses a **Vox AC30** amplifier for clean tones. For distorted tones, he uses effects pedals and a **Fender Deluxe 85**.

Steve Hackett
GUITAR GENIUS AND GENESIS

The guitarist in Genesis from 1970–77, Steve Hackett developed a technical skill and tone control that was a vital factor in shaping the band's music. He also helped to steer the post-Peter Gabriel Genesis towards a new style before leaving to pursue a solo career. An undemonstrative performer, Hackett has been a major influence on guitarists looking beyond the blues tradition.

Essential Recordings

1971 Genesis: *Nursery Cryme*
1977 Genesis: *Wind & Wuthering*
1979 Solo: *Spectral Mornings*
2009 Solo: *Out Of The Tunnel's Mouth*

Hackett was born in 1950 and grew up in Pimlico, London, teaching himself guitar as a teenager. Leaving school at 16, he started placing classified advertisements in music paper *Melody Maker*, seeking 'receptive musicians determined to strive beyond existing stagnant music forms'. In 1970, he was approached by Genesis, who were looking for a new guitarist. He joined singer Peter Gabriel, keyboard player Tony Banks, bassist Mike Rutherford and newly recruited drummer Phil Collins.

His introspective manner suited Genesis' style on **Nursery Cryme** (1971), adding an extra dynamic to 'The Musical Box' and the dominant theme to 'The Fountain Of Salmarcis'. The line-up gelled more effectively on **Foxtrot** (1972), with Hackett's acoustic and electric guitars blending with the tight arrangements and tempo changes on the 23-minute 'Supper's Ready'.

On **Selling England By The Pound** (1973), Genesis reverted to shorter, self-contained songs, and Hackett made some of his strongest contributions with controlled guitar effects on 'Dancing With The Moonlit Knight' and his epic solo on 'Firth Of Fifth'. **The Lamb Lies Down On Broadway** (1974) was a complex concept album and Hackett's guitar, fed through a range of distortion devices, was an evocative part of the musical tapestry on 'In The Cage', 'The Carpet Crawlers' and 'The Lamia'.

When Gabriel left in 1975, the rest of Genesis decided to stay together as Hackett took the opportunity to record his first solo album, **Voyage Of The Acolyte** (1975), expanding on areas he had touched on in Genesis. The next Genesis album, **A Trick Of The Tail** (1976), with Collins handling the vocals, marked a new beginning for the band and Hackett contributed some strident playing on 'Squonk', 'Dance On A Volcano' and 'Los Endos', as well as atmospheric effects on 'Ripples'. He also cowrote 'Entangled' with Banks. But despite several co-writing credits on **Wind & Wuthering** (1977), he was dissatisfied with the level of his contribution and left Genesis while they were preparing the live **Seconds Out** (1977).

Hackett's second solo album, **Please Don't Touch** (1978), was deliberately diverse, using different guest vocalists as Hackett ventured towards folk and soul, while giving a fresh twist to his progressive style on the vibrant 'Narnia'. **Spectral Mornings** (1979) focused on Hackett's own identity with powerful guitar playing on 'Every Day', balanced by the ambient atmospherics of the title track. **Defector** (1980) maintained the same direction, using Hackett's touring band.

Cured (1981) and *Highly Strung* (1983) moved closer to the pop mainstream, and the former gave him a Top 50 UK album, while the latter brought him a minor UK hit with 'Cell 151'. Throughout the 1980s, Hackett consciously varied the style of his albums. *Bay Of Kings* (1983) focused on his acoustic playing; *Till We Have Faces* (1984) was recorded in Brazil with Latin percussionists while Hackett also introduced oriental themes. *Momentum* (1988) was another acoustic album, exploring flamenco themes and classical pieces.

In 1986, Hackett took part in the GTR project, forming a group with Yes and Asia guitarist Steve Howe. GTR undertook a world tour, but disbanded soon afterwards. Hackett released his first live album, *Timelapse*, in 1992, taken from concerts in 1981 and 1990. Since then, his albums have switched between acoustic and electric: *Guitar Noir* (1993) was a contemporary album; *Blues With A Feeling* (1994) revisited the rhythm and blues he had grown up with; *A Midsummer Night's Dream* (1998), based on Shakespeare's play, featured the Royal

Philharmonic Orchestra; *Darktown* (1999) was a personal album; *Sketches Of Satie* (2000) featured arrangements for guitar and flute played by Hackett's brother John, who has appeared on most of his solo albums.

Hackett's prolific solo career continued in the 2000s, with electric- and acoustic-based albums, including *Feedback 86* (2000), *To Watch the Storms* (2003), *Metamorpheus* (2005), *Wild Orchids* (2006), *Tribute* (2008), and *Out Of The Tunnel's Mouth* (2009). In 2009, his official biography, *Sketches Of Hackett*, was published, and the double album *Genesis Revisited II* (2012), containing Hackett's reworkings of Genesis numbers featuring guest vocalists, was released to global acclaim.

Hackett's favourite guitar is a **1957 Gibson Les Paul Goldtop**. He also plays a **Fernandes Monterey Elite**, an **Ovation UK2**, a **Yairi Classical** and a **1975 Zemaitis** acoustic 12-string.

Jimi Hendrix
THE GUITAR EXPERIENCE

Jimi Hendrix remains the most innovative and influential rock guitarist in the world. He changed the way the guitar was played, transforming its possibilities and its image. Other guitarists had toyed with feedback and distortion, but Hendrix turned these and other effects into a controlled, personalized sound that generations of guitarists since have emulated and embellished.

Essential Recordings

1967   Jimi Hendrix Experience:
       Are You Experienced
1967   Jimi Hendrix Experience:
       Axis Bold As Love
1968   Jimi Hendrix Experience:
       Electric Ladyland
1970   Various Artists:
       *Woodstock: Music From
       The Original Soundtrack
       And More*

He was left-handed and played his favourite guitar, a right-handed **Fender Stratocaster**, upside down and re-strung, giving him a different perspective on the **Fender**'s tremolo arm and enabling him to bend notes and chords without the strings going out of tune. He never stopped looking for ways to get new sounds out of the guitar, from electronic gadgets he could plug into it, to the experimental techniques he employed in the studio.

Hendrix's career was remarkably brief. He was born in Seattle in 1942, but there was no hint of success before he moved to England in 1966 after being spotted in a New York club by Chas Chandler, bassist with the recently disbanded Animals. Hendrix had started playing guitar in 1958, three years before he joined the army. He was discharged because of a broken ankle in 1962 and spent the next four years as a touring musician with, among others, Little Richard, the Isley Brothers and Curtis Knight.

Arriving in England, Hendrix formed the Jimi Hendrix Experience with bassist Noel Redding and drummer Mitch Mitchell. He recorded a version of 'Hey Joe', creating a buzz that launched his career. His second single, 'Purple Haze', early in 1967, galvanized the music scene. *Are You Experienced* (1967) was an audacious debut album, drawing on a whole range of styles and influences and opening up a new world of guitar sounds that included flanging, double tracking and variable recording speeds.

Hendrix returned to America in the summer of 1967 to play the Monterey Pop Festival, a stunning debut that was captured on film. Before he returned to England, he recorded 'Burning Of The Midnight Lamp', which showcased the recently introduced wah-wah pedal, making it another weapon in the Hendrix arsenal.

Barely six months after his first album, *Axis: Bold As Love* (1967) pushed the sonic innovations, particularly the phasing technique, still further and fused his rhythm and blues influences with the music he had heard in England. An instant hit album in the UK, the album also spent a year on the American charts, and Hendrix spent much of 1968 touring his home country.

Electric Ladyland (1968) was his most ambitious and successful record, with 16 songs spread across a double album, ranging from the futuristic

Playlists | Links ebooks & more

FlameTree**Rock**.com

funk of 'Crosstown Traffic' to the emblematic style of 'Voodoo Child (Slight Return)'. But if Hendrix's music was peaking, tensions were growing within his band. As Hendrix jammed with a widening circle of musicians in the studio, Redding in particular became irritated. In June 1969, Hendrix disbanded the Experience and formed a new band called Gypsy Sun And Rainbow that included bassist Billy Cox and guitarist Larry Lee, with whom Hendrix had played before heading to England in 1966.

With Mitchell reinstated as drummer, Gypsy Sun And Rainbows made a tentative debut at the Woodstock Festival in August, notable for Hendrix's unaccompanied rendition of 'The Star Spangled Banner', performed against a sustained wall of feedback. In fact, he had been playing it regularly for the past year.

Within a month, the band had disintegrated and little was heard from Hendrix until the end of 1969, when he played two nights at New York's Fillmore East with a new trio called the Band Of Gypsys, featuring Cox and drummer Buddy Miles. ***Band Of Gypsys*** (1970) was the last Hendrix album released before he died.

The Band Of Gypsys lasted no longer than Gypsy Sun And Rainbows, and Hendrix reverted to the Experience with Cox and Mitchell. The first half of 1970 was divided between recording and touring, and the next album was largely complete when Hendrix died of an overdose of sleeping tablets in London in August 1970, after playing a European tour that included a headline appearance at the Isle Of Wight Festival.

In the aftermath of his death, unreleased studio recordings were hurriedly released, bearing no relation to the album he had been planning. It wasn't until 1997 that ***First Rays Of The New Rising Sun***, roughly corresponding to a suggested track listing Hendrix had scrawled on a tape box, was released. In the meantime, over a hundred studio and live albums of varying quality and provenance had come out. It is a tribute to Hendrix's genius that his status as the ultimate guitar hero remains undiminished.

Steve Howe
THE YES MAN

As the guitarist in Yes throughout their heyday in the 1970s, Steve Howe's tasteful, eclectic playing helped to define a new style of rock music. Despite occasional absences during Yes's convoluted history during the 1980s and 1990s, Howe remained a pivotal member of the group and has been a permanent member since 1996. He was also a founding member of progressive supergroup Asia in the 1980s and has released more than a dozen solo albums.

Essential Recordings

1972   Yes:
         Fragile

1973   Yes:
         Yessongs

1982   Asia:
         Asia

1994   Solo:
         Not Necessarily
         Acoustic

Howe was born in 1947 in North London and started playing guitar at the age of 12, incorporating a wide variety of interests including classical, jazz, pop and rhythm and blues. He joined his first professional band, the Syndicate, aged 16, and during the latter half of the 1960s, played with Tomorrow (who were popular on the London underground scene with their hippy anthem, 'My White Bicycle') and Bodast before he was contacted by Yes bassist Chris Squire in 1970 and agreed to join the band.

Yes were redefining their style for their third album, *The Yes Album* (1971), and Howe made an immediate impact with his jangling, jazzy/country playing, adding an atmospheric dimension to tracks like 'Starship Trooper' and 'I've Seen All Good People', and contributing his virtuoso acoustic piece, 'The Clap'.

Fragile (1972) brought together the classic Yes line-up with keyboard player Rick Wakeman joining Howe, Squire, vocalist Jon Anderson and drummer Bill Bruford. The album marked their commercial breakthrough, as the group's combined chemistry brought a new dynamic to their furious riffs, tight harmonies and anthemic refrains on lengthy tracks like 'Roundabout' and 'Long Distance Runaround'. *Close To The Edge* later the same year spread the same verve across even longer songs, and *Yessongs* (1973) demonstrated their live prowess with Howe revealing himself as more of a rock guitarist than he had in the studio.

By the release of *Tales From Topographic Oceans* (1974), Bruford had departed. (He was replaced by Alan White.) Howe and Anderson constructed a double-album concept (based on an Indian philosophy) that succeeded musically but lacked the band's earlier discipline. Wakeman left before *Relayer* (1974), was replaced by Patrick Moraz, and the music became more dissonant, enhanced by frequent tempo changes. Howe released his first solo album, *Beginnings*, in 1975, showcasing a broader range of instruments as well as his own vocals.

The return of Wakeman for *Going For The One* (1977) revived his fruitful partnership with Howe, but it was getting harder to maintain the cohesion within the band and, after another spate of line-up changes, Yes split in 1981. Howe, who had released his second solo album, *The Steve Howe Album*, in 1979, teamed up with ex-King Crimson bassist/vocalist John Wetton, ex-ELP drummer Carl Palmer and keyboardist Geoff Downes (who had been in the final Yes line-up) to form Asia. Their self-titled debut, released in 1982, repackaged the progressive rock sound for the 1980s and became a worldwide hit.

Soon after the follow-up, *Alpha* (1983), Asia was beset by personnel problems and Howe left in 1984 before the next album. For his next project, he teamed up with former Genesis guitarist Steve Hackett and singer Max Bacon for GTR. They released their self-titled album in 1986. It charted in America, and the group undertook a world tour before disbanding.

In 1989, Howe released *Anderson Bruford Wakeman Howe* with former Yes members. An attempt to combine ABWH with the Squire-led Yes on *Union* (1991) was an unsatisfactory compromise, and Howe was not involved in the subsequent Yes line-up. Instead, he focused on his solo career, releasing *Turbulence* (1991), *The Grand Scheme Of Things* (1993), *Not Necessarily Acoustic* (1994) and *Homebrew* (1996), as well as contributing to the Asia album *Aqua* (1992).

In 1995, Howe was involved in another attempt to reunite the 1970s Yes line-up. They played low-key dates the following year and the resulting live album, *Keys To Ascension* (1996), which included additional studio material, encouraged the band to continue recording new material, later releasing *The Ladder* (1999). In latter years, Howe has maintained his solo career while continuing to be a part of Yes – following a brief hiatus in the 2000s, the band released *Fly From Here* (2011). Howe rejoined the three founding members of Asia in a twenty-fith anniversary reunion tour in late 2006 and in the ensuing years, Asia released a DVD, *Fantasia*, and a new CD entitled *Phoenix* in 2008; Howe left the group in 2013.

Throughout his career, Howe has favoured the **Gibson ES-175** guitar (he has a treasured 1964 model) and **Gibson** have made a signature model. His extensive guitar collection has been the subject of a book and several of his instruments have been exhibited in museums.

Brian May
QUEEN'S GUITAR KING

Queen guitarist Brian May is among the most recognizable players in the world. His distinctive tones, created by the home-made guitar he built when he was 16 and has used throughout his career, are integral to the sound of Queen. Many of the sounds he produced were so innovative that the first seven Queen albums pointedly stated that no synthesizers had been used on their records. May has also written some of Queen's most famous hits.

Essential Recordings

1974 Queen:
Sheer Heart Attack

1975 Queen:
A Night At The Opera

1976 Queen:
A Day At The Races

1992 Solo:
Back To The Light

May, born in 1947, grew up in Hampton, South West London. He started playing guitar at the age of seven. Academically gifted, particularly in physics, he made his own guitar with help from his father when he was unable to afford the **Fender Stratocaster** he wanted. The Red Special (also known as the Fireplace Guitar, because the mahogany neck was carved from a 200-year-old fireplace) took 18 months to build at a cost of £18, and he played it with a sixpence rather than a plectrum.

May formed 1984 with bassist friend Tim Staffels prior to entering Imperial College, London in 1965. After 1984 broke up, May and Staffels formed the trio Smile with drummer Roger Taylor. After one failed single, 'Earth', in 1969, Staffels left. Staffels' flatmate Freddie Mercury approached May and Taylor about forming another band. In 1971, bassist John Deacon joined them, completing the Queen line-up. Their debut album, *Queen* (1973), featured a variety of styles and included their first May-composed single, 'Keep Yourself Alive'. *Queen II* (1974) reached No. 5 in the UK charts thanks to extensive touring.

Sheer Heart Attack (1974), recorded while May was suffering from hepatitis and a duodenal ulcer, brought their stylish rock into focus, exemplified by the 'Killer Queen' single that, like the album, reached No. 2 in the charts. May's guitar was also showcased on the opening 'Brighton Rock'. With *A Night At The Opera* (1975), Queen moved beyond conventional rock categories into one of their own, a theatrical pop dominated by multilayered guitars and vocals. The operatic 'Bohemian Rhapsody', with May's memorable solo, became a global hit.

A Day At The Races (1976) kept to the formula, with May drawing on Queen's hard roots for 'Tie Your Mother Down' and contributing one of his finest solos to Mercury's flamboyant 'Somebody To Love'. There was a rockier edge to **News Of The World** (1977), opening with May's anthemic 'We Will Rock You', and a broader sweep to *Jazz* (1978), which featured the May-penned 'Fat Bottomed Girls'. This trend continued on **The Game** (1980), the first Queen album to use synthesizers. May contributed two ballads, 'Sail Away Sweet Sister' and 'Save Me'.

Queen explored a more rhythmic direction on **Hot Space** (1982). May's guitar parts were more succinct, and he wrote three tracks on the album, including the single 'Las Palabras de Amor'. The band took an extended break in 1983, and May recorded a solo project with guitarist Eddie Van Halen that was released as a mini-album, **Star Fleet Project**, later that year. Queen reconvened to record **The Works** (1984), which was pop-oriented, although May's two songs, 'Hammer To Fall' and 'Tear It Up', maintained the band's hard-rock stance.

A Kind Of Magic (1986) followed Queen's show-stopping appearance at Live Aid in 1985, with May writing and arranging the orchestra parts for

Playlists | Links ebooks & more
FlameTreeRock.com

'Who Wants To Live Forever', a single that was also featured in *Highlander*. *The Miracle* (1989) and *Innuendo* (1991) saw all tracks credited to the band, although May was largely responsible for 'Scandal' and 'I Want It All' on the former and 'Headlong' and 'I Can't Live With You' on the latter. In 1991, the band continued recording until Mercury's death from an AIDS-related illness at the end of that year.

May completed his first solo album, *Back To The Light* (1992), which featured the hit singles 'Too Much Love Will Kill You' and 'Driven By You', and embarked on a world tour. He then worked with Deacon and Taylor, completing songs for which Mercury had already recorded vocals, on *Made In Heaven* (1995). His second solo album, *Another World* (1998), was followed by another world tour.

In 2004, May and Taylor began working with former Free and Bad Company vocalist Paul Rodgers, making their debut at Nelson Mandela's 46664 AIDS Awareness Concert in South Africa in 2005 as Queen + Paul Rodgers. They toured Europe, North America and Japan later in 2005 and 2006. They released an album, *The Cosmos Rocks*, in 2008, but Rodgers left the band the following year.

Since 2011, vocalist and 'American Idol' star Adam Lambert has been performing with the band as Queen + Lambert; their first official US tour took place in summer 2014.

May has also produced and played on albums for Kerry Ellis, touring with her in 2011, and collaborated with Meat Loaf and Lady Gaga.

Jimmy Page
YARDBIRDS TO LED ZEPPELIN

The last of the triumvirate of guitar legends who played with the Yardbirds, Jimmy Page became an icon of rock guitarists in the 1970s with Led Zeppelin. Elements of his playing style have been copied to the point of cliché in the years since Led Zeppelin dominated the rock world, but as the originator, Page developed the heavy-metal blueprint for all the guitarists who followed.

Essential Recordings

1969 Led Zeppelin:
Led Zeppelin I

1969 Led Zeppelin:
Led Zeppelin II

1971 Led Zeppelin:
Led Zeppelin IV

1998 with Robert Plant:
Walking Into Clarksdale

Jimmy Page was born in 1944 and grew up in Epsom, south of London. His first electric guitar was a **1958 Resonet Graziola Futurama**, although it was with a **Gibson Les Paul** that he made his reputation as a guitar hero. After leaving school at 16, he briefly played with Neil Christian & the Crusaders before becoming an in-demand session musician.

Between 1962 and 1968, Page played on hundreds of recording sessions for a variety of bands, including the Rolling Stones, the Who, the Kinks, Donovan, Them, Cliff Richard and Burt Bacharach. He was often hired as an insurance policy in case the band's guitarist couldn't cut it in the studio. He played on Jet Harris & Tony Meeham's 'Diamonds', a No. 1 in 1962, and Joe Cocker's 'With A Little Help From My Friends', a No. 1 in 1968.

The joy of sessions was already fading by 1966 when Page joined the Yardbirds, for whom Jeff Beck was lead guitarist. A short but exciting experiment with Beck and Page as twin lead guitarists ended when Beck abruptly left the band. Page soon found himself carrying an increasingly disillusioned band, and after the commercial failure of **Little Games** (1967), he started planning a new band, encouraged by Yardbirds' road manager Peter Grant.

Page, Robert Plant, John Paul Jones and John Bonham came together as the Yardbirds were disintegrating in 1968, and recorded **Led**

Zeppelin I (1969) before manager Peter Grant secured a record contract with Atlantic. The album's raw sound and Page's dynamic range, along with innovative techniques like playing his guitar with a violin bow, made a resounding impact. **Led Zeppelin I** spent 18 months in the charts in the US and UK.

Led Zeppelin II (1969) maintained the same high energy level and topped the charts on both sides of the Atlantic, propelled by Page's signature riff on 'Whole Lotta Love'. With more time to prepare **Led Zeppelin III** (1970), the band broadened their scope, adding more

folk-influenced acoustic songs and putting more emphasis on the arrangements. This approach paid off spectacularly on **Led Zeppelin IV** (1971), which featured the bombastic 'Black Dog' and 'Rock And Roll', the more restrained 'Misty Mountain Hop' and 'Going To California', and the monumental 'Stairway To Heaven', which drew on elements of both. The band's refusal to release singles or appear on TV did not prevent 'Stairway To Heaven' from becoming the most-played album track on radio.

Through the mid-1970s Led Zeppelin swept all before them with **Houses Of The Holy** (1973), **Physical Graffiti** (1975), **Presence** (1976), and an epic live show that was captured in all its rock-god glory on the film and soundtrack album **The Song Remains The Same** (1976). But in the summer of 1977, the band's career came to an abrupt halt when Plant's son died suddenly during yet another successful American tour. They returned in 1979 with two major British shows at the Knebworth Festival, but the following year, while rehearsing for a US tour, Bonham died after a drinking binge and Led Zeppelin was at an end.

During the 1980s, Page occupied himself with the film soundtracks **Death Wish II** (1982) and **Lucifer Rising** (1987), a solo album **Outrider** (1988), the Robert Plant collaboration **The Honeydrippers Volume One** (1984), and **The Firm** project with singer Paul Rodgers. In the 1990s, he worked with former Deep Purple singer David Coverdale on **Coverdale Page** (1993) before reuniting with Plant for **No Quarter** (1994) and **Walking Into Clarksdale** (1998). In 2000, he worked with the Black Crowes on **Live At The Greek**.

One-off Led Zeppelin reunions at Live Aid (1985) and Atlantic Records' twenty-fifth anniversary (1988) proved unsatisfactory, but towards the end of 2007, the band reformed with Bonham's son Jason on drums to play a spectacular show at London's O2 Arena to benefit the late Atlantic founder Ahmet Ertegun's charitable trust.

At the closing ceremonies of the 2008 Olympics, Jimmy Page represented Britain in a performance marking the change in Olympic venue to London in 2012. The same year, he co-produced a documentary film on the history of the electric guitar, entitled **It Might Get Loud**. Page's limited-edition autobiography was published in September 2010 by Genesis Publications, and in December 2012, along with Robert Plant and John Paul Jones, Page was awarded the Kennedy Center Honors by US President Barack Obama in recognition of Led Zeppelin's contribution to American culture.

Joe Satriani
GUITAR GIANT

American guitarist Joe Satriani is widely credited with pioneering the rock-instrumental style in the 1980s, opening up the genre for guitarists like Steve Vai, Eric Johnson and Yngwie Malmsteen. His talent for creating highly evolved music, using a pop-song structure with tuneful melodies before applying his own virtuoso skills, has made him one of the most successful guitar instrumentalists.

Satriani was born in 1956 and brought up in Westbury, New York, the youngest of five siblings, who all played musical instruments. He played piano and drums until he first heard Jimi Hendrix's 'Purple Haze' and picked up the guitar. Three years later, he was told of Hendrix's death, and the hobby became a compulsion. 'I went home and played my Hendrix records,' he told the *Los Angeles Times*. 'Then I had to play.'

He acquired a **Hagstrom III** solid-body guitar and, although he never had any formal lessons, he studied music theory at high school. By the age of 17, he was giving guitar lessons to students, one of whom was his classmate Steve Vai. In the mid-1970s, he was on a Rolling Stones list of possible replacements for Mick Taylor before they opted for Ron Wood. Unsure what musical direction to take, Satriani spent two months studying with jazz pianist Lennie Tristano and six months living alone in Japan, practising constantly. In 1977, he returned to America, settled in Berkeley, California, and resumed teaching. Among his students were Vai (again), Kirk Hammett (Metallica), David Bryson (Counting Crows), Larry Lalonde (Primus, Possessed), Alex Skolnick (Testament) and Charlie Hunter.

In 1986, he released his first, self-financed album, **Not Of This Earth**, focusing on sound textures rather than technique. **Surfing With The Alien** (1987) was his major breakthrough, highlighting his composing, production and playing talents, including two-handed tapping, sweep picking, whammy-bar effects, frenetic legato runs and volume swell. The album became the most successful rock instrumental album since Jeff Beck's **Wired** a decade earlier, with 'Satch Boogie' and 'Always With Me, Always With You' getting extensive airplay. On the back of his new profile, Satriani was recruited by Mick Jagger for his solo tour of Japan and Australasia in 1988.

Flying In A Blue Dream (1989) felt more experimental, introducing Satriani's vocals and displaying a sense of humour on 'The Phone Call'. **The Extremist** (1992) put more emphasis on melodic rock, with catchy hooks on 'Friends', 'Why' and the stirring 'Cryin''.

In the early 1990s, Satriani guested on albums by Alice Cooper and Spinal Tap, and in 1993, he joined Deep Purple at short notice when Ritchie Blackmore quit the band in the middle of a tour, but he turned down the offer to join them permanently. **Time Machine** (1993) consisted of studio tracks from earlier EPs together with recent live material, while **Joe Satriani** (1995), produced by Glyn Johns, took a more relaxed, bluesier approach.

Essential Recordings

1987   Solo:
Surfing With The Alien

1992   Solo:
The Extremist

1997   with Eric Johnson
& Steve Vai:
G3: Live In Concert

2006   Solo:
Super Colossal

Playlists | Links
ebooks & more

FlameTreeRock.com

In 1996, Satriani set up the first G3 tour of North America with Steve Vai and Eric Johnson, putting three guitarists on the same bill, performing separately and together. The success of the tour and subsequent CD/DVD *G3: Live In Concert* (1997) ensured that G3 became a regular event, with Satriani and (usually) Vai choosing a third guitarist (Robert Fripp, Yngwie Malmsteen, John Petrucci, Uli Jon Roth and Paul Gilbert have all taken part). The tours have also expanded into Europe, Asia and South America.

Meanwhile, Satriani continued his own career. *Crystal Planet* (1998) evoked comparisons with *Surfing With The Alien*, with its signature power ballads, anthems and rockers. *Engines Of Creation* (2000) was more experimental, incorporating techno and electronica. *Strange Beautiful Music* (2002), *Is There Love In Space* (2004) and *Super Colossal* (2006) have all brought the guitar back to the fore, showing that the Hendrix flame still burns, and that Satriani's flair for great hooks is intact.

Satriani's album *Professor Satchafunkilus And The Musterion Of Rock* was released in 2008. He released the *Live In Paris: I Just Wanna Rock* DVD and a companion two-CD set in 2010. The same year, Satriani joined other guitarists in the Experience Hendrix tribute tour, performing music written and inspired by Jimi Hendrix. His sixteenth studio album, *What Happens Next*, was released in 2018, on which he collaborated with Chad Smith and Glenn Hughes to produce 'pure rock and soul'.

Satriani has had a long association with **Ibanez** guitars (with **DiMarzio** pickups) and **Peavey** amplifiers, and both companies have made customized equipment for him.

Eddie Van Halen
HAIL TO HEAVY METAL

Eddie Van Halen redefined the sound of heavy metal at the end of the 1970s. His high-velocity solos, distinguished by his finger-tapping technique and tremolo-bar effects, on Van Halen's 1978 debut album heralded a new era in hard-rock guitar that rejected the clichés of a jaded genre. His solo on Michael Jackson's 'Beat It' in 1982, which effectively compressed his style into one 30-second explosive burst, took Van Halen's guitar sound into the mainstream.

Essential Recordings

1978	Van Halen: *Van Halen*
1982	Van Halen: *Diver Down*
1984	Van Halen: *1984*
1986	Van Halen: *5150*

Born in Holland in 1955, Van Halen moved to Pasadena, California with his family and older brother Alex in 1962. His father had played clarinet and saxophone in Dutch jazz bands, and both sons studied classical piano before Alex took up drums and Eddie started playing guitar at the age of 12. They formed a band in 1972, recruiting bassist Michael Anthony and singer David Lee Roth. They played the competitive Los Angeles rock scene as Mammoth until they changed their name to Van Halen.

The album *Van Halen* (1978) made an immediate impact on the heavy metal scene. Eddie poured 10 years of obsessive practising into his solo instrumental, 'Eruption', with its innovative use of two-handed tapping, high-speed fretwork, vibrato and tremolo picking. His 'Frankenstrat' guitar (pictured on the album cover), made from a **Charvel** body and neck with a modified **Gibson** humbucker pickup and **Fender** tremolo arm, provided his distinctive tone. The band's swaggering, high-energy rock style was vigorously displayed on 'Running With The Devil', 'Ain't Talkin' 'Bout Love' and a cover of the Kinks' 'You Really Got Me', and the album went platinum by the end of the year, turning Eddie into an instant guitar hero.

Van Halen II (1979) capitalized on their initial success with Eddie's singular riff providing the compelling component to 'Dance The Night

Away' – their first hit single – while his acoustic playing on the instrumental 'Spanish Fly' and use of harmonics on the introduction to 'Women In Love' broadened his scope. *Women And Children First* (1980) and *Fair Warning* (1981) consolidated Van Halen's position as a guaranteed Top 10 album band in America – as well as a stadium-filling live act – and *Diver Down* (1982) brought them another hit single with a cover of Roy Orbison's '(Oh) Pretty Woman', while Eddie refined and developed his own style on the instrumentals 'Cathedral' and 'Intruder'.

Following Eddie's groundbreaking solo on Michael Jackson's 'Beat It', the album *1984* (1984) propelled Van Halen to superstardom with their No. 1 hit 'Jump'. He also expanded his repertoire of riffs and runs on 'Panama' and 'Hot For Teacher'. Ironically, *1984* was kept off the top of

the US album charts by Michael Jackson's *Thriller*, and the simmering competitive tension that had been growing between Eddie and Roth led to the singer's departure in 1985.

Van Halen's success continued with new vocalist Sammy Hagar. The album *5150* (1986) finally gave them a No. 1 album. The band overhauled their sound mix, and the chemistry between Eddie's riffs and Hagar's vocals was evident on 'Best Of Both Worlds' and the hit singles 'Why Can't This Be Love', 'Dreams' and 'Love Walks In'. The albums *OU812* (1988) and *For Unlawful Carnal Knowledge* (1991) also hit No. 1, along with the live *Right Here, Right Now* (1993). The studio rapport between Eddie and Hagar was still strong on *Balance* (1995), but personality clashes over recording a song for the film soundtrack to *Twister* led to Hagar's departure.

Roth was recalled to sing two new tracks for a Greatest Hits collection (1996), but the band then replaced him with Extreme vocalist Gary Cherone for *Van Halen III* (1998) amid controversy, and the reaction to the longer songs and less bombastic style was mixed. The album also featured Eddie taking lead vocals on one track, 'How Many Say I'. The

band played a world tour with Cherone, but he left the band amicably during recording for the next (unreleased) album. Eddie had a hip replacement operation and was also treated for tongue cancer.

Van Halen stayed dormant until 2004, when Hagar rejoined to record three tracks for another Greatest Hits compilation (2004) and toured North America with the band. Afterwards, he resumed his solo career. In March 2007, Van Halen were inducted into the Rock and Roll Hall of Fame, but neither Van Halen brother attended the ceremony. Eddie announced that he was in rehab for alcohol addiction. In September 2007, Van Halen with Roth (but without Anthony, who was replaced by Eddie's son Wolfgang) began an American tour, which continued into 2008.

In 2009, Eddie guest-starred as himself in an episode of the American television series *Two and a Half Men*, in a scene in which he was shown playing his guitar in a mens' room. Van Halen released their twelfth studio album, *A Different Kind Of Truth*, in 2012; it was their first album to feature David Lee Roth since *1984*.

Eric Johnson
INSTRUMENTAL IDEAL

Defying categorization with his blend of rock, blues, country and melodic pop styles, Eric Johnson is highly revered by guitarists of all genres for his skill and perfectionism on stage and in the studio, and for his uniquely rich, overdriven tone.

Born in 1954, Johnson grew up in Austin, Texas. Encouraged by his parents, he started playing piano aged five and guitar at the age of 11. After hearing Jimi Hendrix's *Are You Experienced* (1967), he began experimenting with new sounds on the guitar. He formed a fusion band, the Electromagnetics, building a reputation around Texas in the mid-1970s, but his prospects were badly damaged when he signed a six-year contract with a production company that failed to release his album, *Seven Worlds*, recorded in 1977.

Playing local gigs and recording sessions with Cat Stevens, Carole King and Christopher Cross, Johnson resumed his career in 1984, signing to Warner Brothers (reportedly recommended by Prince) and releasing his first album, *Tones* (1986). Despite critical praise for his range of playing, the album did not sell commercially.

Essential Recordings

1986 Solo:
Tones
1990 Solo:
Ah Via Musicom
1996 Solo:
Venus Isle
1997 with Joe Satriani
& Steve Vai:
G3: Live in Concert

Johnson's next album, *Ah Via Musicom* (1990), saw sales that matched the reviews. He won a Grammy for Best Instrumental with 'White Cliffs Of Dover'. *Venus Isle* (1996) featured rock instrumentals, blues and jazz. In 1996, he was part of the first G3 guitarists tour of North America with Joe Satriani and Steve Vai. Johnson has since taken part in G3 tours of Asia (2000) and South America (2006). In 2006, Johnson took part in a theatrical production entitled 'Primal Twang: The Legacy of the Guitar', an examination of the guitar's history. This was followed in 2007 by 'Love-In: A Musical Celebration', in which Johnson performed a set of Jimi Hendrix songs. Further homage to his hero came in 2014's Experience Hendrix tour, when he appeared alongside Buddy Guy, Zakk Wylde and Johnny Lang, among others.

Johnson's quest for perfection has enhanced his cult status. *Live & Beyond* (2000), recorded with power trio Alien Love Child, was blues-oriented. *Bloom* (2005) was a reflection of his nomadic musical styles. Johnson mostly plays a **Stratocaster**, although he also plays vintage **Gibson** guitars and a **Flying V**. 'I like them all,' he told a journalist. 'They're all just different.'

Playlists | Links ebooks & more
FlameTreeRock.com

Mark Knopfler
DIRE STRAITS TO MASTER

From the unlikeliest of beginnings in the British new wave of the late 1970s, Dire Straits became one of the biggest bands of the 1980s, due in large part to Mark Knopfler's finger-picking guitar style, which has continued to define the sound of his solo work.

Born in Glasgow in 1949, Knopfler spent his teenage years in Newcastle, playing in a number of local schoolboy bands. After attending college, he came to London and formed Dire Straits in 1977, with his brother David on rhythm guitar, bassist John Illsley and drummer Pick Withers, and took to playing the pub circuit. A demo tape of 'Sultans Of Swing' sent to DJ Charlie Gillett stirred up interest and the band secured a contract with Vertigo Records.

Dire Straits (1978) attracted little attention in Britain but took off in Europe, followed by America, where 'Sultans Of Swing' was a hit. *Communiqué* (1979) maintained the stripped-down sound, while *Making Movies* (1980) and *Love Over Gold* (1982) stretched out their country-rock groove. But it was 1985's *Brothers In Arms* that hit the Zeitgeist, becoming the first ever million-selling CD, propelled by the hit 'Money For Nothing' and a massive world tour. Afterwards, Knopfler switched to solo projects, including soundtracks (having had success with *Local Hero* in 1983) and the low-key Notting Hillbillies. Dire Straits appeared at the Nelson Mandela Tribute Concert in 1988.

Dire Straits reformed for *On Every Street* (1991) and played another world tour that produced a live album, *On The Night* (1993), before Knopfler dissolved the band for good and pursued a solo career that has included *Golden Heart* (1996), *Sailing To Philadelphia* (2000), *The Ragpicker's Dream* (2002) and *Shangri-La* (2006).

Knopfler released *Kill To Get Crimson* in 2007 and a tour of Europe and North America followed in 2008. *Get Lucky* was released in 2009, with Knopfler

Essential Recordings

1978	Dire Straits: *Dire Straits*
1985	Dire Straits: *Brothers In Arms*
1983	Solo: *Local Hero*
2000	Solo: *Sailing To Philadelphia*

embarking on a world tour in 2010. Knopfler then toured with Bob Dylan, in 2011, and his seventh studio album, *Privateering*, was released in 2012. He continues to tour and record. Although Knopfler is left-handed, he plays right-handed guitars, usually **Fender Stratocasters** and **Telecasters**. He used a **National Steel Resonator Guitar** on 'Romeo & Juliet' (pictured on the cover of *Brothers In Arms*).

Yngwie Malmsteen
A GUITAR FORCE

A leading figure of 1980s 'neo-classical' rock guitarists, Yngwie Malmsteen (b. 1963) learned his breakneck arpeggios and baroque composing style from classical composers and performers as well as rock artists. His own sweep-picking technique, his use of harmonic scales and pedal tones and his aggressive playing have helped create his distinctive style.

Essential Recordings

1984	Alcatrazz: *Live Sentence*
1985	Rising Force: *Marching Out*
1988	Rising Force: *Odyssey*
2005	Rising Force: *Unleash The Fury*

Born in Stockholm, Sweden, Malmsteen's interest in the guitar started, like many of his contemporaries, with the death of Jimi Hendrix in 1970. Also influenced by Ritchie Blackmore's style, which was influenced by the classics, Malmsteen studied classical composers like Bach and flamboyant nineteenth-century violinist Niccolò Paganini. Malmsteen practised intently and by the age of 18, was playing in various bands around Sweden.

A demo tape that Malmsteen unsuccessfully sent around to Swedish record companies was picked up by US label Shrapnel, and he was invited over to join metal band Steeler. He played on their self-titled debut album (1983) before moving on to Alcatrazz, where he had more input, recording **No Parole For Rock & Roll** (1984) and **Live Sentence** (1984). However, he still felt stifled, so he formed his own band, Rising Force, with keyboard player Jens Johansson. **Rising Force** (1984) showcased Malmsteen's writing and playing abilities and charted in the US. The band released **Marching Out** (1985), **Trilogy** (1986) and **Odyssey** (1988), which featured 'Heaven Tonight'. Malmsteen disbanded the group and recruited Swedish musicians for his next band. **Eclipse** (1990), **Fire & Ice** (1992), **The Seventh Sign** (1994) and **Magnum Opus** (1995) were major successes in Japan. **Inspiration** (1996) featured covers of songs by Deep Purple, Hendrix and Rush. In 1998, he recorded the 'Concerto Suite For

Electric Guitar And Orchestra' with the Czech Philharmonic Orchestra. He also revived Rising Force for **Unleash The Fury** (2005). Malmsteen added singer Tim Owens for **Perpetual Flame** (2008). In 2009, Malmsteen released **Angels Of Love**, featuring acoustic arrangements of some of his best-known ballads. This was followed by **Relentless** (2010) and **Spellbound** (2012). He signed a new record deal with Mascot in 2018.

Malmsteen's best-known guitar is his 1972 blond **Fender Stratocaster**. Bought when he was a teenager, he has used it throughout his career. In 2009, *Time* magazine named him ninth on their list of the 10 best electric guitar players of all time.

Steve Morse
DIXIE DREGS TO DEEP PURPLE

A consummate guitarist in an extraordinary variety of styles, including jazz, classical, country, rock and heavy metal, Steve Morse also has the compositional skills and the improvising genius to match. He has played with, among others, Dixie Dregs, Kansas and Deep Purple, while also maintaining his own band.

Morse was born in 1954 into a musical family and learned piano, clarinet and violin before picking up the guitar. He met bassist Andy West at high school and formed Dixie Grit, a heavy-metal covers band, in the late 1960s. Morse and West went on to the University of Miami, where they took part in a musical lab project called Rock Ensemble II, which became the Dixie Dregs, playing a mixture of jazz rock and Southern rock.

Free Fall (1977), *What If* (1978) and *Dregs Of The Earth* (1980) were critically praised, but even Grammy nominations couldn't generate commercial sales, and the group disbanded in 1983. Morse formed his own trio out of the Dixie Dregs and released *The Introduction* (1984) and *Stand Up* (1985) before he joined the reformed Kansas for *Power* (1986) and *In The Spirit Of Things* (1988). Resuming his solo career, Morse expanded his own parameters on *High Tension Wires* (1989), *Southern Steel* (1991) and *Coast To Coast* (1992), while participating in the Dixie Dregs revival on *Bring 'Em Back Alive* (1992) and *Full Circle* (1994).

In 1994, Morse joined Deep Purple, replacing Ritchie Blackmore for *Purpendicular* (1996). He has remained their guitarist ever since, consolidating his role on *Abandon* (1998), *Total Abandon* (1999), *Bananas* (2003) and *Raptures Of The Deep* (2005). Live releases include *They All Came Down To Montreux* (2007). Morse has also maintained his solo career with *Major Impacts* (2000), featuring

his own compositions that pay tribute to his own guitar heroes, *Split Decision* (2002) and *Major Impacts II* (2004). In addition to Deep Purple and his solo work, Morse has performed and recorded with other outfits, including Living Loud, formed in 2003; Angelfire, with vocalist Sarah Spencer; and US supergroup Flying Colors, formed in 2012.

During his time with the Dixie Dregs, Morse played a customized **Fender Stratocaster** with a **Telecaster** neck that he assembled himself. He now has a signature model made by **Ernie Ball Music Man**.

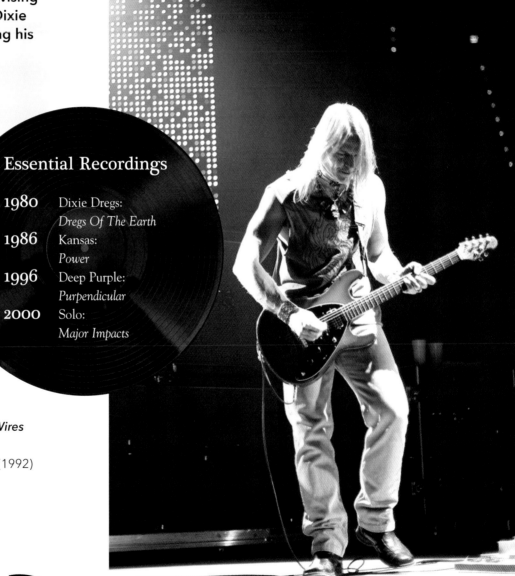

Essential Recordings

1980	Dixie Dregs: *Dregs Of The Earth*
1986	Kansas: *Power*
1996	Deep Purple: *Purpendicular*
2000	Solo: *Major Impacts*

Playlists | Links
ebooks & more
FlameTreeRock.com

John Petrucci
DREAM THEATER TO G3

The guitarist in Dream Theater, John Petrucci (b. 1967) brought his virtuoso style – lengthy syncopated lines, complex rhythmic variations and grinding tones – into the progressive-metal scene. In the past decade, he has been involved in several extracurricular projects, often with other members of Dream Theater.

Essential Recordings

1992 Dream Theater:
Images And Words

1994 Dream Theater:
Awake

1998 Liquid Tension Experiment:
Liquid Tension Experiment

2005 Solo:
Suspended Animation

Raised in Long Island, New York, Petrucci started playing guitar at the age of 12 and assiduously practised and emulated his heroes, working his way through the acknowledged masters, from Steve Howe to Randy Rhoads. At 18, he attended Berklee College of Music in Boston with his school friend, bassist John Myung. There, they met drummer Mike Portnoy and formed the basis of Dream Theater.

Recruiting keyboard player Kevin Moore and singer Charlie Dominici, they released **When Dream And Day Unite** (1989). *Images And Words* (1992) with new singer James LaBrie broke them to the MTV audience with the epic 'Pull Me Under'. **Live At The Marquee** (1993) and **Awake** (1994) consolidated their following, with an emphasis on lengthy but concisely written pieces. **Metropolis Part 2: Scenes From A Memory** (1999) was a concept album that featured new keyboard player Jordan Rudess. **Six Degrees Of Inner Turbulence** (2002) balanced heavy, experimental songs with progressive pieces. **Train Of Thought** (2003) had an underlying theme of anger, **Octavarium** (2005) was fixated around the number eight, and **Systematic Chaos** (2006) was dramatic and aggressive.

Petrucci's first side project was **Liquid Tension Experiment** (1998) with Portnoy, Rudess and bassist Tony Levin. Its success resulted in **Liquid Tension Experiment 2** (1999). In 2001, Petrucci joined the G3 tour of North America with guitarists Joe Satriani and Steve Vai. He toured with them in 2005, the first of several times through to 2018.

Dream Theater signed with Roadrunner Records in 2006, and their releases since then include **Systematic Chaos** (2007), **Black Clouds & Silver Linings** (2009), **A Dramatic Turn Of Events** (2011) and **Dream Theater** (2013).

Petrucci mainly plays **Ernie Ball Music Man** guitars and has two signature models; he also plays a seven-string guitar. His complex stage rig is based around **Mesa Boogie** amps and speakers.

Playlists | Links
ebooks & more
FlameTreeRock.com

Randy Rhoads
QUIET RIOT TO OZZY

Randy Rhoads (1956–82) had a career that lasted only six years. He played with Quiet Riot and Ozzy Osbourne before dying in a plane crash in 1982. But his guitar style, which included classical influences, opened up new directions in heavy metal, and he was an acknowledged influence on a subsequent generation of guitarists, including Zakk Wylde. Rhoads also played with Warren DeMartini (Ratt), George Lynch (Dokken) and Alex Skolnick (Testament).

William Randall Rhoads, born in Santa Monica, California, grew up with a strong musical background. His mother owned a music school in Hollywood. Rhoads was learning acoustic guitar by the age of seven and played in various bands from the age of 14. He formed Quiet Riot in 1976 with friend and bassist Kelly Garni and vocalist Kevin DuBrow. The band gained a strong following in Los Angeles, but they were unable to get a US record deal, signing instead with Columbia in Japan. Neither *Quiet Riot* (1977) nor *Quiet Riot II* (1978) was released in America. In 1979, Rhoads successfully auditioned for Ozzy Osbourne, who was recruiting for a new band, and came to the UK to record *Blizzard Of Ozz* (1980). Rhoads cowrote seven tracks, including 'Mr Crowley' with its 'neo-classical' guitar solo, and 'Crazy Train', with a guitar riff that has been regularly used on American sports programmes. He also wrote the intricate acoustic solo 'Dee'.

The band toured Britain, where the album went Top 10. Rhoads cowrote every track on their second album *Diary Of A Madman* (1981), including 'Flying High Again', on which his compact solo ushered in a new style of 1980s metal guitar. The band toured the US during the summer of 1981 and commenced another four-month schedule at the end of the year as sales of both albums took off. On 19 March 1982, Rhoads was killed when a plane in which he was a passenger clipped the tour bus and crashed in Leesburg, Florida. A live album, *Tribute*, recorded in 1981, was released in 1987 and Joel McIver's Rhoads biography, *Crazy Train: The High Life and Tragic Death of Randy Rhoads*, was published in 2011.

During his career Rhoads had three guitars custom-made for him. The first was a black and white polka dot **Flying V** made by **Karl Sandoval**, the second was a white **Flying V** made by **Grover Jackson of Charvel Guitars**, the third was a variation of the first **Jackson guitar** in black. As a tribute to Rhoads, **Marshall Amplification** released the **1959RR** in 2008. The amp is a limited-edition, all-white **Marshall Super Lead 100-watt head** modeled after Randy's own **Super Lead amp**.

Essential Recordings

1977	Quiet Riot: *Quiet Riot*
1980	with Ozzy Osbourne: *Blizzard Of Ozz*
1981	with Ozzy Osbourne: *Diary Of A Madman*
1987	with Ozzy Osbourne: *Tribute*

Steve Vai
LEGEND AMONG LEGENDS

Schooled by Joe Satriani, trained by Frank Zappa and turned into a guitar hero by David Lee Roth, Steve Vai (b. 1960) has combined an energetic technique with a distinctive and often unusual sense of tone.

Born and raised in North Hempstead, New York, Vai began taking guitar lessons from his schoolmate Satriani when he was 14. He attended the Berklee College of Music in Boston, where he developed an obsession with transcribing Frank Zappa guitar solos. Zappa hired him in 1979, and he appeared on *Tinsel Town Rebellion* (1981), *Shut Up 'N Play Your Guitar* (1981), *You Are What You Is* (1981), *Ship Too Late To Save A Drowning Witch* (1982) and *The Man From Utopia* (1983).

Essential Recordings

1981   with Frank Zappa:
You Are What You Is
1988   with David Lee Roth:
Skyscraper
1990   Solo:
Passion And Warfare
2001   Solo:
*Alive in An
Ultra World*

He left Zappa's band in 1982 and recorded his first solo album, *Flex-Able* (1984). That year, he joined Alcatrazz, replacing Yngwie Malmsteen. After *Disturbing The Peace* (1985) Vai accepted an offer to join Roth's post-Van Halen band. *Eat 'Em And Smile* (1986) and *Skyscraper* (1988) combined the band's fire with Roth's showmanship, and both albums went platinum. Vai left Roth's band in 1989 and temporarily joined Whitesnake before recording a solo album, *Passion And Warfare* (1990), which went gold. He formed a conventional rock band for *Sex & Religion* (1993), but returned to his standard format for *Alien Love Secrets* (1995) and *Fire Garden* (1996). In 1996, he also took part in the first G3 tour with Satriani and Eric Johnson and has played on almost every tour since.

Vai has continued to release studio albums like *Real Illusions: Reflections* (2005); live albums like *Alive In An Ultra World* (2001); and compilations like *Elusive Light And Sound* (2002), which featured his film work for *Crossroads*, *PCU*, and *Bill And Ted's Excellent Adventure*. He has taken part in classical projects with the Netherlands Metropole Orchestra and the Tokyo Metropolitan Symphony Orchestra and created music for the video game Halo 2 and Guitar Hero 3. In March 2011, together with Boston's Berklee College of Music, Vai set the Guinness World Record for the largest online guitar lesson, attracting thousands of participants. And in 2016 he took the *Passion And Warfare* album on a 25th anniversary world tour.

Like Satriani, Vai favours **Ibanez** guitars with a **DiMarzio** pickup. In the 1990s he pioneered the use of seven-string guitar, which was used by Korn and other bands to create the nu-metal sound.

Playlists | Links
ebooks & more

FlameTreeRock.com

Frank Zappa
FATHER OF HARMONY

Renowned as the leader of avant-garde satirical group the Mothers Of Invention in the 1960s, Frank Zappa developed a singular guitar prowess that emerged in the 1970s as his band became increasingly adventurous, drawing on a wide variety of classical, jazz and rock forms while maintaining their razor-sharp wit. His approach to playing influenced many guitarists, including band members Steve Vai and Adrian Belew.

Zappa's guitar style was unique – based more around harmony than melody – because he approached the instrument as a composer and arranger rather than as a player only. 'There are plenty of people who play faster than I do, never play a wrong note and have a lovely sound,' Zappa told an interviewer in 1984. 'But there isn't anyone else who will take the chances that I will take with a composition onstage in front of an audience.'

Born in 1940, Zappa grew up in Los Angeles and wrote film scores in the early 1960s before forming the Mothers Of Invention in 1965. His guitar playing on *Freak Out!* (1966), *Absolutely Free* (1967) and *We're Only In It For The Money* (1968) was succinct, but he began stretching out on solo albums like *Hot Rats* (1969), *Apostrophe (')* (1974), *One Size Fits All* (1975) and *Zoot Allures* (1978). Zappa's reputation was enhanced by extended guitar solos on a succession of live albums through the 1970s – *Live At The Fillmore East* (1971), *Roxy & Elsewhere* (1974), *Live In New York* (1977) and *Sheik Yerbouti* (1979).

In 1981, Zappa encouraged his guitar fan club with a triple-album set called *Shut Up 'N Play Yer Guitar*, that featured 'solos and nothing else'. And he continued to push his own boundaries with the rock musical *Joe's Garage Acts I, II & III* (1979), *Ship Arriving Too Late To Save A Drowning Witch* (1982) – featuring 'Valley Girl', the closest he came to a hit single – and *Jazz From Hell* (1987), which won a Grammy for Best Rock Instrumental Performance.

By the time of his death from prostate cancer in 1993, Zappa had amassed a catalogue of over 60 albums.

Essential Recordings

1966	The Mothers of Invention: *Freak Out!*
1969	Solo: *Hot Rats*
1974	with the Mothers: *Roxy & Elsewhere*
1987	Solo: *Jazz From Hell*

The day you open your mind to music, you're halfway to opening your mind to life.

Pete Townshend

From Blues
to Rock

Chuck Berry
ROCK'N'ROLL'S PIONEER

One of the founding fathers of rock'n'roll, Charles Edward (Chuck) Berry was born in 1926 in St Louis, Missouri, to a middle-class family. His interest in the blues began in high school, where he gave his first public performance. In 1944, he was convicted of armed robbery and sentenced to three years in an Intermediate Reformatory for Young Men. He was released on his twenty-first birthday. Before his career in music, Berry worked as a hairdresser.

Essential Recordings

1955   Solo:
        Maybellene
1956   Solo:
        Roll Over Beethoven
1958   Solo:
        Johnny B. Goode
1964   Solo:
        No Particular Place To Go

Influenced by the guitar styles of Carl Hogen, T-Bone Walker, Charlie Christian and Elmore James, by 1953 Berry was playing in the Johnnie Johnson Trio. The group mixed the blues with ballads and hillbilly music, and played the songs of Nat King Cole alongside those of Muddy Waters. These combinations, along with Berry's natural showmanship, began to attract a mixed black and white audience. A meeting with Muddy Waters in Chicago led to Berry contacting Leonard Chess, who had ambitions to expand his Chess label beyond the blues. Berry seemed the ideal artist to help achieve this.

Released in July 1955, Berry's single 'Maybellene', based on an old country song, was one of the first rock'n'roll singles and became a Top 5 hit in America. The string of hits that followed were all self-penned, something that set Berry apart from the majority of his contemporaries. His songs defined rock'n'roll with their teen-oriented themes about cars, girls and dancing. The exciting, driving yet loose guitar sound came courtesy of Berry's **Gibson ES 350T**. The opening riff of 'Johnny B. Goode' typifies Berry's style and set the template for rock'n'roll for many years to come, exerting a fundamental influence on the Rolling Stones and the Beatles. Even the fledgling Sex Pistols used to practise with the song.

In 1959, Berry was sentenced to a second term in prison, this time under the US Mann Act for transporting a minor across the state line for immoral purposes. The charge involved a hatcheck girl at his nightclub in St Louis. On his release in 1963, Berry's career prospered as the Beatles and the Stones recorded versions of his songs. Berry also inspired surf rock; he received a cowriting credit on the Beach Boys' 'Surfin' USA' because of its close resemblance to 'Sweet Little Sixteen'. His recording career resumed in 1964, producing more standards, including 'No Particular Place To Go' and 'You Never Can Tell'. Although he remained a popular live draw, Berry's records became less successful as the 1960s progressed.

Playlists | Links
ebooks & more

FlameTreeRock.com

A return to Chess in 1970 resulted in Berry's only No. 1 single, the suggestive novelty ditty 'My Ding-A-Ling', which was recorded live in England and reached the top of the charts in both the US and the UK. Berry remained unrepentant in the face of criticism, delighted at the money it made for him. The song did rekindle interest in Berry's music and a live version of 'Reelin' And Rockin'', issued shortly afterwards, also charted.

For the rest of the 1970s, Berry would hire a local band to back him at each performance, confident in the expectation that they would be familiar with his material. This led to criticisms of his gigs as slapdash and out of tune, although Berry has sometimes been known to deliberately detune his guitar for effect. His insistence on being paid in cash by promoters led to a third stint in prison when he was convicted of tax evasion in 1979.

In 1986, a sixtieth-birthday celebration concert was filmed by Taylor Hackford as **Hail! Hail! Rock'n'Roll**. Berry disciple Keith Richards acted as musical director, finding the curmudgeonly Berry difficult to work with. Amongst those paying homage were Eric Clapton and Robert Cray. The film sees Berry playing a **Gibson ES-355**, a deluxe version of the guitar he used on his 1970s tours.

The irascible Berry continued managing legal troubles – in 1991, he negotiated a plea bargain for installing a video camera in the women's restroom of his restaurant – and performing, well into his 80s. He received Kennedy Center Honors in 2000. He died, aged 90, of a cardiac arrest at his home in Wentzville, Missouri, in March 2017. He was buried with his cherry red **Gibson Lucille** signature guitar bolted to the inside of his coffin lid. In 2009, *Time* placed Berry seventh on its list of the 10 best electric guitar players of all time.

Keith Richards
ICON OF EXCESS

Veteran Rolling Stones guitarist Keith Richards (b. 1943) was born in Dartford, Kent. After being expelled from technical school in 1958, Richards attended Sidcup Art College. The art-school environment was crucial to Richards' development, as it was for many of his generation. He was able to nurture his passion for rhythm and blues, finding many fellow enthusiasts and hearing Big Bill Broonzy and Little Walter for the first time there.

Essential Recordings

1965   The Rolling Stones:
Out Of Our Heads

1968   The Rolling Stones:
Beggars Banquet

1972   The Rolling Stones:
Exile On Main Street

1988   Solo:
Talk Is Cheap

Richards acquired an acoustic guitar, and after some help from his grandfather who schooled him in the rudiments, Keith set about mastering the instrument by listening to records. Chuck Berry was a defining influence on the young Richards, who soon graduated to playing a cheap electric guitar. 'To me, Chuck Berry's style is one of the loosest and most exciting to play,' said Richards. 'When I started, I pinched virtually all of his riffs.'

A chance meeting with Mick Jagger revealed a shared interest in the blues. Jagger invited Richards to join the group in which he sang, Little Boy Blue & the Blue Boys. In 1962, Richards successfully auditioned for a rhythm and blues outfit which Brian Jones, a blues fanatic from Cheltenham, was putting together in London and which would ultimately evolve into the Rolling Stones.

Richards took Jagger along, although the singer initially was also working with Blues Incorporated, led by British blues pioneer Alexis Korner. The foundations for the Rolling Stones were laid by Richards and Jones spending days together practising and trying to figure out how bluesmen like Robert Johnson, Elmore James and Muddy Waters achieved the sounds on their records. 'The Rolling Stones are basically a two-guitar band. That's how we started off. And the whole secret, if there is a secret behind the sound of the Rolling Stones, is the way we work two guitars together,' said Richards. The interlocking lead and

rhythm guitars can be heard to good effect on the first three Stones albums: *Rolling Stones* (1964), *Rolling Stones No. 2* (1965) and *Out Of Our Heads* (1965).

The recruitment of Bill Wyman (bass) and Charlie Watts (drums) completed the Stones line-up. Astutely marketed by manager Andrew Loog Oldham as the polar opposites of the wholesome Beatles, the Stones were second only to their Merseyside rivals in the 1960s. Oldham's insistence that Jagger and Richards provide original material for the band changed its dynamic, leading eventually to the marginalization of the increasingly dissolute and unreliable Jones. The first Jagger-Richards A-side, 'The Last Time', featured a menacing, repeated four-note phrase from Richards. Although Oldham was credited as producer on early Stones records, in practical terms, it was Richards who carried out the role.

With Jones too out of it to contribute, Richards was at his most creative on *Beggars Banquet* (1968), playing almost all the guitar parts on the album, which restored the Stones' fortunes after an unconvincing flirtation with psychedelia. Jones left in 1969, replaced by former Bluesbreakers guitarist Mick Taylor, a skilled blues and jazz player.

Playlists | Links
ebooks & more

FlameTreeRock.com

The high point of Taylor's time in the Stones was *Exile On Main Street* (1972), on which his and Richards' guitars combined and interplayed effortlessly. Former Face Ronnie Wood was recruited after Taylor's departure late in 1974. Wood proved the ideal foil for Richards, both visually and musically. 'We both become one instrument,' said Richards.

Richards was and is an innovative player, claiming the first chart hit to feature a fuzzbox, '(I Can't Get No) Satisfaction', in 1965, while his use of open tunings from the late 1960s became a trademark. He has a collection of over 1,000 guitars and was associated with the **Fender Telecaster**,

although in 1964, he was one of the first stars in Britain to own a **Les Paul**. In recent years, he has favoured the **Gibson ES-345**. Richards' look, lifestyle and guitar playing has influenced many musicians, some of whom, like Mick Jones (The Clash) and Johnny Thunders (New York Dolls, The Heartbreakers), apparently wanted to be Richards, not just sound like him. His longevity remains a source of surprise and delight.

Richards underwent cranial surgery in 2006 after a head injury, but returned to the Stones in 2007. His autobiography, *Life*, was published in October 2010.

Carlos Santana
SANTANA'S SEARING COLOSSUS

Multitalented guitarist Carlos Santana was born the son of a mariachi musician in the Mexican town of Autlan de Navarro in 1947. The family moved to Tijuana when he was nine, and Carlos, who first played violin before changing to guitar, became interested in rock'n'roll and blues. At 13, he was earning money playing in cantinas and strip joints. When his family emigrated to San Francisco, he stayed behind to continue working as a musician, but was persuaded to join them and soon became involved in the city's burgeoning music scene.

Essential Recordings

1970	Santana: *Abraxas*
1971	Santana: *Santana*
1972	Santana: *Caravanserai*
1999	Santana: *Supernatural*

In 1966, the Santana Blues Band was formed. Despite the name, they operated as a collective, and Carlos was not regarded as the leader, a situation which persisted for several years, even after the name was shortened to Santana in 1968. Embarking on a two-month tour of colleges and universities in California, the band developed their distinctive sound, incorporating the Afro-Cuban rhythms of Latin America, which complemented Santana's lyrical guitar style.

Carlos quickly made a name for himself; his first appearance on record was as a guest on *The Live Adventures Of Mike Bloomfield And Al Kooper* (1968), which came about as a result of legendary promoter Bill Graham taking the band under his wing. Graham pulled off a remarkable coup in securing Santana a slot at the Woodstock Festival in August 1969. By then, they had signed to CBS and recorded their debut album *Santana* (1969), a collection of free-form jams with which the band were largely dissatisfied. Woodstock proved a turning point for Santana; their rendition of the 11-minute instrumental 'Soul Sacrifice' was one of the highlights of the movie, making the band internationally famous. Santana were also on the bill at the Rolling Stones' disastrous free gig at Altamont later in the year. Their second album, *Abraxas*

(1970), went to No. 1, and its mix of salsa, rock'n'roll, Latin and jazz was more successful for being compressed into structured songs. The album featured Santana's expressive guitar on two well-known pieces, Peter Green's 'Black Magic Woman' and 'Samba Pa Ti'.

The recruitment of teenage prodigy Neal Schon gave the band a harder-edged dual-guitar sound for *Santana* (1971), also known as *Santana III* to avoid confusion with the first album. *Caravanserai* (1972) veered into jazz-rock fusion territory, and Santana's commercial fortunes started to decline. Next came *Amigos* (1976). By returning to the Latin feel and adding a dose of funk, Carlos Santana arrived at a formula that served him for many years.

Santana made an acclaimed appearance during the American leg of Live Aid in 1985. The year 1988 saw a reunion tour with various former members of the Santana band. During the 1990s, however, his career was at a low point, and he was without a record contract, but he pulled off a remarkable comeback by signing to Arista Records and assembling an all-star cast for *Supernatural* (1999), which won nine Grammy Awards. It was followed by *Shaman* (2003) and *All That I Am* (2005), which mined the same vein, mixing hip-hop and pop with Santana's familiar lyrical Latin guitar.

In 2008, Santana worked with Marcelo Vieira on the album *Marcelo Vieira's Acoustic Sounds*. Santana is featured as a playable character in the video game Guitar Hero 5. An album of mainly instrumental tracks, *Shape Shifter*, was released in 2012. In 2016 Carlos teamed up with past Santana members Gregg Rolie, Michael Carabello, Nichael Shrieve and Neil Schon to release *Santana IV*, a "What-if" album that could have followed *Santana III*.

Carlos Santana is famous for his searing lead lines and, largely thanks to the Woodstock movie, his gurning facial expressions as he wrings every drop of emotion from his instrument. He tends not to use many effects pedals other than wah-wah and delay. He was associated with **Gibson** guitars for a long time, endorsing them in advertisements during the 1970s. At Woodstock, he played a red **Gibson SG Special**, and on *Supernatural* he used a **Gibson Les Paul**. Carlos now favours **Paul Reed Smith** guitars, and the company has produced a signature series in his honour, including the **Santana SE** and **Santana III**, the necks and fretboards of which are made of Brazilian rosewood to help create his trademark smooth tone. For classical guitar, Santana favours an **Alvarez Yairi**.

Pete Townshend
THE WHO'S WHO
OF ROCK

A pioneering guitarist and the principal creative force behind the Who, Pete Townshend was born in Chiswick, London in 1941. The Townshends were a musical family – Pete's grandfather was a musician, his father a dance-band saxophonist and his mother a singer. Consequently, a career in music seemed natural for Pete, and his parents encouraged him.

Essential Recordings

1965	The Who: *My Generation*
1969	The Who: *Tommy*
1971	The Who: *Who's Next*
1980	Solo: *Empty Glass*

His first instrument was the banjo, which he played as a teenager in Dixieland outfit the Confederates with school friend John Entwistle. After leaving school, he attended Ealing Art College, where the bohemian atmosphere and emphasis on the exploration of new ideas left an indelible imprint on Townshend. When bassist Entwistle joined the Detours, a rhythm and blues group fronted by singer Roger Daltrey, Townshend, who had switched to guitar at the age of 12, followed him. With the recruitment of drummer Keith Moon, the classic Who line-up was complete.

Townshend's reputation as a destroyer of guitars began by accident in September 1964, when he broke the neck of his guitar on the low ceiling of the Railway Tavern in Harrow, and then smashed the rest of it in frustration. The routine soon became part of the act, with Moon enthusiastically joining in by destroying his drum kit. The other aspects of Townshend's physical approach – the windmilling arm, assaults on the strings and leaps into the air – Townshend claimed to have developed to hide the fact that he could not play the blues properly.

The Who's unique sound was unleashed on their 1965 Kinks-influenced debut single 'I Can't Explain'. The song's signature riff would be widely imitated. The second single, 'Anyway, Anyhow, Anywhere', featured the innovative use of feedback, as Townshend nailed down the rhythm and Moon fired out short drum solos. The

Who's first album, *My Generation* (1965), was a mix of rhythm and blues and pop, while the follow-up, *A Quick One* (1966), was significant in that it contained in the title track Townshend's first conceptual piece. In Britain, the Who were regarded as a singles band, and they had yet to crack America. After an uncertain year in 1968, the band released *Tommy* (1969), which was hailed as the first rock opera and was a major success in the United States. *Live at Leeds* (1970, reissued with extra tracks in 1995) captured the original line-up at its peak. Townshend's blues riffs and solos on Mose Allison's 'Young Man Blues' and his extended soloing on 'My Generation' are driving forces in the performances.

The Who were established as one of the 1970s' major rock bands, and they consolidated their position with the acclaimed *Who's Next* (1971) and a second rock opera, *Quadrophenia* (1973), which looked back to the band's mod roots. In between, Townshend made his first solo album, *Who Came First* (1972). Shortly after the release of *Who Are You* (1978), Moon died and the future of the Who was thrown into uncertainty, but the band continued with ex-Small Faces and Faces drummer Kenney Jones for two more albums. Townshend pursued a parallel solo career, achieving notable success with *Empty Glass* (1980). In 1983, he declared that the Who were finished, although they reunited for occasional live performances, including Live Aid, during the 1980s. Since 1996, Townshend has worked with various incarnations of the band (not initially billed as the Who), a practice that continued after the death of Entwistle in 2002. With Daltrey, Townshend made the first new Who album in 24 years, *Endless Wire* (2006). The Who continue to perform critically acclaimed sets in the twenty-first century, including the Concert For New York City (2001), Isle of Wight Festival (2004), Live 8 (2005), Glastonbury Festival (2007), the 2010 Super Bowl halftime show and the closing ceremony of the 2012 Summer Olympics in London.

Townshend's early inspirations were John Lee Hooker, Bo Diddley, Eddie Cochran, Link Wray and Hank Marvin. His use of the guitar as a sonic tool as much as a melodic device was influential to many punk guitarists. A prime example of his powerful strumming is the intro to 'Pinball Wizard'. In the Who's early days, he played an **Emile Grimshaw SS Deluxe**, plus six- and 12-string **Rickenbackers**. He began using **Fender Stratocasters** and **Telecasters**, as these were less expensive to replace. From the late 1960s, he favoured **Gibson** guitars for live work, using a **Gretsch** in the studio. Since the late 1980s, he has preferred the **Fender Eric Clapton Stratocaster** to his own signature model.

Playlists | Links ebooks & more
FlameTreeRock.com

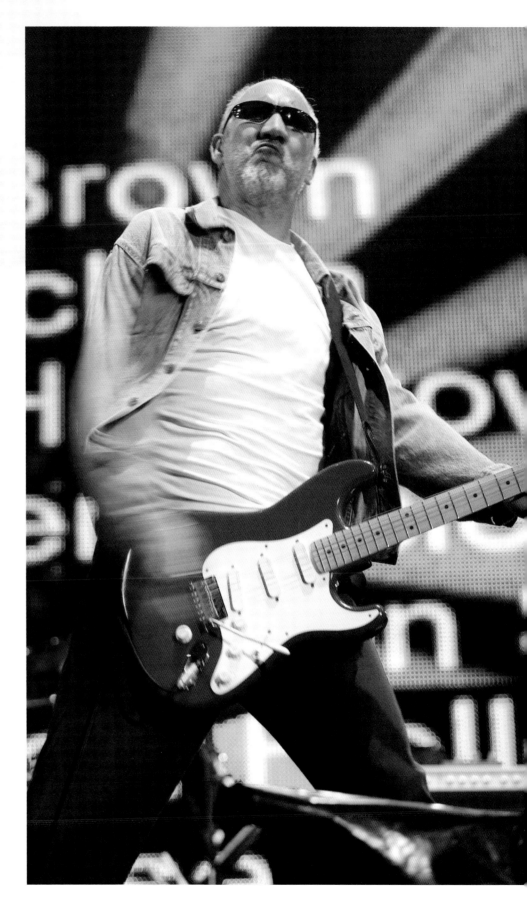

Duane Allman
SOUTHERN SLIDE STAR

Southern-rock guitarist Duane Allman was born in Nashville, Tennessee in 1946. Allman was inspired to take up the guitar by his brother Gregg. At first, they played country music, their initiation into the blues coming when the brothers saw B.B. King performing in Nashville. The pair began playing professionally in 1961, first in the Allman Joys and then the Hour Glass, who made two albums before splitting up in early 1968. Around this time, Allman began playing electric slide, inspired by Jesse Ed Davis, and using an empty glass medicine bottle as a slide, a technique later adopted by Rory Gallagher and Lynyrd Skynyrd's Gary Rossington.

Essential Recordings

1969 The Allman Brothers Band:
The Allman Brothers Band

1970 The Allman Brothers Band:
Idlewild South

1970 Derek & the Dominos:
Layla And Other Assorted Love Songs

1971 The Allman Brothers Band:
At Fillmore East

The Hour Glass recording led to Allman being offered session work on Wilson Pickett's *Hey Jude* (1968) album, which in turn led to him becoming a full-time session musician at Muscle Shoals Studio in Alabama, where he contributed to albums by Aretha Franklin, Percy Sledge and Boz Scaggs. Frustration at the limitations of session playing led Allman to form the Allman Brothers Band in March 1969 with Gregg (organ, vocals), Dickey Betts (second lead), Berry Oakley (bass) and twin drummers Butch Trucks and Jai Johanny 'Jaimoe' Johanson. The band became one of America's most influential in the early 1970s, pioneering Southern rock and paving the way for Lynyrd Skynyrd and the Marshall Tucker Band. After gigging extensively, they made their recorded debut on the largely overlooked *The Allman Brothers Band* (1969), building momentum with *Idlewild South* (1970). Allman also played with Eric Clapton in Derek & the Dominos, memorably on the classic 'Layla'. He returned to the Allman Brothers Band as they recorded one of the seminal live albums, *At Fillmore East* (1971), which captured their incendiary double-lead guitar attack at its peak. A few months after its release, Allman was killed in a motorcycle accident. The band elected to carry on without him.

Allman is remembered as one of the greatest guitarists of all time, admired not only for his slide technique but also for the improvisatory skills he displayed on his **1959 Gibson Darkburst Les Paul** and **1968 Gibson Cherry SG**.

Syd Barrett
FLOYD'S DESTRUCTIVE GENIUS

Legendary 'lost' psychedelic genius Syd Barrett was born Roger Keith Barrett in Cambridge in 1946. He learned to play guitar at the age of 14 and formed his first band in 1965. While attending art college in London, he joined the embryonic Pink Floyd.

Floyd began by playing blues and rhythm and blues covers, but soon developed the improvisational style that made them the premier band of London's underground scene. In January 1967, their debut single 'Arnold Layne' was a minor hit and was followed by the Top 10 success 'See Emily Play'. Barrett penned both, but neither was truly representative of the band in concert. Similarly, Barrett's short whimsical songs dominate *Piper At The Gates Of Dawn* (1967), although 'Astronomy Dominé' and the free-form 'Interstellar Overdrive' were more representative of the band's live sound.

By the time of *Piper*'s release, Barrett's behaviour had become increasingly unpredictable. He was often unable to function onstage and, ultimately, too difficult to work with. His breakdown was caused by a combination of deep unease with the trappings of fame and an excessive intake of LSD. Barrett's old Cambridge friend David Gilmour was drafted at first to cover for him, replacing him altogether early in 1968. Barrett was an innovative guitarist who was influenced by the improvisatory technique of Keith Rowe of underground band AMM. Although no virtuoso, Barrett achieved unique effects by playing through a Binson echo unit and employing a Zippo lighter or plastic ruler as bottlenecks. This experimental approach heralded new ways of playing rock guitar. His favoured instrument was a **Telecaster Esquire** decorated with mirrors.

Barrett's solo career was short, consisting of *The Madcap Laughs* and *Barrett* (both 1970), and *Opel* (1988), a collection of outtakes and unreleased material. After some ill-fated live outings as a member of Stars in 1972 and an abortive return to the studio in 1974, Barrett gave

up music and retreated to Cambridge, where he spent his time painting and gardening. His reclusiveness fuelled the legend, and successive generations of musicians from David Bowie to the Damned to Kasabian have cited his influence. Barrett died in July 2006 of pancreatic cancer.

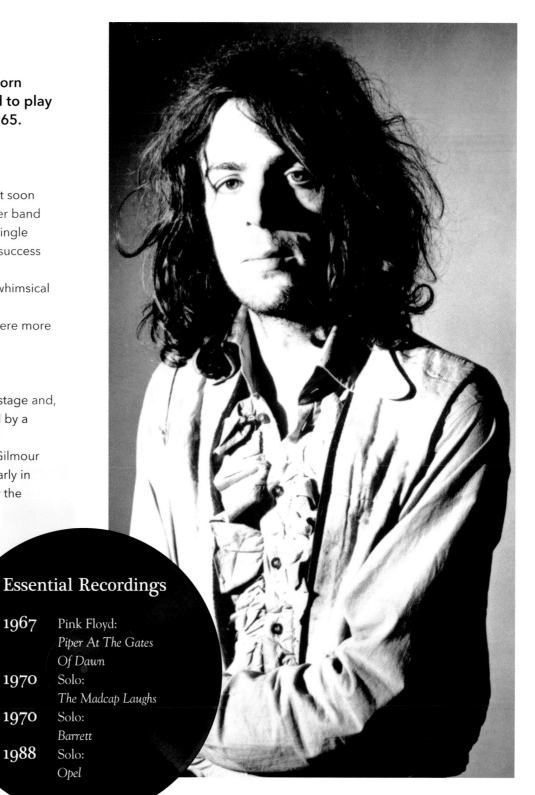

Essential Recordings

1967	Pink Floyd: *Piper At The Gates Of Dawn*
1970	Solo: *The Madcap Laughs*
1970	Solo: *Barrett*
1988	Solo: *Opel*

Dickey Betts
THE 'GOLDIE' TOUCH

Southern blues-rock guitarist Dickey Betts was born in West Palm Beach, Florida in 1943. Betts was leading a group called the Second Coming when he met and jammed with the other members of what soon became the Allman Brothers Band. His role as second lead guitarist and his partnership with Duane Allman gave the band their trademark dual-lead sound, which was captured at its most potent on the Allmans' seminal double live album *At Fillmore East* (1971), particularly the side-long epic 'Whipping Post'.

Essential Recordings

1971   The Allman Brothers Band:
At Fillmore East

1974   Solo:
Highway Call

1977   with Great Southern:
*Dickey Betts And
Great Southern*

1978   with Great Southern:
*Atlanta's Burning
Down*

Following Allman's death in 1971, Betts became sole lead guitarist and took on more of the lead vocals. He wrote many of the Allmans' most celebrated songs, including 'In Memory Of Elizabeth Reed', 'Blue Sky', 'Ramblin' Man' – the band's biggest US hit – and 'Jessica', which has served as the theme to British motoring programme 'Top Gear' for many years.

Betts released his first solo album, *Highway Call* (1974), and when the Allmans split in 1976, he resumed his solo career with *Dickey Betts And Great Southern* (1977) and *Atlanta's Burning Down* (1978). The release of a box-set retrospective helped rekindle interest in the Allman Brothers Band, leading to them re-forming, with a revised line-up, in 1978, which marked the start of a cycle of splits and reunions. The band made three more studio albums and released several live sets, remaining a popular attraction in concert. In the mid-1990s, Betts was suffering problems with alcohol, which necessitated his replacement on some dates. In 2000, he was suspended by his colleagues for 'personal and professional reasons' and, following legal action on his part, the separation became permanent. Betts relaunched his solo career, forming the Dickey Betts Band, which turned into Dickey Betts & Great Southern. His son, Duane, joined the band on lead guitar. In 2009, Betts announced his retirement from touring and live performances, although he has since resumed touring with Great Southern.

Early in his career, Betts played a **1961 Gibson SG**, which he subsequently gave to Allman for slide work. He replaced this with a **1957 Gibson Les Paul Goldtop**, nicknamed 'Goldie', which became synonymous with him. He has also played **Fender Stratocasters** and **PRS** guitars.

Mike
Bloomfield
BLENDING IN
WITH THE BLUES

Blues-rock guitarist Mike Bloomfield was born in Chicago, Illinois in 1943, to an affluent Jewish family. He possessed an innate ability on guitar, which he began playing at the age of 13, initially influenced by Scotty Moore. Despite his background, Bloomfield quickly became a devotee of Chicago's indigenous blues scene, frequently visiting clubs on the city's South Side. He often jumped on to the stage, asking to sit in on guitar.

Bloomfield's empathy for blues performers saw him accepted in an area where white faces were rare. He encountered CBS producer John Hammond, who signed him to the label, but Bloomfield's solo work remained unreleased until after his death. An equally important meeting was with harmonica player and singer Paul Butterfield, whose Paul Butterfield Blues Band Bloomfield joined in 1964. Their eponymous 1965 debut was one of the first blues albums to feature a white singer, anticipating the British blues boom of the late 1960s.

Essential Recordings

1965	Bob Dylan: *Highway 61 Revisited*
1966	The Paul Butterfield Blues Band: *East-West*
1968	The Electric Flag: *A Long Time Comin'*
1968	Bloomfield / Kooper / Stills: *Super Session*

East-West (1966) was a groundbreaking work that saw Bloomfield hailed for his fluid lead guitar, particularly on the epic, improvisational title track's blend of blues, psychedelia and Indian raga. Bloomfield switched between a **Fender Telecaster** and a **Gibson Les Paul** on this album, and he would use both guitars throughout his career. His **Les Paul** work was particularly influential for the way he created long, sustained notes on the instrument. He preferred a clean sound with plenty of reverb and vibrato, rarely using distortion or feedback. Bloomfield's session work for CBS was equally groundbreaking as he accompanied Bob Dylan's first, famously controversial steps into electric rock on *Highway 61 Revisited* (1965).

Weary of touring, Bloomfield left Butterfield in 1967 to form the short-lived Electric Flag, which disbanded after one album. He teamed up with Al Kooper, who had played organ with Dylan, and the pair made *Super Session* (1968) with Stephen Stills and *The Live Adventures Of Mike*

Bloomfield And Al Kooper (1968). Bloomfield's career in the 1970s was a lower-profile affair. He continued to record and undertake session work, but he had descended into drug addiction and suffered from arthritis in his hands. In February 1981, he died of a heroin overdose.

Joe **Bonamassa**
KEEPING THE BLUES ALIVE

Joe Bonamassa, born in 1977, began playing guitar at the age of four on a small instrument given to him by his father. By the age of seven, he was playing Stevie Ray Vaughan songs on a full-size guitar. Bonamassa began performing in upstate New York at the age of 10 and was discovered by the blues great B.B. King, who said: 'This kid's potential is unbelievable. He's one of a kind.' By the age of 12, Bonamassa was touring with King, Buddy Guy, George Thorogood and Robert Cray, among others.

Essential Recordings

2000 Solo:
A New Day Yesterday
2002 Solo:
So, It's Like That
2003 Solo:
Blues Deluxe
2008 Solo:
Live From Nowhere In Particular

Bonamassa's influences are British and Irish blues acts. He has cited the three albums that had the biggest influence on his playing: John Mayall's **Bluesbreakers With Eric Clapton** (1966), Rory Gallagher's **Irish Tour '74** (1974) and Cream's **Goodbye** (1969). He also cited Jethro Tull as one of his influences, naming Martin Barre and Mick Abrahams specifically. His first solo album is named for his cover version of 'A New Day Yesterday', from Jethro Tull's **Stand Up** (1969).

Bonamassa's recording career began during the early 1990s with the band Bloodline, formed with Berry Oakley, Jr. (son of the original Allman Brothers bassist), Waylon Krieger (son of Doors keyboardist Robby Krieger) and Erin Davis (son of jazz great Miles Davis). Bloodline released a single self-titled album of hard-edged blues rock in 1994.

Bonamassa's 2000 solo debut *A New Day Yesterday* hit No. 9 on *Billboard* magazine's blues chart. He followed with 2002's *So, It's Like That*, which would become his first No. 1 album. He released *A New Day Yesterday Live*, the following year. In 2003, Bonamassa also released *Blues Deluxe*, a collection of originals and classic blues numbers. *Blues Deluxe* hit No. 1 on the blues charts, a feat that Bonamassa would

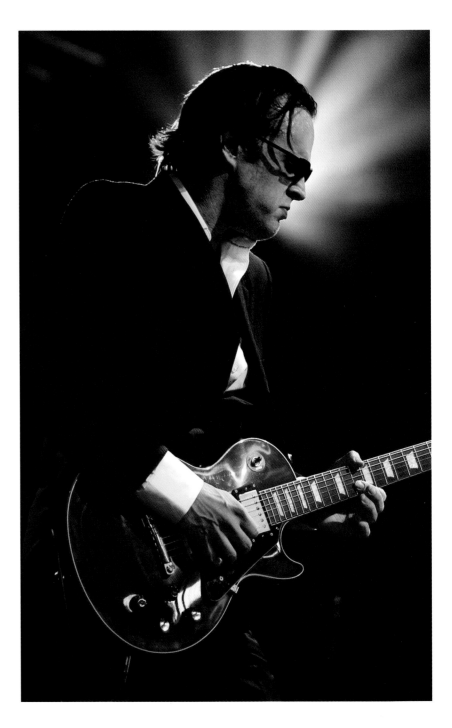

accomplish with three of his four following studio albums, as well as 2008's *Live From Nowhere In Particular*. Since 2010 he has released an astonishing 30 albums: six solo studio albums, 11 live, five with Black Country Communion (featuring Glenn Hughes and Jason Bonham), four with Beth Hart and four with jazz funk band Rock Candy Funk Party.

Bonamassa also founded and oversees the nonprofit Keeping The Blues Alive Foundation.

Playlists | Links ebooks & more
FlameTreeRock.com

Eddie Cochran
INNOVATION PERSONIFIED

One of rock'n'roll's most influential guitarists, Eddie Cochran was born in Albert Lea, Minnesota in 1938. Eddie wanted to join the school band as a drummer, but opted for trombone when he was told that he would have to learn piano before being allowed to play drums. When advised that he didn't have the 'lip' for trombone, he asked his brother to show him some chords on guitar, and from there, taught himself to play.

The family moved to California, where he formed his first group in high school. He later teamed up with Hank Cochran and the duo played country music as the Cochran Brothers (although they were not related) and made some recordings. On seeing Elvis Presley in late 1955, Eddie was inspired to switch to rock'n'roll, and the Cochran Brothers split up soon afterwards.

The year 1956 proved to be pivotal for Cochran. He recorded the Elvis-influenced 'Twenty Flight Rock' and performed it in the classic rock'n'roll movie *The Girl Can't Help It*. The following year, he recorded what would be the only LP issued in his lifetime, *Singin' To My Baby* (1957). He went on to create three seminal and frequently covered rock'n'roll songs 'C'mon Everybody', 'Somethin' Else' and 'Summertime Blues'.

Cochran was hugely popular in Britain. While on tour with Gene Vincent in April 1960, he was killed in a car crash in Chippenham, Wiltshire. He was 21 years old. Also in the car were his fiancée and songwriting partner Sharon Sheeley, who was not seriously injured, and Vincent, who was left with a permanent limp. 'Three Steps to Heaven' became a posthumous No. 1 in Britain. Cochran was a fundamental influence on the first generation of British rock'n'rollers. Paul McCartney showed John Lennon how to play 'Twenty Flight Rock' at their first meeting.

Cochran's distinctive rhythmic approach both puzzled and fascinated listeners. One of his innovations was aligning the bass and guitar to equivalent harmonic frequencies. Cochran began by using a **Gibson** guitar, but is most closely associated with a modified **1956 Gretsch 6120 Chet Atkins Western** model.

Essential Recordings

1957	Solo: *Twenty Flight Rock*
1958	Solo: *Summertime Blues*
1958	Solo: *C'mon Everybody*
1959	Solo: *Somethin' Else*

Ry Cooder
SESSION AND SOLO SUPREMO

Versatile American roots guitarist Ry Cooder was born in Los Angeles, California in 1947. As a child, he mastered the fundamentals of guitar, and at the age of 17, played in a blues outfit with singer/songwriter Jackie DeShannon. In 1965, Cooder teamed up with blues legend Taj Mahal and future Spirit drummer Ed Cassidy in the Rising Sons. The project was short-lived, falling apart when the release of their album was vetoed by CBS.

Essential Recordings

1967 Captain Beefheart & the Magic Band: *Safe As Milk*

1974 Solo: *Paradise And Lunch*

1979 Solo: *Bop Till You Drop*

1984 Solo: *Paris, Texas*

Producer Terry Melcher later employed Cooder as a session player on many records, including some by Paul Revere & the Raiders. This led to his unique slide-guitar work gracing Captain Beefheart & the Magic Band's first album *Safe As Milk* (1967). Cooder turned down the Captain's offer to join the band permanently and continued his session career, working with Randy Newman, Van Dyke Parks and Little Feat. Cooder was a candidate to replace Brian Jones in the Rolling Stones, but clashes with Keith Richards precluded that, although he did contribute to the Stones' albums *Let It Bleed* (1969) and *Sticky Fingers* (1971).

His solo debut *Ry Cooder* (1971) featured covers of blues songs, while subsequent albums such as *Into The Purple Valley* (1971) and *Paradise And Lunch* (1974) showcased his guitar work, exploring folk music and establishing his place within the industry. *Chicken Skin Music* (1976) and *Show Time* (1977) blended Tex-Mex and Hawaiian, and Cooder turned his hand to Dixieland on *Jazz* (1978). *Bop Till You Drop* (1979), the first rock album to be recorded digitally, was more mainstream and yielded his biggest American hit, a cover of Elvis Presley's 'Little Sister'. Cooder has composed numerous soundtracks, notably for Wim Wenders' 1984 movie *Paris, Texas*. The title piece's haunting, atmospheric slide guitar, recorded on a 1950s **Martin 000-18**, was evocative of the American South.

He has continued to release live and studio albums, as well as collaborating on a number of world music crossover projects such as *A Meeting By The River* (1993) with V.M. Bhatt and the highly acclaimed Cuban recording, *Buena Vista Social Club* (1997).

Cooder's main acoustic is a 1930s **Gibson Roy Smeck** model. His other guitars include a **Fender Stratocaster** (his foremost bottleneck guitar) and a **Gibson ES-P**. He has also played Japanese **Guyatone** models and a **Ripley Stereo Guitar**.

Playlists | Links ebooks & more
FlameTreeRock.com

Steve Cropper
THE COLONEL

Steve 'The Colonel' Cropper is an American guitarist, songwriter, producer and soul musician, best known for his work creating the trailblazing soul records produced by Memphis's Stax label as a member of its studio band, which became Booker T. & the MGs, in the mid-1960s.

Stephen Lee Cropper was born on a farm outside Dora, Missouri in 1941. In 1950, his family moved to Memphis. Cropper received his first guitar at the age of 14, and started playing with local musicians.

Cropper and guitarist Charlie Freeman formed the Royal Spades, who eventually became the Mar-Keys, named for the marquee outside the Stax (at the time called Satellite Records) offices. The Mar-Keys began playing on sessions there and eventually had a hit single of their own with 1961's 'Last Night'. Also in the band were future legends bassist Donald 'Duck' Dunn and trumpeter Wayne Jackson. Cropper eventually became an A&R man for the label. Along with Booker T. Jones on organ and piano, bassist Dunn and drummer Al Jackson, Jr., Cropper went on to record several hits. As a house guitarist, he played on hundreds of records, from '(Sittin' On) The Dock Of The Bay', cowritten with Otis Redding, to Sam and Dave's 'Soul Man', on which Sam Moore shouts, 'Play it, Steve!' Cropper also cowrote 'Knock On Wood' with Eddie Floyd and 'In The Midnight Hour' with Wilson Pickett.

Cropper left Stax in 1970 and played on or produced records by Jeff Beck, Tower Of Power, John Prine and Jose Feliciano. He played on Ringo Starr's 1973 album *Ringo* and John Lennon's *Rock'n'Roll* (1974). In the late 1970s, Cropper and Duck Dunn became leaders of the Blues Brothers Band. In 1998, he released *Play It, Steve!*, on which he described the inspirations behind his creation of some of soul music's most enduring songs.

In 1996, *Mojo* named Cropper the greatest living guitar player (second of all time behind Jimi Hendrix). In June 2005, Cropper was inducted into the Songwriters Hall of Fame alongside Bill Withers, John Fogerty, David Porter and Isaac Hayes. He has continued to perform and

record with other artists, including the Rascals' Felix Cavaliere for 2008's *Nudge It Up A Notch*, as well as releasing solo albums *Midnight Flyer* (2010) and *Dedicated - A Salute To The 5 Royals* (2011).

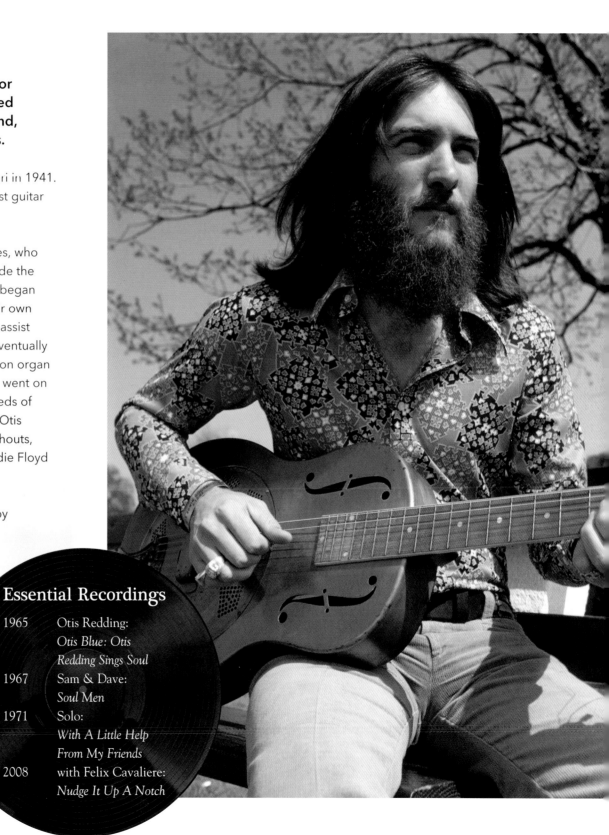

Essential Recordings

1965	Otis Redding: *Otis Blue: Otis Redding Sings Soul*
1967	Sam & Dave: *Soul Men*
1971	Solo: *With A Little Help From My Friends*
2008	with Felix Cavaliere: *Nudge It Up A Notch*

Dick Dale
SURF'S SUPERSTAR

'King of the Surf Guitar' Dick Dale was born Richard Monsour in Boston, Massachusetts in 1937. Dale learned to play drums, ukulele and trumpet before taking up the guitar, inspired by country music. His first break in music was winning an Elvis Presley soundalike contest. Dale began playing guitar in clubs, solo at first, but later backed by the Del-Tones. He was an early enthusiast of the surfing scene that arose on the beaches of southern California in the early 1960s, his family having moved there in 1954.

Essential Recordings

1962   with his Del-Tones:
Surfers' Choice

1963   with his Del-Tones:
King Of The Surf Guitar

1964   with his Del-Tones:
Mr. Eliminator

1993   Solo:
Tribal Thunder

His recording career began in 1961 with the single 'Let's Go Trippin'', regarded as the first surf-rock song, and he achieved national popularity in the States with *Surfers' Choice* (1962). Diagnosed with cancer in 1966, he was forced to retire, although he made a full recovery. After almost losing a leg to a surfing injury sustained in polluted water, he became an environmental activist. He is best known for 'Misirlou' (1962), which brought him to a new audience when used in the movie *Pulp Fiction* (1994) and led to his comeback.

Dale is left-handed but learned to play on a right-handed guitar without re-stringing it, effectively playing the instrument upside down. He was notorious for using strings of the heaviest gauge possible but still regularly breaking them and wearing out plectrums because of his forceful playing. This rhythmic, percussive attack was influenced by jazz drummer Gene Krupa.

Dale aimed to recreate the experiences of surfing in his music; his trademark twang was intended to simulate the sound of breaking waves. He is credited with inventing surf music and has been hailed as 'the father of heavy metal' due to his work with Leo Fender in increasing the power of amplifiers. He uses a signature-model **Stratocaster**, given to him by **Fender**. Dale used the first 100-watt amp. Jimi Hendrix and Stevie Ray Vaughan were among the admirers of his unique style.

In 2008, he was once more diagnosed with cancer and underwent surgery, but by 2009, he was on tour again. His backing band is anchored by son Jimmy Dale on drums.

Playlists | Links ebooks & more

FlameTreeRock.com

Dave Davies
RIFFING LEGEND FROM THE KINKS

Trailblazing Kinks lead guitarist Dave Davies was born in Muswell Hill, London in 1947. The Davies were a close-knit, musical family and Dave acquired his first guitar, a Harmony Meteor, at the age of 11. He taught himself to play, citing blues pioneer Big Bill Broonzy as his earliest influence. Other inspirations were James Burton, Chuck Berry, Muddy Waters, Scotty Moore and jazz guitarist Tal Farlow.

The teenage Dave was a rebel, frequently truanting from the secondary school where the Kinks came together with elder brother Ray on rhythm guitar and vocals and Pete Quaife on bass (drummer Mick Avory was recruited later). The Kinks' third single 'You Really Got Me' proved their breakthrough. Davies played its famous two-chord riff on his **Harmony Meteor**, creating the distortion effect by slashing his speaker with a razorblade. His work on the song is often credited as establishing the blueprint for heavy metal. A more reflective, melancholic vein soon crept into the Kinks' work, which developed into a unique Englishness, perhaps a side effect of the Musicians' Union ban that prevented the band from visiting America from 1965 to 1969.

Davies' occasional solo career got under way with the single 'Death of a Clown', cowritten with Ray, which subsequently appeared on *Something Else By The Kinks* (1967). Three other singles followed, but it was not until 1980 that he issued his first solo album, *Dave Davies* (also known by its catalogue number *AF1-3603*). In the 1970s and 1980s, the Kinks became a major live attraction in America and with Ray playing less onstage, Dave adopted a dual-purpose rhythm-lead style, primarily on a **Gibson L5-S**, using very few effects. Other instruments played in his lengthy career include a **Gibson Flying V Futura**, a **Gibson Les Paul** and a **Fender Telecaster**, plus an **Ovation** and a **Martin** for acoustic work.

Although a split was never formally announced, the Kinks last performed together in 1996, after which both brothers began work on solo projects.

In 2004, Davies suffered a stroke, which has affected his ability to sing and play, although he has since recorded two solo albums, *Fractured Mindz* (2007) and *I Will Be Me* (2013), and in 2010 a DVD, *Mystical Journey*.

Essential Recordings

1966	The Kinks: *Face to Face*
1967	The Kinks: *Something Else By The Kinks*
1971	The Kinks: *Muswell Hillbillies*
1980	Solo: *Dave Davies*

Bo Diddley
INFLUENTIAL RHYTHM MASTER

A pivotal figure in the transition from blues to rock'n'roll, Bo Diddley was born Elias Bates in McComb, Mississippi in 1928. When he was seven, the family relocated to Chicago, where he took violin lessons before switching to guitar, inspired by John Lee Hooker. He began by playing on street corners, then in the Hipsters. In 1951, he secured a regular gig at the 708 Club in Chicago's South Side, the cradle of the blues. Here, he adopted the stage name Bo Diddley, which was also the title of the first single he recorded for Checker (a subsidiary of Chess) in 1955. The song featured the distinctive jerky rhythm based on the 'patted juba', an African tribal beat adopted by street performers in Chicago, but known subsequently as the 'Bo Diddley beat'.

Diddley was also known for his rectangular-bodied **Gretsch**, which he adapted himself. Nicknamed 'The Twang Machine', the guitar was at Diddley's side throughout his career, along with similar instruments made by other companies. The modifications made the guitar smaller and less restrictive onstage. Diddley's hard-driving rhythmic style was a major influence on the development of rock'n'roll. Songs such as 'Who Do You Love?' and 'Hey! Bo Diddley' were based on one chord, de-emphasizing harmony in favour of rhythm. He often used a capo at G to help achieve his staccato sound.

Diddley made 11 albums between 1958 and 1963, while touring relentlessly. In the late 1960s, he added funk to his repertoire, and greatly influenced successive generations of musicians. Buddy Holly adapted the Diddley beat for 'Not Fade Away', covered by the Rolling Stones. Diddley was one of the godfathers of the 1960s British rhythm and blues movement. Artists as diverse as George Michael and Guns N' Roses have used the Bo Diddley beat as a basis for songs. The Clash invited him to open for them on their 1979 American tour. He was inducted into the Rock and Roll Hall of Fame and the Rockabilly Hall of Fame in 1987, and in 1998 received lifetime achievement awards from the Rhythm and Blues Foundation and NARAS.

In 2008, Diddley died of heart failure at his home in Florida.

Essential Recordings

1955   Solo:
            Bo Diddley
1955   Solo:
            Mona
1956   Solo:
            Who Do You Love?
1960   Solo:
            Road Runner

Duane Eddy
THE REBEL ROUSER

Rock'n'roll guitarist Duane Eddy was born in Corning, New York in 1938. His interest in the guitar began when he was five, inspired by singing film-cowboy Gene Autry. In 1951, the family moved to Arizona. While playing guitar in a country duo, Duane met songwriter, producer and disc jockey Lee Hazelwood. The pair embarked on a writing and production partnership, pioneering the rock'n'roll instrumental. 'Movin' 'N' Groovin'' was a minor hit for Eddy in 1958. It was followed by the Top 10 success of 'Rebel Rouser', the first of a string of similar hits.

Eddy achieved his unique twangy guitar sound by bending the bass strings and using a combination of echo chamber and tremolo arm. The twang evoked the sound of hot-rod engines revving up and had echoes of the Wild West. Eddy credited Hazelwood with creating the big sound on his records by mixing them specifically for AM radio. His backing band, the Rebels, consisted of top session players, many of whom became members of Phil Spector's Wrecking Crew in the 1960s. He later introduced female backing vocalists, the Rebelettes, on '(Dance With The) Guitar Man'.

Eddy's biggest hit, the theme to the movie *Because They're Young*, brought strings into the repertoire. Eddy was the first rock'n'roll guitarist with a signature model, the **Guild DE-400** and deluxe **DE-500**. For a long time, he was associated with the **Gretsch Chet Atkins 6120**.

Eddy's chart success started to dry up in 1962, but he remained an innovative performer, recording many albums, including one of instrumental versions of Dylan songs. He returned to the British charts in 1975 with 'Play Me Like You Play Your Guitar'; in 1986, he recorded a new version of 'Peter Gunn' with avant-garde outfit Art of Noise. The album *Duane Eddy* (1987) followed. It featured guest appearances by many of the musicians he had influenced, including Paul McCartney, George Harrison, Jeff Lynne, Ry Cooder and John Fogerty.

Essential Recordings

1958	Solo: *Rebel Rouser*
1959	Solo: *Peter Gunn*
1960	Solo: *Because They're Young*
1987	Solo: *Duane Eddy*

Eddy was inducted into the Rock and Roll Hall of Fame in 1994. A further album, *Road Trip*, was released by Mad Monkey Records in 2011, and he played the Glastonbury Festival the same year.

Playlists | Links ebooks & more

FlameTreeRock.com

Rory Gallagher
KEEPING THE FAITH

Highly respected blues guitarist Rory Gallagher was born in Ballyshannon, Ireland In 1948, and grew up in Cork. After learning his trade as a teenager playing in Irish show bands, Gallagher formed the power trio Taste in 1966. The band released two studio and two live albums. Shortly after their appearance at the 1970 Isle of Wight Festival, Taste split acrimoniously. Gallagher, already established as a virtuoso, went solo.

The 1970s were prolific years for Gallagher, with 10 albums to his name. *Live In Europe* (1972) captured his high-octane live show, and a second live album, *Irish Tour* (1974), sold in excess of two million copies worldwide. His later output was more sporadic, but he remained a hugely popular live attraction and toured constantly.

Essential Recordings

1969   Taste:
Taste

1971   Solo:
Rory Gallagher

1974   Solo:
Irish Tour

1976   Solo:
Calling Card

His formative influences were Lonnie Donegan, Chuck Berry, Muddy Waters, Leadbelly and Woody Guthrie. In turn, he influenced many other guitarists, including Johnny Marr, Slash, Glen Tipton, the Edge and Brian May. Gallagher was closely identified with his sunburst **Fender Stratocaster**, believed to have been the first in Ireland, which he bought in 1961, impressed with its appearance and swayed by Buddy Holly's use of the same model. He modified the guitar several times, and after extensive use, it was extremely battered and had virtually lost its sunburst finish. The **Strat** was invaluable to Gallagher for its bright tone and because he could achieve a wah-wah effect by manipulating its tone control rather than using a pedal. Soloing on the **Stratocaster**, Gallagher created an exquisite flurry of notes on 'Daughter Of The Everglades' from *Blueprint* (1973). His other guitars included a **Fender Esquire** and **Telecaster**, **Danelectro Silvertone**, **Gretsch Corvette** and **National Resophonic**. A **Martin D-35** was his favoured acoustic. Gallagher's bottleneck technique was widely admired by his peers and was showcased on the title track of *Calling Card* (1976).

Having been in poor health for several years, Gallagher died in June 1995 from complications following a liver transplant. He is remembered as a talented singer and songwriter as well as an uncompromising musician who, although he dabbled in country, hard rock and folk, remained a bluesman at heart.

Jerry Garcia
GRATEFUL'S GREATNESS

A leading figure on America's West Coast music scene, Jerry Garcia was born in San Francisco in 1942. His father was a retired professional musician, his mother a pianist. The musically inclined Jerry began taking piano lessons as a child. The emergence of Chuck Berry, Buddy Holly and Eddie Cochran inspired him to learn guitar at 15, his first instrument being a Danelectro. He took an arts course at San Francisco Institute of Arts, where he encountered the city's Bohemian subculture for the first time. In the early 1960s, he met future Grateful Dead bassist Phil Lesh and lyricist Robert Hunter. Garcia began playing guitar in earnest around this time, also taking up the banjo.

Essential Recordings

1969	The Grateful Dead: *Live/Dead*
1970	The Grateful Dead: *Workingman's Dead*
1991	Jerry Garcia Band: *Jerry Garcia Band*
2001	Jerry Garcia Band: *Shining Star*

Garcia began performing in a bluegrass outfit and subsequently a jug band, which evolved into the Warlocks and ultimately into the Grateful Dead. The band fused such diverse elements as bluegrass, folk, blues, country, Celtic music and jazz, all of which were evident in their long, improvised live jams and in Garcia's extended solos. Rarely captured adequately in the studio, early Dead is best represented on *Live/Dead* (1969). Their commercially successful albums, *Workingman's Dead* and *American Beauty* (both 1970) featured more conventional, country-flavoured songwriting and musicianship. Garcia was an accomplished pedal-steel player, and his achievements are all the more remarkable for the fact that he lost two-thirds of his right middle finger in a childhood accident.

Throughout his career, Garcia used a variety of guitars, sometimes favouring the **Gibson SG** or **Les Paul**, at other times the **Fender Stratocaster**. In 1973, he acquired his first custom-built guitar, and later added two more, all from the innovative guitar and bass company **Alembic**.

Although the Dead gigged relentlessly, Garcia found time for extracurricular activity, notably the Jerry Garcia Band, some Grateful Dead spin-offs and sessions for other musicians such as Crosby, Stills, Nash & Young, Jefferson Airplane and New Riders of the Purple Sage. After struggling with heroin addiction for many years and surviving a near-fatal diabetic coma in 1988, Garcia died of a heart attack in August 1995. Many tributes have been paid to him since, including Soundgarden's 1996 B-side track 'Jerry Garcia's Finger'.

Playlists | Links ebooks & more
FlameTreeRock.com

Billy Gibbons
ZZ TOP'S TALENT

Billy F. Gibbons (b. 1949), also known as the Reverend Willie G, led his Texas boogie band, ZZ Top, to international superstardom in the early days of MTV, combining a unique image with driving Southern rock and a series of eye-catching videos. At the music's core was Gibbons' tasteful blend of rhythmic crunch and fiery soloing, created on his 1959 Gibson Les Paul, named 'Miss Pearly Gates'.

Gibbons grew up in Houston, Texas. In the 1960s, he formed the psychedelic group the Moving Sidewalks, which recorded *Flash* (1968), and opened for the Jimi Hendrix Experience during the Texas leg of Hendrix's first American tour. He formed ZZ Top in 1969 with bassist-vocalist Dusty Hill and drummer Frank Beard. They released *ZZ Top's First Album* on London Records in 1971. The follow-ups *Rio Grande Mud* (1972) and *Tres Hombres* (1973), with its driving paean to a Texas bordello 'La Grange', combined with extensive touring, cemented the band's reputation as a hard-rocking power trio.

Essential Recordings

1973   ZZ Top:
        Tres Hombres
1983   ZZ Top:
        Eliminator
1985   ZZ Top:
        Afterburner
1990   ZZ Top:
        Recycler

It was in the 1980s, however, that ZZ Top really exploded. The band changed record labels, and Gibbons and Hill, during a hiatus from recording, each grew chest-length beards, unbeknownst to each other. The band also updated its sound, incorporating synthesizers into the music. The results were their three biggest albums, *Eliminator* (1983), *Afterburner* (1985) and *Recycler* (1990). A series of videos for the hit singles 'Legs', 'Gimme All Your Lovin'', and 'Sharp Dressed Man', among others, became staples of the young music video channel MTV.

Although ZZ Top lost some of their early fans with their more radio-friendly sound and missteps like the effects-laden remixed box set *Six Pack* (1987), the band's unique blend of boogie and funny, sometimes raunchy lyrics, anchored by Gibbons' blues-based virtuosity, continued to draw fans. In 2004, ZZ Top were inducted into the Rock and Roll Hall of Fame.

In recent years, Gibbons has made appearances with other bands and acted on television shows. ZZ Top played at the 2007 Orange Bowl game in Miami. The *Eliminator Collector's Edition* CD/DVD, celebrating the twenty-fifth anniversary of the album was released in 2008 and a new album, *La Futura*, in 2012. Gibbons also continues to perform and guest on the albums of various artists.

Playlists | Links
ebooks & more

FlameTreeRock.com

Peter Green
FLEETWOOD MAC'S FOUNDER

in the 1990s in the Peter Green Splinter Group, making nine albums up to 2003, but then took a break, stating that his medication was affecting his concentration and ability to play. He has since resumed touring as Peter Green and Friends.

Blues-rock guitarist Peter Green was born Peter Greenbaum in Bethnal Green, London in 1946. He began playing guitar at the age of 10. Among his early influences were Hank Marvin, Muddy Waters and B.B. King. After Green played bass in several semi-pro outfits, keyboardist Peter Bardens invited him to play lead in his band. Three months later, he joined John Mayall's Bluesbreakers, initially filling in for Eric Clapton for three gigs and becoming permanent when the guitarist left altogether. Replacing Clapton, of whom he was a great admirer, was a formidable task, but Green quickly established himself, developing an economical, sweetly melancholic style on his favoured Gibson Les Paul. His album with the Bluesbreakers, *Hard Road* (1967), contains two Green compositions, including the instrumental 'The Supernatural'.

Originally billed as 'Peter Green's Fleetwood Mac', his next band utilized Bluesbreakers' rhythm section Mick Fleetwood (drums) and John McVie (bass), with Jeremy Spencer (slide guitar, vocals) and Green on lead guitar and vocals. Debut album *Fleetwood Mac* (1968) was a mix of blues classics and original material. *Mr Wonderful* (1968) was straight-ahead blues, recorded live in the studio. Additional guitarist Danny Kirwan joined shortly before the 1968 No. 1 single 'Albatross', which showcased Green's stately, mournful blues playing.

Green struggled with fame and success, and his personality changed after a three-day LSD trip. He began appearing onstage in long robes, wearing crucifixes, and demanded that the band give all their money away to charity. After the chilling 'Green Manalishi', which seemed to address his mental struggles, he left Fleetwood Mac in May 1970. After an experimental jam session was released as a solo album, *The End Of The Game* (1970), Green disappeared, taking a succession of menial jobs, undergoing electroconvulsive therapy and spending time in mental institutions. He re-emerged as a recording artist in 1979, but suffered a relapse in 1984, living like a tramp for several years until rescued by his family. He made another comeback

Essential Recordings

1967	John Mayall & the Bluesbreakers: *Hard Road*
1968	Fleetwood Mac: *Fleetwood Mac*
1968	Fleetwood Mac: *Mr Wonderful*
1997	Peter Green Splinter Group: *Peter Green Splinter Group*

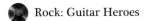
Warren Haynes
ALLMAN BROTHER TO GOV'T MULE

Warren Haynes was born in Asheville, North Carolina in 1960. He began to play the guitar at age 12. Jimi Hendrix, Eric Clapton and Johnny Winter were early influences. 'I would read interviews with all these people and find out who they listened to,' Haynes has said. 'And they all listened to B.B. King and Freddie King and Albert King and Howlin' Wolf and Muddy Waters and Elmore James. So I would go back and discover that stuff.'

Essential Recordings

1993	Solo: *Tales Of Ordinary Madness*
1994	The Allman Brothers Band: *Where It All Begins*
2009	Gov't Mule: *By A Thread*
2011	The Warren Haynes Band: *Man In Motion*

Haynes joined country veteran David Allan Coe's band in 1980 when he was 20 years old, and remained with the band for four years. While playing with local musicians and doing session guitar and vocal work, he cowrote 'Two Of A Kind, Workin' On A Full House', which became a No. 1 single for Garth Brooks.

Around 1987, Haynes was hired by Dickey Betts of the Allman Brothers Band and cowrote the title track for Gregg Allman's solo album, *Just Before The Bullets Fly* (1988). In 1989, the reunited Allman Brothers Band recruited Haynes. He has since played on four studio albums, including the gold-certified *Where It All Begins* (1994).

Haynes and bassist Allen Woody left the group in March 1997 to focus solely on their side project, Gov't Mule, which released three albums and became known for powerful live performances. Shortly after Woody's death in 2000, Haynes began appearing with the Allman Brothers again, alongside guitarist Derek Trucks. Haynes has performed and toured with many of the remaining members of the Grateful Dead, first with Phil Lesh and Friends, and then with the other remaining members, now performing as the Dead.

In 1993, Haynes' first solo album, *Tales Of Ordinary Madness*, was produced by former Allman Brothers keyboardist Chuck Leavell. In 2003 and 2004 respectively, Haynes released two solo acoustic works, *The Lone EP* and *Live From Bonnaroo*. After recording Gov't Mule's *By A Thread* album, Haynes formed The Warren Haynes Band. The album *Man In Motion* was released in May 2011 and the *Live At The Moody Theater* package came out in April 2012 on Stax Records.

Starting in 1988, Haynes put together an annual charity benefit show to benefit Habitat for Humanity, inviting musicians originally from his hometown of Asheville, North Carolina.

Playlists | Links ebooks & more

FlameTreeRock.com

Buddy Holly
STRUMMING SAVIOUR

Buddy Holly helped define and popularize rock'n'roll in its earliest days, when its future was in doubt and its existence was under attack. Strumming a Fender Stratocaster, he brought an extra dose of country to a sound that was still closely related to pure blues and rhythm and blues. He blazed a trail for white artists who, unlike Elvis, could write their own songs. His death at the age of 22 made him an American cultural icon in the order of James Dean and Marilyn Monroe.

Charles Hardin Holley was born in Lubbock, Texas in 1936. The Holleys were a musical family, and as a young boy, Holley learned to play several instruments. He sang in a bluegrass duo and in the Lubbock High School choir. Holly turned to rock music after seeing Elvis Presley sing live in Lubbock in early 1955. A few months later, he appeared on the same bill with Presley, and later opened for Bill Haley & His Comets.Offered a deal with Decca Records, he changed his name from Holley to Holly because of a typo on the contract.

He cut an early version of 'That'll Be The Day', which secured his deal with the Decca subsidiary Coral. Along with that classic, he had a string of hit singles with 'Everyday', 'Peggy Sue', 'Maybe Baby' and 'Rave On'. With his new band the Crickets he won over the crowd at Harlem's Apollo Theater and toured the UK in 1958.

The Crickets left Holly as he became a national figure, and he toured with a new backing band. On a tour with Ritchie Valens and the Big Bopper, Holly chartered a plane to fly him from a performance in Clear Lake, Iowa, to Fargo, North Dakota, in February 1959. The plane crashed, killing the three young stars. The prolific Holly had recorded so many songs that 'new' records were released for the next ten years.

Holly's influence has been felt throughout rock's history, from the ubiquitous **Stratocaster** (a carving of which adorns his headstone) to his songs, which influenced a generation of songwriters and inspired legions to take up the guitar.

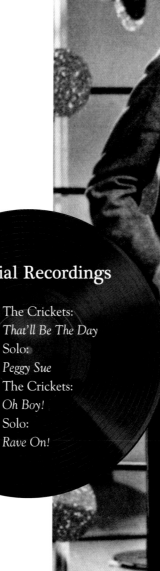

Essential Recordings

1957 The Crickets:
That'll Be The Day
1957 Solo:
Peggy Sue
1957 The Crickets:
Oh Boy!
1958 Solo:
Rave On!

Paul Kossoff
FREE FOR ALL

Blues and hard-rock guitarist Paul Kossoff, son of British actor David Kossoff, was born in Hampstead, London in 1950. He studied classical guitar as a child, but had given it up by his early teens. Inspired by John Mayall's Bluesbreakers, featuring Eric Clapton, he resumed playing and teamed up with drummer Simon Kirke in the rhythm and blues band Black Cat Bones in 1966.

Essential Recordings

1969   Free:
        Tons Of Sobs
1969   Free:
        Free
1970   Free:
        Fire And Water
1973   Solo:
        Back Street Crawler

The band often supported Fleetwood Mac, and a friendship arose between Peter Green and Kossoff, based on their shared enthusiasm for the blues. Kossoff saw singer Paul Rodgers singing in the band Brown Sugar, which led to the formation of Free at the height of the British blues boom in 1968. Bassist Andy Fraser, another former Bluesbreaker, was recruited at the suggestion of pioneering blues musician Alexis Korner, who also came up with the band's name. All four members of Free were in their teens at the time.

Korner helped broker a deal with Island Records, and Free's debut **Tons Of Sobs** (1969) was recorded on a minimal budget. The album showcased the band's blues rock at its most raw, driven by Kossoff's guitar. 'Goin' Down Slow', one of only two non-originals on the album, featured his long, complex solo. **Free** (1969) was more polished, with Fraser's rhythmic bass coming to the fore and providing a springboard for Kossoff's lead. Before **Fire And Water** (1970), Kossoff was disillusioned by the band's lack of commercial success, until the classic single 'All Right Now' rectified that. Kossoff's aggressive riff, played on his trademark **Gibson Les Paul**, remains his best-known work. Free temporarily split after the failure of **Highway** (1971), but reconvened for **Free At Last** (1972). But Kossoff's drug problems spiralled out of control, and he had minimal input into the final Free album **Heartbreaker** (1973).

Playlists | Links
ebooks & more

FlameTreeRock.com

The guitarist was able to complete a solo album, *Back Street Crawler* (1973), and subsequently assembled a band of the same name, which made two albums with him. Still struggling with drug addiction, he almost died in rehab in 1975, and on a flight from Los Angeles to New York in March 1976, Kossoff suffered a fatal, drug-induced heart attack.

Robby Krieger
OPENING DOORS

Eclectic guitarist Robby Krieger was born in Los Angeles in 1946. Krieger started to play the blues on piano, and began to learn guitar at the age of 17 on a flamenco model. 'I switched around from folk to flamenco to blues to rock'n'roll,' he recalled. The Paul Butterfield Blues Band was an important influence. 'If it hadn't been for Butterfield going electric, I probably wouldn't have gone rock'n'roll.'

For Krieger, rock'n'roll offered almost as much musical freedom as jazz, but with greater earning potential. While playing in the Psychedelic Rangers with drummer John Densmore, they hooked up with keyboardist Ray Manzarek and singer Jim Morrison to form the Doors. The band was unusual in having no bassist; in concert, Manzarek played keyboard bass with his left hand while session musicians were used in the studio. Their debut album *The Doors* (1967) was an instant sensation. 'Light My Fire' became a massive Summer of Love hit in America and featured Krieger's guitar sparring with Manzarek's swirling organ in the jazzy middle section. His discordant solo on 'When The Music's Over' from *Strange Days* (1967) anticipated Robert Fripp's style, while his vibrato on the introduction to 'Riders on the Storm' from *LA Woman* (1971) evoked gentle rainfall. He generally favoured a **Gibson SG**, although he has also used a **Les Paul Sunburst** and a **Fender Stratocaster**.

Essential Recordings

1967	The Doors: *The Doors*
1967	The Doors: *Strange Days*
1971	The Doors: *LA Woman*
1974	The Butts Band: *The Butts Band*

After Morrison's death in 1971, the Doors made two more albums, with Manzarek and Krieger sharing the vocal duties. They reunited in 1978 for *An American Prayer*, adding music to recently discovered tapes of Morrison reading his poetry. Krieger has also made several jazz-tinged solo albums. The Doors' enduring popularity and influence on successive generations of bands, starting with the Stranglers and Echo & the Bunnymen, inspired Krieger and Manzarek to assemble a new version of the band in 2002 with former Cult singer Ian Astbury but without Densmore, who subsequently took legal action to prevent the use of the Doors name. The move forced the outfit to tour as Riders On The Storm. Krieger later took part in the Experience Hendrix tribute concerts (2008–09), and in 2012, toured with the Roadhouse Rebels.

Albert Lee
TRIUMPH ON A TELECASTER

Rock guitarist Albert Lee was born in Leominster, Herefordshire in 1943. The son of a musician, Lee started his musical career on piano, but like many of his generation, took up the guitar upon the arrival of rock'n'roll, inspired in particular by Buddy Holly. He played in various bands after leaving school at the age of 16, before becoming lead guitarist with Chris Farlowe and the Thunderbirds.

Essential Recordings

1972   Heads Hands & Feet: *Tracks*
1980   Emmylou Harris: *Roses In The Snow*
1983   Eric Clapton: *Money And Cigarettes*
2003   Solo: *Heartbreak Hill*

Preferring country to the soul-influenced music of Farlowe, he left in 1968 to join country-rock outfit Heads Hands & Feet. While playing with the band, Lee made his name as a guitarist, gaining a reputation for the amazing speed at which he played his **Fender Telecaster**. Heads Hands & Feet were a popular live attraction in Britain and Europe, but their critically acclaimed albums failed to reach a mainstream audience.

In 1974, Lee relocated to Los Angeles, where he found himself very much in demand as a session musician but unable to progress his solo career satisfactorily. He joined Emmylou Harris's Hot Band in 1976 as a replacement for one of his idols, James Burton. Two years later, he linked up with Eric Clapton, with whom he played for the next five years. Lee has also worked with the Everly Brothers, having masterminded their 1983 reunion concert and served as its musical director. In 1987, he fronted a band for the first time, Hogan's Heroes, with whom he still tours regularly. Although not well known to the general public, Hogan's Heroes regularly attracts star names to jam with them. Lee has also worked frequently with Bill Wyman's Rhythm Kings.

Because of his long association with the **Fender** instrument, Lee has become known as 'Mr **Telecaster**', although he has also played **Gibson** guitars, an **Ernie Ball Music Man** and a **Stratocaster** from time to time.

Lee has not been rewarded with great commercial success or fame, but is widely admired by his peers and acknowledged as the guitarist's guitarist, particularly renowned for his fingerstyle and hybrid picking techniques. While his trademarks are speed and virtuosity, he is equally adept at slower, melodic passages.

Playlists | Links ebooks & more
FlameTreeRock.com

Alvin Lee
TITAN OF TEN YEARS AFTER

Blues-rock guitarist Alvin Lee was born Graham Barnes in Nottingham in 1944. Inspired by rock'n'roll guitarists Chuck Berry and Scotty Moore, Lee began to play at the age of 13, and formed his first band, Ivan Jay and the Jaymen, in 1960. Lee became lead vocalist in 1962 when the band changed their name to the Jaybirds and played Hamburg's Star Club. They moved to London in 1966, eventually settling on the name Ten Years After. A residency at the Marquee Club led to an invitation to play at the Windsor Jazz and Blues Festival in 1967, which in turn led to a record contract with Deram.

Debut album *Ten Years After* (1967) showcased Lee's soulful, nimble-fingered guitar-playing and the band's trail-blazing mix of swing jazz, blues and rock, earning them a cult following in America, where they toured on the first of many occasions in 1968. An appearance at the Woodstock

Festival in 1969 provided their breakthrough in the States. Lee's virtuoso guitar on what would become his signature tune, 'I'm Going Home', was featured in the film and hailed as a highlight of the event. The band also played the Isle of Wight Festival in 1970, the year of their only British hit single, 'Love Like A Man'. After nine studio albums, Lee's dissatisfaction with the group's limitations prompted him to disband Ten Years After in 1974.

Lee's career outside the band had already begun with *On The Road To Freedom* (1973), a country-rock collaboration with Mylon LeFevre that boasted George Harrison, Ronnie Wood and Steve Winwood amongst its superstar guests. In 1978, he put together a new version of Ten Years After, and he toured under the name again in 1989. In between, he worked with Steve Gould of Rare Bird and former Rolling Stone Mick Taylor. In the 1990s, he recorded with rock'n'roll pioneers Scotty Moore and D.J. Fontana. Lee's last album, *Still On The Road To Freedom*, was released in 2012. He died from complications following surgery in March 2013.

Lee's favourite guitar was his long-serving **Gibson Custom Shop 335**, affectionately dubbed 'Big Red'. As it was too valuable to take on the road, the company made him a copy of it.

Essential Recordings

1967   Ten Years After:
         Ten Years After

1970   Various Artists:
         Woodstock: Music
         From The Original
         Soundtrack And More

1973   with Mylon LeFevre:
         On The Road
         To Freedom

2012   Solo:
         Still On The
         Road To Freedom

Hank Marvin
OUT OF THE SHADOWS

Britain's first home-grown guitar hero, Hank Marvin (pictured below, right) was born Brian Rankin in Newcastle-upon-Tyne in 1941. His first instruments were piano and banjo, but he switched to guitar upon discovering Buddy Holly. Marvin formed a skiffle band, the Railroaders, with school friend Bruce Welch, and they travelled to London in 1958 to compete, unsuccessfully, in a talent contest. Welch and Marvin opted to remain in London and gravitated to the legendary 2i's coffee bar, where they were recruited to play in the Drifters, the backing band for singer Cliff Richard.

In addition to working with Richard, the band recorded in its own right. After a change of name to the Shadows, their fourth single, 'Apache', reached No. 1 in 1960, the first of a string of instrumental hits characterized by Marvin's echoing

Essential Recordings

1961 The Shadows:
The Shadows

1973 The Shadows:
Rocking With Curly Leads

1979 The Shadows:
String Of Hits

2002 Solo:
Guitar Player

lead lines and manipulation of the tremolo arm. He was the first British guitarist to play a **Fender Stratocaster** (owned by Cliff Richard) and did so much to popularize the model that in 1961, the company supplied the group with matching red fiesta **Stratocasters**. Richard and the Shadows' combined output dominated the British pop charts in the period immediately prior to the Beatles, and while the Shadows survived the arrival of Merseybeat, their popularity began to wane in the mid-1960s.

After the Shadows split up in 1968, Marvin made a self-titled solo album in 1969, and then formed the vocal-harmony trio Marvin, Welch & Farrar, which developed into a revived version of the Shadows. The new line-up's debut, *Rocking With Curly Leads* (1973), saw Marvin experimenting with a vocoder. By the 1980s, the Shadows' output consisted mainly of cover versions. In 1990, Marvin resumed his occasional solo career, and the Shadows reunited for a farewell tour in 2004-05.

Marvin is a melodic guitarist and a tunesmith whose approach remained consistent throughout his career. In addition to his **Fender Stratocaster**, he worked with **Burns of London** to develop his signature brand, the **Burns Marvin**, which he played from 1964 until the Shadows' final tour. Marvin inspired countless guitarists, including Pete Townshend, Neil Young, Carlos Santana, Jeff Beck and Mark Knopfler.

Gary Moore
SKID ROW TO SOLO

Blues and hard-rock guitarist Gary Moore was born in Belfast, Northern Ireland in 1952. He began playing the acoustic guitar at the age of eight, acquiring his first electric model at 14. Moore learned to play right-handed, despite being naturally left-handed. In 1969, he joined Skid Row, an Irish blues-rock group that featured Phil Lynott on vocals. When the latter was sacked, Moore took over as singer of the slimmed-down power trio.

Skid Row supported Fleetwood Mac, then featuring Peter Green, who was a massive influence on the young guitarist. With Green's help, the band signed a contract with CBS, releasing two albums that were very influential on Irish rock, before Moore left in 1971. His debut album *Grinding Stone* (1973) was credited to the Gary Moore Band, but his initial solo career was short-lived, as he was reunited with Phil Lynott, replacing Eric Bell as Thin Lizzy's lead guitarist for a short spell. Moore returned to the band briefly in both 1976 and 1978. In between, he was a member of Colosseum II, the second version of the British jazz-fusion band that featured a heavier sound than its original incarnation, largely because of Moore's guitar work.

Essential Recordings

1973	The Gary Moore Band: *Grinding Stone*
1979	Thin Lizzy: *Black Rose: A Rock Legend*
1987	Solo: *Wild Frontier*
1990	Solo: *Still Got The Blues*

With a little help from Lynott on vocals, Moore's solo career resumed in 1979, when his distinctive bluesy, wailing guitar graced the singles chart on 'Parisienne Walkways'. The pair charted again with the heavier 'Out In The Fields' in 1985. The 1980s saw him concentrating on rock, but he returned to his first love on *Still Got The Blues* (1990). After some puzzling experiments with dance beats, he went back to basics once more on *Back To The Blues* (2001), following which he released *Close As You Get* (2007) and his final album, *Bad For You Baby* (2008). Moore died in his sleep from a heart attack in February 2011.

Of the many guitars that he used in his lengthy career, Moore was probably most attached to the **Gibson Les Paul** that he bought from his mentor Peter Green when the latter quit the music business.

His fondness for **Gibson** guitars was recognized by the company when he became one of the first artists to have a signature model. Moore also played the **Fender Stratocaster** and guitars by **Charvel**, **Paul Reed Smith** and **Ibanez**.

Playlists | Links ebooks & more
FlameTreeRock.com

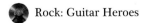
Scotty Moore
LEADING THE FIELD

The original rock'n'roll lead guitarist, Scotty Moore (1931–2016) was born near Gadsden, Tennessee. Moore began playing guitar at the age of eight, largely self-taught. Although he aspired to playing jazz like Barney Kessel and Tal Farlow, he was also influenced by country guitarists like Merle Travis and, in particular, Chet Atkins.

After Navy service, Moore formed a hillbilly group, the Starlite Wranglers, in 1952, with Bill Black on upright bass. After Moore struck up a rapport with Sam Phillips, the proprietor of Sun Records, Phillips suggested that Moore and Black accompany his protégé, Elvis Presley. Initially, the sessions were unproductive, until the trio began playing 'That's All Right (Mama)', which captured the chemistry between them and became Presley's first single in 1954.

Moore and Black, along with drummer D.J. Fontana, backed Elvis on his greatest records. Before Chuck Berry and Bo Diddley, Moore fused various strands of American music to create the language of rock'n'roll lead guitar, establishing it as the main instrument and inspiring countless guitarists. His style was clean, simple and economical, primarily at the insistence of Sam Phillips. Moore favoured **Gibson** guitars, using the semi-acoustic **ES-295** on early Sun recordings with Presley, and switching in 1955 to an **L5** and later to a **Super 400 CES**.

Essential Recordings

1956	Elvis Presley: *Elvis Presley*
1956	Elvis Presley: *Elvis*
1964	Solo: *The Guitar That Changed The World*
1976	Elvis Presley *The Sun Sessions*

Moore continued to back Elvis until 1958. He made his only solo album, the all-instrumental *The Guitar That Changed The World* (1964), and worked with Presley again during the 1960s, appearing with the singer for the last time in the ''68 Comeback Special' television performance. Afterwards, Scotty virtually retired from playing for 23 years, founding his own recording studio in Memphis. He was reunited with D.J. Fontana on *All The King's Men* (1997), an all-star celebration of Elvis's music.

Moore spent most of his last 10 years performing tribute shows with disciples such as Eric Clapton and Mark Knopfler, and accepting awards for his legendary contribution to rock'n'roll. He was inducted into the Rock and Roll Hall of Fame in 2009. He died in 2016, aged 84, in Nashville, Tennessee.

Playlists | Links
ebooks & more

FlameTreeRock.com

Martin Pugh
STEAMHAMMER
ARMAGEDDON

Martin Pugh grew up in England during the 1960s and 1970s. As a young musician influenced by rock'n'roll, Pugh developed his progressive, blues-and-folk-influenced style with his first band, known as the Package Deal, who performed in Devon and Cornwall in the early 1960s. Martin soon moved to London and joined Carl Douglas ('Kung Fu Fighting') and the Big Stampede for a year, before joining Steamhammer, the blues-rock band from Worthing, England founded in 1968 by Martin Quittenton (guitar) and Kieran White (vocals, guitar, harmonica).

Pugh remained with Steamhammer through five years and four albums. Their debut album, **Steamhammer**, was released in 1969 and yielded a minor hit record in Europe, 'Junior's Wailing'. While the album was not commercially successful, the band's sound became popular live, especially in West Germany. The second version of the band recorded the album **Mk II**, released in 1969. Blues-guitar legend Freddie King invited Steamhammer to back him on two tours in Britain. Martin cited King as an enormous influence on his own sound: raw, wailing tones that come from creative improvisation, intuition and aggressive finger attack. During this period, Rod Stewart came to watch Steamhammer at a London club and hired Martin to handle lead-guitar work, along with Quittenton, who cowrote 'Maggie May' and 'You Wear It Well' on Stewart's first solo record, **An Old Raincoat Won't Ever Let You Down** (US: **The Rod Stewart Album**, 1969).

Steamhammer's final album, **Speech** (1972), was produced by ex-Yardbird and Renaissance frontman, Keith Relf. After Steamhammer's break-up, Pugh and Relf formed Armageddon with bassist Louis Cennamo (also formerly of Renaissance and Steamhammer). The band's debut album was released in 1974 to favourable reviews and significant airplay, but Relf's sudden death dissolved the band. Pugh, disenchanted with changes in the music business, settled down in the rustic town of Three Rivers in central California, with his wife and two daughters. Since that time, Pugh has immersed himself in American blues, making electric guitars and working on his original music.

Essential Recordings

1969	Steamhammer: *Steamhammer*
1969	Steamhammer: *Mk II*
1969	Rod Stewart: *An Old Raincoat Won't Ever Let You Down*
1975	Armageddon: *Armageddon*

Bonnie Raitt
COUNTRY BLUES CLASS

Blue-eyed soul and country guitarist and singer-songwriter Bonnie Raitt was born in Burbank, California in 1949, the daughter of Broadway vocalist John Raitt and pianist-singer Marge Goddard. At the age of eight, she was given a Stella guitar as a Christmas present, which her parents insisted she play at family gatherings. Raitt became a devotee of blues and folk music at 14 upon hearing an album recorded at the Newport Blues Festival.

Essential Recordings

1977 Solo:
Sweet Forgiveness

1989 Solo:
Nick Of Time

1991 Solo:
Luck Of The Draw

1994 Solo:
*Longing In
Their Hearts*

She began studying at Harvard in 1967 and started to play clubs and coffee houses in the Boston area, supporting blues legends like Muddy Waters, Son House and John Lee Hooker. Leaving college for a full-time career in music, she was opening for Mississippi Fred McDowell in New York in 1970 when word began to spread of her talents, which led to a recording contract with Warner. Her debut album, *Bonnie Raitt* (1971), mixed covers of blues standards with Bonnie's own material. Subsequent albums matched its critical acclaim, but sold in modest quantities until she achieved a breakthrough with 'Runaway' from *Sweet Forgiveness* (1977). Her momentum stalled, however, and she was dropped by Warner in 1983.

Without a record contract for much of the 1980s, Bonnie was struggling with alcohol and drugs, but kept touring and remained politically active, singing on the anti-apartheid song 'Sun City' and appearing at Amnesty International benefit concerts. After signing to Capitol in 1989, Bonnie finally achieved commercial success with three chart-topping albums: *Nick Of Time* (1989), *Luck Of The Draw* (1991), and *Longing In Their Hearts* (1994), which earned her an armful of Grammy Awards. Raitt was inducted into the Rock and Roll Hall of Fame in 2000. Since then, she has mixed recording and performing with political activism. *Silver Lining* was released in 2002, *Souls Alike* in 2005 and *Slipstream* in 2012.

Since 1969, Bonnie has used her **Fender Stratocaster** at every gig, backed up by her signature-model **Stratocasters**, to avoid constant retuning. She also has a **Gibson ES-175** and a **Guild F-50**. Bonnie likes to adapt her playing style to suit each song.

Francis Rossi & Rick Parfitt
MORE THAN THE STATUS QUO

The twin-guitar partnership of Francis Rossi (b. 1949) and Rick Parfitt (1948–2016) was at the heart of Status Quo from 1967. Francis Rossi (originally known as Mike) was born in Forest Hill, London. He formed the band that evolved into Status Quo with bassist Alan Lancaster while at school in 1962. Rick Parfitt, born Richard Harrison in Woking, Surrey, was playing in the Highlights on the same bill as Quo at Butlin's, Minehead in 1965 when he first encountered Rossi.

The pair struck up a friendship and Parfitt was invited to join Status Quo as rhythm guitarist to Rossi's lead shortly before the fashionably psychedelic 'Pictures Of Matchstick Men' became their first British (and only American) hit early in 1968. Two years later, the single 'Down The Dustpipe' heralded an abrupt change of direction and third album *Ma Kelly's Greasy Spoon* (1970) confirmed that Quo had swapped psychedelia for 12-bar boogie, taking their lead from the Doors' 'Roadhouse Blues'.

As the 1970s progressed, Quo honed their accessible hard rock, finding mainstream acceptance via a string of hit singles and well-received albums. The image of Rossi and Parfitt, long-haired, clad in denims and plimsolls, legs astride and heads down hammering out three-chord crowd-pleasers like 'Caroline' is as iconic as any in rock'n'roll. Both have long been associated with the **Fender Telecaster** – Rossi has played his green 1957 model since 1968, whilst Parfitt's favoured white guitar hailed from 1965.

Shortly before famously opening Live Aid in London with 'Rockin' All Over The World' in July 1985, Quo had apparently retired, but the Wembley gig proved the catalyst for re-formation and the band remained active. Although singles like 'Living On An Island' and 'In The Army Now' amply demonstrated their versatility, Rossi and Parfitt relished playing up to the cartoon image of Quo, as the title of their 2007 album, *In Search Of The Fourth Chord*, attests. However, the rock and roll lifestyle was catching up with Parfitt, who suffered the first of a number of heart attacks in 1997. He died on Christmas Eve 2016 in a hospital in Marbella, Spain, of sepsis caused by an infected shoulder injury. Rossi and Parfitt were awarded the OBE in the New Year Honours 2010 for their services to music.

Essential Recordings

1970	Status Quo: *Ma Kelly's Greasy Spoon*
1973	Status Quo: *Hello!*
1976	Status Quo: *Blue For You*
1982	Status Quo: *1+9+8+2*

Neal Schon
JOURNEY'S SOUL

Rock and jazz guitarist Neal Schon, son of a jazz saxophonist and composer, was born in Oklahoma in 1954. A precocious talent, he learned guitar at the age of 10 and joined Santana at 15, turning down an invitation to join Eric Clapton in Derek and the Dominos. Schon made two albums with the band, *Santana III* (1971), on which he was credited as co-producer, and *Caravanserai* (1972), a departure into jazz fusion. In 1972, he played with Azteca, a Latin jazz-rock fusion ensemble that onstage consisted of up to 25 members.

Essential Recordings

1971 Santana:
       Santana

1981 Journey:
       Escape

1989 Bad English:
       Bad English

1996 Journey:
       Trial By Fire

In 1973, Schon formed Journey with former Santana band member Greg Rolie on keyboards and vocals. The band was originally intended to serve as a back-up outfit for musicians in the San Francisco area, but this notion was quickly abandoned and Journey made their first live appearance at the city's Winterland Ballroom. Signed to Columbia Records, the debut album *Journey* (1975), the follow-up *Look Into The Future* (1976) and *Next* (1977) were all firmly in the jazz-rock mould, featuring long tracks and lengthy instrumental workouts. The albums sold poorly, prompting a change in direction on *Infinity* (1978) to a pomp-rock sound similar to Boston and Foreigner.

This marked the start of a run of success for Journey that would bring them to a whole new audience, peaking with their bestselling work *Escape* (1981). Schon also recorded two albums with keyboardist Jan Hammer in 1981 and 1982, and has issued sporadic solo recordings since, the most of recent of which, *So U*, was released in 2014. After Journey split, he joined forces with former Babys singer John Waite to form Bad English in 1988. Journey reunited in 1995 and released *Trial By Fire* in 1996, followed by *Arrival* (2001), *Generations* (2005), *Revelation* (2008) and *Eclipse* (2011).

Schon was inspired by bluesman B.B. King and jazz-fusionist Al Di Meola. His first guitar was an acoustic **Stella**, followed by a **Gibson ES-355**, and a **Les Paul Goldtop**. He currently uses **Gibson** guitars, and the company produced a limited-edition signature-model **Les Paul**. In the 1980s, he inaugurated his own brand, the **Schon**, manufactured by **Jackson Guitars** and later **Larrivee**. Schon suffers from tinnitus after many years of playing live.

Mick Taylor
BLUESBREAKING STONE

Blues-rock guitarist Mick Taylor was born in Hatfield, Hertfordshire in 1949. A guitarist from the age of nine, he was in his teens when he formed a group with some school friends that subsequently evolved into the Gods. Taylor made two singles with the band. When Eric Clapton failed to turn up for a Bluesbreakers gig in Welwyn Garden City, the 16-year-old Taylor stood in for Clapton for the second half of the set. When Peter Green left the Bluesbreakers in 1967, John Mayall signed Taylor as his replacement.

He became known for a style that is based on the blues with overtones of Latin and jazz. His reputation as a slide guitarist was second to none. These attributes made him ideally qualified to replace Brian Jones in the Rolling Stones. Under the impression he was doing session work, Taylor attended a Stones recording, soon realizing that he was auditioning. He contributed to 'Country Honk' and 'Live With Me' from **Let It Bleed** (1969) and was hired. His live debut was the free Hyde Park concert in 1969. On Taylor's first full album with the Stones, **Sticky Fingers** (1971), he worked with Mick Jagger on 'Moonlight Mile' and 'Sway' when Keith Richards was absent from the studio. The classic **Exile On Main Street** (1972) featured Taylor and Richards' guitar interplay at its peak. He left the Stones in 1974, frustrated at not receiving songwriting credits and convinced that the band was about to collapse.

Regarded as one of the finest guitarists in the world, Taylor was expected to pursue a high-profile solo career, but instead he joined Jack Bruce's band Cream. His first solo work was the largely overlooked blues and jazz-tinged album **Mick Taylor** (1978). He spent much of the 1980s battling heroin addiction, a legacy from his time in the Stones, and he guested for Bob Dylan and Mark Knopfler. A second solo album, **A Stone's Throw**, was released in 2000, and he has since toured with John Mayall, Stephen Dale Petit and the Rolling Stones.

Taylor is usually associated with the **Gibson Les Paul**. He used a **Gibson ES-355** for the recording of *Sticky Fingers* and *Exile On Main Street*, a **Gibson SG** on tour and, on occasion, a **Fender Stratocaster** and **Telecaster**.

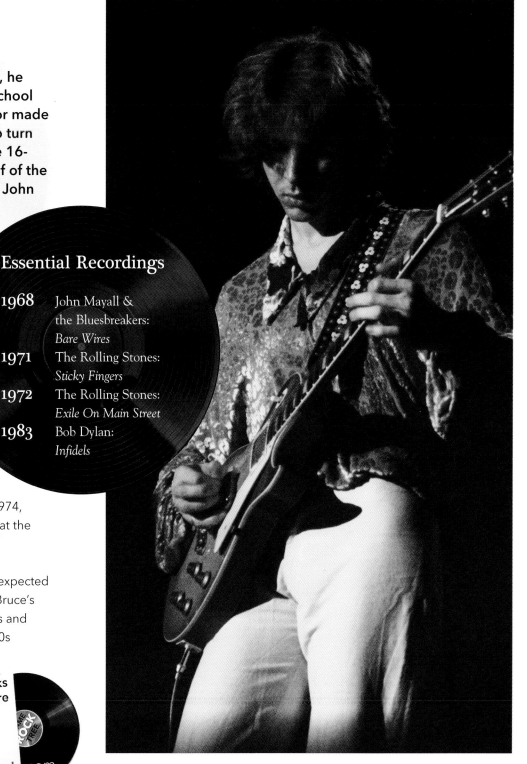

Essential Recordings

1968	John Mayall & the Bluesbreakers: *Bare Wires*
1971	The Rolling Stones: *Sticky Fingers*
1972	The Rolling Stones: *Exile On Main Street*
1983	Bob Dylan: *Infidels*

Playlists | Links ebooks & more
FlameTreeRock.com

Derek Trucks
SLIDE SENSATION

Derek Trucks was born in Jacksonville, Florida in 1979. Trucks bought his first guitar at a yard sale for $5 at age nine and became a child prodigy, playing his first paid performance at age 11. Trucks began playing the guitar using a 'slide' bar because it allowed him to play the guitar with his small hands. By his thirteenth birthday, Trucks had played alongside Buddy Guy and gone on tour with Thunderhawk. Trucks formed the Derek Trucks Band in 1996, and by the time he was 20, he had played with such artists as Bob Dylan, Joe Walsh and Stephen Stills.

Essential Recordings

2003 The Allman Brothers Band: *Hittin' The Note*

2006 J.J. Cale & Eric Clapton: *The Road To Escondido*

2009 Derek Trucks Band: *Already Free*

2011 Tedeschi Trucks Band: *Revelator*

Trucks credits guitarist Duane Allman and bluesman Elmore James as the two slide guitarists who influenced his early style. He was inspired by blues greats John Lee Hooker, Howlin' Wolf, Freddie King, B.B. King and Albert King, as well as the jazz players Miles Davis, Sun Ra, John Coltrane, Charlie Parker, Django Reinhardt, Charlie Christian and Wayne Shorter.

After performing with the Allman Brothers Band for several years as a guest musician, Trucks became a formal member in 1999 and appeared on the albums **Live At The Beacon Theater** and **Hittin' The Note** (both 2003). In 2006, Trucks began a studio collaboration with J.J. Cale and Eric Clapton called **The Road To Escondido** and that year performed with three bands in 17 different countries. Trucks was invited to perform at the 2007 Crossroads Guitar Festival, and after the festival, he toured as part of Clapton's band.

Trucks built a studio in his home in January 2008, and he and his band recorded the album **Already Free** (2009). Trucks and his wife, guitarist Susan Tedeschi, combined their bands to form the Soul Stew Revival in 2007 and performed at the Bonnaroo Music Festival in June 2008. In late 2009, Trucks and his band went on hiatus and then dissolved. In 2010, Trucks formed the Tedeschi Trucks Band with his wife. That same year, The Derek Trucks Band won the Grammy Award for Best

Contemporary Blues Album for **Already Free**. In 2012, the Tedeschi Trucks Band won the Grammy Award for Best Blues Album for the band's debut album **Revelator**.

On 12 February 2012, Trucks accepted a Grammy Lifetime Achievement Award, along with 10 other members of The Allman Brothers Band. On 8 January 2014, Trucks announced that he and fellow guitarist Warren Haynes planned to leave the Allman Brothers Band at the end of that year.

Playlists | Links ebooks & more

FlameTreeRock.com

Ike Turner
THE RHYTHM KING

Rock'n'roll pioneer Ike Turner was born in Clarksdale, Mississippi in November 1931. He displayed an early interest in music while working for a local radio station. He was taught to play boogie-woogie piano by one of his idols, blues musician Pinetop Perkins. Inspired by other bluesmen like Howlin' Wolf, Sonny Boy Williamson II, Muddy Waters and Elmore James, he took up the guitar. Turner formed the Rhythm Kings in the late 1940s, and in 1951, they made what many consider to be the first rock'n'roll record, 'Rocket 88', credited on the label to Jackie Brenston (the band's singer) and his Delta Cats. Produced by Sam Phillips at Sun Studios, the single contained the first recorded example of distorted guitar, caused by Ike's faulty amp.

The Rhythm Kings relocated to St Louis, where Turner acted as an A&R man for local independent record companies and played guitar with many of his blues heroes. It was here that Turner established a reputation as a hard-hitting guitarist who used the whammy bar of his **Fender Stratocaster** to good effect. In 1957, during a Kings of Rhythm 'open mic' spot, a teenage girl, Anna Mae Bullock, so impressed Turner that he recruited her as a backing singer. Renamed Tina, she soon became lead vocalist and, within a year, Turner's wife (although he later questioned the validity of the Mexican ceremony). The Rhythm Kings morphed into the Ike & Tina Turner Revue. As simply Ike & Tina Turner, they created an explosive live act that was never adequately captured on vinyl. Their magnum opus 'River Deep, Mountain High' (in which Turner did not participate) failed in the States, and after 1973's **Nutbush City Limits**, their star began to wane.

After many years of physical and mental abuse, Tina walked out mid-tour in 1976. Turner continued to work, but after Tina's 1980s comeback, her autobiography cast him in the role of wife-beating villain. In 1989, he was imprisoned on drugs charges. On his release in 1993, Turner returned to touring and recording, slowly attempting to repair his tarnished reputation, and appeared on the Gorillaz album **Demon Days** (2005). He died in December 2007 of a cocaine overdose.

Essential Recordings

1951	Jackie Brenston and his Delta Cats: *Rocket 88*
1961	with Tina Turner: *The Soul Of Ike And Tina Turner*
1966	with Tina Turner: *River Deep, Mountain High*
1971	with Tina Turner: *Workin' Together*

Stevie Ray Vaughan
REVIVING THE BLUES

Exploding on to a generally lethargic blues scene in 1983 with his *Texas Flood* album, Stevie Ray Vaughan, born in Texas in 1954, administered a high-voltage charge that revitalized the blues with his stunning playing and imagination. He took inspiration from Jimi Hendrix, Buddy Guy, Howlin' Wolf and Albert King, but it was the wild style of 1950s blues-rocker Lonnie Mack that gave him his aggressive swagger.

Essential Recordings

1983   David Bowie:
Let's Dance

1983   with Double Trouble:
Texas Flood

1984   with Double Trouble:
*Couldn't Stand
The Weather*

1985   with Double Trouble:
Soul To Soul

It was Vaughan's older brother Jimmie who introduced him to the blues, and when Jimmie left their home in Dallas, Texas to form the Fabulous Thunderbirds in Austin, Stevie followed him. In 1975, he cofounded Triple Threat with singer Lou Ann Barton, and when the band broke up three years later Vaughan took over the vocals and brought in bassist Tommy Shannon to join drummer Chris Layton, renaming the trio Double Trouble.

The band's reputation gradually spread, and in 1982, they played the Montreux Jazz Festival, attracting the attention of David Bowie, who recruited Vaughan to play on **Let's Dance** (1983), and Jackson Browne, who offered his studio for recording. *Texas Flood* (1983), recorded in three days, revelled in Vaughan's influences while also spotlighting his own compositions. ***Couldn't Stand The Weather*** (1984) confirmed Vaughan's promise, and for ***Soul To Soul*** (1985), he added keyboard player Reese Wynans to the band.

Vaughan also recorded with Albert King, Johnny Copeland and Lonnie Mack, but his health suffered due to drug abuse, and in 1986, he collapsed during a European tour. He resumed touring in 1988, and ***In Step*** (1989) showed renewed vigour and commitment, winning a Grammy for Best Contemporary Blues Album.

In 1990, Vaughan recorded another Grammy-winning album with his brother Jimmie, *Family Style*, but before its release, he was killed in a helicopter crash returning from a concert in Wisconsin. He was inducted into the Blues Hall of Fame in 2000.

Vaughan generally played **Fender Stratocasters**, and **Fender** has released two tribute models, the **Stevie Ray Vaughan Signature Stratocaster** in 1992 and in 2007, the **Lenny**. He also played a **Hamiltone Custom** guitar and a semi-hollow **Groove Master**.

Johnny Winter
BLUES DEVOTION

Blues guitarist Johnny Winter (1944–2014) was born in Beaumont, Texas. Albino and cross-eyed from birth, Johnny showed a precocious talent for music, taking up the clarinet at the age of five and switching to guitar after a brief flirtation with the ukulele. Inspired by bluesmen like B.B. King, Muddy Waters and Bobby Bland, he formed his first group, Johnny & The Jammers, with brother Edgar. Winter went on to play in several blues bands during the mid- to late 1960s. His break came in 1969 when an album he had recorded as part of a trio came to the attention of two *Rolling Stone* journalists who raved about it in the magazine, leading to its release as *Johnny Winter* (1969) on CBS.

Hailed as the new superstar blues guitarist, Winter played the Woodstock Festival in August 1969. His third album, ***Johnny Winter And*** (1970), confirmed his success and featured the song that became his signature tune, Rick Derringer's 'Rock'n'Roll Hoochie Koo'. Derringer was added to the band on second guitar as a foil for Johnny on ***Live Johnny Winter And*** (1971), a milestone in hard-rocking blues. Suffering from drug addiction and depression, Winter took a break, returning for ***Still Alive And Well*** (1973). He produced two albums for Muddy Waters, ***Hard Again*** (1977) and Waters' final work ***King Bee*** (1980). His own ***Nothin' But The Blues*** (1977) was made with members of Waters' touring band.

Essential Recordings

1969	Solo: *Johnny Winter*
1970	Solo: *Johnny Winter And*
1971	Solo: *Live Johnny Winter And*
1977	Solo: *Nothin' But The Blues*

Renowned for his fiery style, Winter used various guitars. In his early days, he played a **Gibson ES-125**, but switched to an **SG** for Woodstock, although his first album was made with a **Fender Mustang**. His early slide work was done on a **National Steel Standard**, but for *Live Johnny Winter And*, he used a **Gibson Firebird**. For the next phase of his career, an **Erlewine Lazer** was his primary guitar. Johnny has also played an **Epiphone Wiltshire** extensively. Still touring despite health problems (he could only play while sitting), Winter concentrated on the blues. A new studio album, *Roots*, was released in 2011 and featured a range of guest artists. He died in a hotel near Zurich, Switzerland, in July 2014, two days after playing the Cahors Blues Festival in France. The cause was believed to be emphysema and pneumonia.

Playlists | Links ebooks & more

FlameTreeRock.com

I think heavy metal is therapeutic – it's music that blows the tension away.

Kirk Hammett

Hard Rock
& Metal

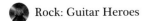

Jason Becker
A TRUE HERO

Jason Becker, born in 1969, is an American neo-classical metal guitarist and composer whose steady rise to the top of the guitar world was cut short by illness. Becker was born and raised in Richmond, California. In high school, he performed Yngwie Malmsteen's 'Black Star' with his band at a talent show. At 16, he formed Cacophony with his friend Marty Friedman. Produced by Mike Varney, the duo released *Speed Metal Symphony* in 1987 and *Go Off!* in 1988, touring the US and Japan in support. By 1989, Becker was a solo act, having recorded *Perpetual Burn* on his own in 1988.

Essential Recordings

1987   Cacophony:
        Speed Metal Symphony
1988   Solo:
        Perpetual Burn
1991   David Lee Roth:
        A Little Ain't Enough
1996   Solo:
        Perspective

At the peak of his abilities, Becker was known as a shredder with exceptional technique who demonstrated his mastery at clinics. He studied the works of violinist Niccolò Paganini, arranging the composer's **Fifth Caprice**, and performing it in an instructional guitar video. Becker's compositions feature high-speed scalar and arpeggio passages.

At 20, Becker replaced Steve Vai in David Lee Roth's band. While recording **A Little Ain't Enough** in 1989 and preparing for a tour, Becker began to feel limpness in his left leg. He was diagnosed with Amyotrophic Lateral Sclerosis (Lou Gehrig's Disease) and given a grim prognosis. Becker finished the album, but quickly lost the ability to perform onstage. As the disease progressed, Becker turned to composing, using a keyboard after he was unable to use both hands, and controlling a computer system – eventually with his eyes – as his mental acuity remained unaffected by the disease.

In 1996, Becker released **Perspective**, an instrumental album composed by him (with the exception of Bob Dylan's song 'Meet Me In The Morning'). The writing of the music had begun before ALS completely crippled his abilities. Later, Becker released **Raspberry Jams** (1999) and **Blackberry Jams** (2003), collections of demos and alternative versions of songs that were later reworked and released on his albums. Two tribute

albums, **Warmth In The Wilderness** (I and II), featuring guitarists Steve Vai, Paul Gilbert, Marty Friedman and others, have been released, with profits aiding Becker with his medical expenses. Becker's **Collection** (2008) featured three new songs as well as previously unreleased material, while **Boy Meets Guitar: Volume One Of The Youngster Tapes** (2012) contains some of Becker's home recordings from his teenage years.

Playlists | Links
ebooks & more
FlameTreeRock.com

Nuno Bettencourt
EXTREME GUITAR STAR

As a guitarist and songwriter, Nuno Bettencourt draws from many styles and influences. Born in the Portuguese archipelago of the Azores in 1966, Bettencourt grew up in Boston, Massachusetts. As a teenager, he began playing drums, bass and keyboards, but ultimately chose guitar as his primary instrument, drawing heavy influence from Eddie Van Halen as well as the Beatles, Led Zeppelin and Queen.

Bettencourt joined Extreme in 1985, and the band released its self-titled debut album in 1989. In 1991, the band released **Pornograffitti**, which included the acoustic hits 'More Than Words' and 'Hole Hearted'. But it was the extraordinary technical prowess Bettencourt displayed on such tunes as 'Get The Funk Out' and 'He-Man Woman Hater' – from speed picking to string skipping to tapped arpeggios – that solidified him as one of the era's top guitarists. It was also during this time that **Washburn** guitars unveiled the **Nuno Bettencourt N4** signature-model guitar, a model that endures today.

After Extreme disbanded in 1996, Bettencourt released his solo debut, **Schizophonic** (1997), on which he played all the instruments. He next assembled a new group, Mourning Widows, which incorporated a variety of alternative-rock styles. The band released its self-titled debut CD in 1998, and followed up with **Furnished Souls For Rent**, which was released in Japan in 2000. In 2002, Bettencourt formed the recording entity Population 1, and released the self-titled and self-produced 2002 album, **Population 1**. **Sessions From Room 4** followed in 2004, and in 2005, the band changed its name to the DramaGods and released **Love**. In 2007, Bettencourt teamed up with singer Perry Farrell in Satellite Party, releasing **Ultra Payloaded** that same year, but departed soon after its release. He then rejoined Extreme and continues to tour with them today.

In addition, Bettencourt can be heard and seen on the Universal/Japan CD and DVD release of **Guitar Wars** (2004). He has also written, recorded and toured with several artists, including Tantric, BBMak, Toni Braxton, Wyclef Jean and Rhianna, among numerous others.

Essential Recordings

1991   Extreme:
       Pornograffitti
1997   Solo:
       Schizophonic
1998   Mourning Widows:
       Mourning Widows
2002   Population 1:
       Population 1

Ritchie Blackmore
RULER OF THE RIFF

His contemporaries Eric Clapton, Jimmy Page and Jeff Beck might receive more time in the spotlight, but guitarist Ritchie Blackmore has been similarly influential and innovative during his 40-plus-year career.

Born in Weston-Super-Mare, England, in April 1945, Blackmore was given his first guitar at the age of 11 and began taking classical lessons, an education that would later reveal itself in both his neoclassical rock leanings and his Renaissance work in Blackmore's Night. His early influences include rockers Hank Marvin and Cliff Gallup, as well as country legend Chet Atkins. In the mid-1960s, Blackmore began working as a session guitarist with legendary producer Joe Meek, appearing on tracks such as Heinz's Top 10 1963 hit 'Just Like Eddie'. In 1968, Blackmore joined forces with keyboardist Jon Lord and formed Deep Purple. Later that same year, the band released its first album, **Shades Of Deep Purple**. After a few more albums and a line-up change, Deep Purple released **Machine Head** (1972), which would become not only the band's high-water mark, but also one of the most influential hard-rock and heavy-metal albums of all time. The album contained their signature hit 'Smoke On The Water', which contains arguably the greatest – and most widely recognized – guitar riff ever written. Blackmore's solo in 'Highway Star', another standout track, is even more significant; with his fiery double-picked lines, Blackmore ushered in the neo-classical shred style of guitar playing.

Following **Machine Head**, Deep Purple's reign began to dissolve. Blackmore hooked up with Elf singer Ronnie James Dio and formed Rainbow in 1975. Their first album together, **Ritchie Blackmore's Rainbow** (1975), produced the iconic rock hit 'Man On The Silver Mountain'. In 1984, Blackmore rejoined Deep Purple, and released

Essential Recordings

1972	Deep Purple: *Machine Head*
1975	Rainbow: *Ritchie Blackmore's Rainbow*
1984	Deep Purple: *Perfect Strangers*
2013	Blackmore's Night: *Dancer and the Moon*

Perfect Strangers. The record produced major rock radio hits with both its title track and the rock anthem 'Knockin' At Your Back Door'.

In 1997, Blackmore formed Blackmore's Night, a primarily acoustic stew of Renaissance, folk, world and new-age music featuring lyricist and vocalist Candice Night. In 2016 he reformed Rainbow with none of the earlier members and played a **Greatest Hits** tour (also featuring Deep Purple classic) in Europe and the UK.

Playlists | Links
ebooks & more

FlameTreeRock.com

Vito Bratta
WHITE LION'S LEGEND

When 1980s hair-metal band White Lion released the video for their breakthrough hit 'Wait' in 1987, guitar fans saw arguably the second coming of Eddie Van Halen. Guitarist Vito Bratta brought forth tasty rhythm-guitar parts, masterly single-note technique, and above all, a two-hand tapping technique that, while in the style of Van Halen, found a new direction and thus provided Bratta with his own identity.

Born in Staten Island, New York in 1961, Bratta took up the guitar at the age of 12. Five years later, he heard Van Halen, and it changed his world for ever. Prior to joining White Lion, Bratta played in a New York band called Dreamer, where he earned the respectful nickname 'Vito Van Halen', for his own amazing tapping technique.

In 1983, Bratta teamed up with Danish singer Mike Tramp and formed White Lion, releasing their debut album, *Fight To Survive* (1985), on Grand Slamm Records. After several personnel changes in their rhythm section, the band signed a major-label deal with Atlantic Records in 1987 and released *Pride*. The single 'Wait' exploded on MTV, and White Lion was quickly thrust into the spotlight. But their biggest success would come more than a year after the album's release, when the tender acoustic ballad 'When The Children Cry' would take the band to the top of the hair-metal genre. For Bratta, the exposure brought well-deserved recognition for his instrumental prowess. He also received critical acclaim as a guitarist whose playing had substance and direction in an era of 'guitar wars' repetitiveness. He further set himself apart via his preference for a **Steinberger** guitar, while his contemporaries remained primarily in the **Charvel**, **B.C. Rich** and **Kramer** camps.

The band's follow-up album, *Big Game* (1989), while a commercial success, didn't measure up to the expectations set by *Pride*. They released one more album, *Mane Attraction*

Essential Recordings

1985	White Lion: *Fight To Survive*
1987	White Lion: *Pride*
1989	White Lion: *Big Game*
1991	White Lion: *Mane Attraction*

(1991). In 1995, Bratta decided to take a break from the instrument he had played every day since the age of 12, finally picking it up again in 1997, only to experience a wrist injury that would prevent him from playing again for several years. He has released no new music since 1992.

Dimebag Darrell
CUT OFF IN HIS PRIME

Despite a life cut tragically short by violence, Darrell Lance Abbott (1966-2004), known as 'Dimebag Darrell,' achieved stardom not only as a founding member of the bands Pantera and Damageplan, but also in death as an icon who succumbed onstage and carried his passions to the grave.

Darrell Abbott took up guitar when he was 12. He was a devoted fan of Black Sabbath and KISS. (He later had an autograph on his chest by KISS guitarist Ace Frehley tattooed in place.) Abbott formed Pantera in 1981 with his brother, drummer Vinnie Paul. Influenced by metal acts from Iron Maiden to Slayer, Pantera became a force in the subgenre 'groove' metal. Pantera scored with *Cowboys From Hell* in 1990 and cemented their reputation with *Vulgar Display Of Power* in 1992, as the band adopted

Essential Recordings

1990   Pantera:
        Cowboys From Hell
1992   Pantera:
        Vulgar Display Of Power
1994   Pantera:
        Far Beyond Driven
2004   Damageplan:
        New Found Power

a heavier vocal and guitar sound. However, by 2003, frictions with vocalist Phil Anselmo caused the group to split.

A year later, Dimebag and Vinnie formed Damageplan with guitarist Pat Lachman and Bob Zilla on bass, and released the hit album **New Found Power**. Throughout the runs of Pantera and Damageplan, Dimebag performed as a guest on multiple projects, including cuts for Nickelback, country singer David Allen Coe and the Dallas Stars hockey team. He was called 'the sixth member of Anthrax', because of his many guest appearances on the band's albums.

In 2004, Abbott was performing with Damageplan at a club in Columbus, Ohio. Nathan Gale, a paranoid schizophrenic, approached the stage and shot Abbott five times, killing him instantly, along with three others, and wounding seven more. Gale was shot and killed by police officer James Niggemeyer. Dimebag was buried in a KISS Kasket with Eddie Van Halen's **Charvel Hybrid VH2** – a black and yellow **Frankenstrat** guitar, known as 'Bumblebee', that was on the cover of **Van Halen II**.

Dimebag wrote a column for **Guitar World**, and three of his solos, 'Walk,' 'Cemetery Gates' and 'Floods', are ranked among the magazine's 100 Greatest Guitar Solos of all time.

Lita Ford
ROCKING RUNAWAY

Lita Rossana Ford (b. 1958) was born in London. After her family settled in Los Angeles in the 1960s, she took up guitar at the age of 11, inspired by Deep Purple's Ritchie Blackmore. When she was 16, she met novelty-music producer Kim Fowley, who helped recruit her, along with Joan Jett, Sandy West, Cherie Currie and Jackie Fox, for the all-girl rock band the Runaways.

Propelled by Ford's guitar and their unique image, the Runaways released their self-titled first album in 1976. Steady touring led to a string of sold-out shows and follow-up albums, with the band enjoying enormous popularity in Japan. After four albums and hits including 'Cherry Bomb', 'Hollywood' and 'Queens Of Noise', the band's factions split on musical direction, with Jett preferring the path of punk rockers like the Ramones and Blondie, while Ford and West wanted to continue with their hard rock/metal approach. The Runaways finally disbanded in 1979.

After the breakup, Ford's solo debut, **Out For Blood** (1983), was a commercial disappointment, but 1984's **Dancin' On The Edge** helped establish her with heavy-metal fans. The single 'Fire In My Heart' hit the Top 10 in several countries, and the follow-up, 'Gotta Let Go', reached No. 1 on mainstream rock charts. Ford's third album for Mercury, **The Bride Wore Black**, produced by Tony Iommi, was never released, and she kept busy touring until signing with RCA Records and manager Sharon Osbourne. In 1988, Ford released the self-produced **Lita**, which included the singles 'Kiss Me Deadly' and 'Back To The Cave'. The ballad 'Close My Eyes Forever', a duet with Ozzy Osbourne, reached No. 8 on the US **Billboard** Hot 100. After three minor follow-up albums in the 1990s, Ford began a hiatus from music to concentrate on raising her two sons.

Almost 15 years later, in 2009, she re-emerged with a new band behind her and released the album **Wicked Wonderland**. In 2012, Ford returned to her roots with **Living Like A Runaway**. Ford is featured extensively in the 2005 documentary film **Edgeplay: A Film About The Runaways**. In 2016 she released **Time Capsule**, a collection of songs she'd recorded in the 80s with Billy Sheehan, Gene Simmons, Rick Nielson and others.

Essential Recordings

1976	The Runaways: *The Runaways*
1984	Solo: *Dancin' On The Edge*
1988	Solo: *Lita*
2009	Solo: *Wicked Wonderland*

Playlists | Links ebooks & more
FlameTreeRock.com

Marty Friedman
SHREDDING SUPERSTAR

Many guitarists of the 'shred' variety unfortunately stick to scalar lines and diatonic arpeggios in straight major or minor keys. Marty Friedman (b. 1962) is not one of them. Indeed, Friedman's tendency towards Eastern, Middle Eastern and other ethnic sounds has distinguished him as one of the most musically gifted super-pickers the guitar world has ever seen.

Essential Recordings

1988   Solo:
Dragon's Kiss

1990   Megadeth:
Rust In Peace

1992   Megadeth:
Countdown To Extinction

1992   Solo:
Scenes

Martin Adam Friedman grew up in the Baltimore area. He began playing guitar at the age of 15, shortly before his family moved to Hawaii. While there, he played in several local bands and began seeking out Asian and Middle Eastern music to incorporate their exotic sounds into his own. His constant practising and unquenchable thirst for musical knowledge paid off in 1982, when he hooked up with Shrapnel Records. Five years later, working with fellow shredder Jason Becker, the duo recorded **Speed Metal Symphony** under the moniker Cacophony. It was a hit in the shred community, and Friedman's solo debut, **Dragon's Kiss**, followed a year later, in 1988.

The exposure, combined with Friedman's virtuosity, led to his joining thrash giants Megadeth in 1990. Their first album together, **Rust In Peace** (1990), is generally recognized as one of the most technically accomplished thrash albums in history. Friedman's fretboard explorations on such tracks as 'Holy Wars … The Punishment Due' and 'Tornado Of Souls' ably demonstrate how effective shred stylings can be when phrased appropriately. His second album with Megadeth, **Countdown To Extinction** (1992), further demonstrated the chemistry that had seemingly eluded singer/leader Dave Mustaine for most of his career, thanks largely to Friedman's fretwork.

Around this time, Friedman began to seek outlets for his non-metal, exotic compositions. He formed a partnership with new-age musician

Kitaro and released the Asian-themed instrumental record **Scenes** (1992). In the coming years, he released two other solo-guitar albums in the same vein, before recording his final album with Megadeth, **Risk**, in 1999. Since then, he has moved to Japan, where he regularly appears with various Japanese artists and continues to record exotic-rock instrumental guitar albums. In 2008, his eighth solo album, **Future Addict**, was released in Japan, featuring reworked versions of some of his past work. Other solo albums followed, with the most recent, **Wall of Sound**, released in 2017.

Playlists | Links ebooks & more

FlameTreeRock.com

Paul Gilbert
RACER X'S MR BIG

Too often, the music created by so-called 'shred' guitarists comes across as too cerebral and serious to elicit enjoyment from any but the most die-hard shred fan. Fortunately for all other fans of instrumental guitar, Paul Gilbert (b. 1966) prefers to dish out his hungry-man portions of notes with humour and irreverence matched only by his technical ferocity.

Gilbert first picked up the guitar at the age of five, but did not fully understand music until he was nine. In 1982, he sent a tape of his band Missing Lynx to Shrapnel Records' head Mike Varney, who, upon hearing it put Gilbert into his Spotlight column in *Guitar Player* magazine (Yngwie Malmsteen also appeared in that issue's column). In 1984, Gilbert moved to Hollywood, California, to attend the Guitar Institute of Technology, where he met the future members of Racer X. The band recorded their debut album, *Street Lethal*, in 1985, with such tracks as 'Y.R.O.' helping Gilbert quickly become one of the most talked-about guitarists on the scene. By the time they released their second album, *Second Heat* (1987), which featured the downright terrifying guitar instrumental 'Scarified', the band was selling out all the big clubs on the LA scene and Gilbert was being recognized as one of the most technically proficient guitarists of the 1980s.

Whereas Racer X was essentially one giant adrenaline rush, Gilbert's next band, Mr. Big, offered him the opportunity to stretch his songwriting wings, and the band's 1989 self-titled debut reached No. 46 on the *Billboard* Top 200 album chart. But it was 1991's *Lean Into It*, featuring the No. 1 acoustic ballad 'To Be With You', as well as 'Just Take My Heart' and 'Green-Tinted 1960s Mind', that brought Gilbert more widespread acclaim.

In 1997, Gilbert left Mr. Big to pursue a solo career. He has since released 10 studio albums, including the all-instrumental *Get Out Of My Yard* (2006). His signature-model **Ibanez PGM** guitars continue to be top-sellers, and his instructional videos, particularly *Intense*

Rock I and *Intense Rock II* are generally considered in the guitar-playing community to be among the best ever produced. In 2009, Gilbert reunited with the original Mr. Big band members Eric Martin, Billy Sheehan and Pat Torpey for a reunion world tour. In 2010, Gilbert released an instrumental album, *Fuzz Universe*.

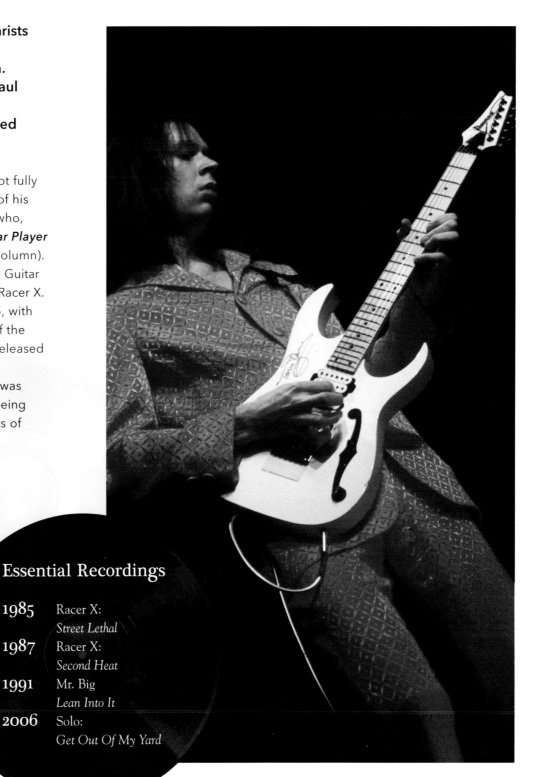

Essential Recordings

1985	Racer X: *Street Lethal*
1987	Racer X: *Second Heat*
1991	Mr. Big *Lean Into It*
2006	Solo: *Get Out Of My Yard*

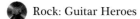

Kirk Hammett
METALLICA'S MASTER OF GUITAR

When singer-guitarist Dave Mustaine was dismissed from the original Metallica line-up, it opened the door for a young Bay Area-based guitarist named Kirk Hammett (b. 1962) to come in and lead the thrash-metal charge. What Hammett and his mates in Metallica would accomplish from that point, no one could have predicted.

Essential Recordings

1984   Metallica:
        Ride The Lightning
1986   Metallica:
        Master Of Puppets
1988   Metallica:
        … And Justice For All
1991   Metallica:
        Metallica

Born in San Francisco, California, Hammett benefited from his older brother's extensive hard-rock record collection, which included albums by Jimi Hendrix, Led Zeppelin and UFO. Inspired, Hammett picked up a **Montgomery Ward** catalogue guitar at the age of 15. He soon upgraded to a **1978 Fender Stratocaster**, and then a **1974 Gibson Flying V**, matching it to a **Marshall** amp. With his powerful new rig, the guitarist soon hooked up with vocalist Paul Baloff and formed Exodus. The pioneering thrash band would later support Metallica twice, in late 1982 and early 1983.

In the spring of 1983, after giving guitarist Mustaine the boot, Metallica called Hammett and invited him to audition in New York. He hopped on a flight, nailed the gig and before long was in the studio recording the band's debut, *Kill 'Em All* (1983). After the ensuing tour, Hammett began taking lessons from virtuoso Joe Satriani. His hard work paid off, and Hammett began to make a name for himself in the guitar community via his incendiary scalar lines in solos such as 'Fade To Black' from 1984's *Ride The Lightning*. Two years later, in 1986, the band released what many believe to be their magnum opus, *Master Of Puppets*.

In 1987, Hammett began an association with **ESP** guitars, becoming their biggest endorser. With his signature guitar in hand, Hammett

laid down some of his scariest lines to date on Metallica's 1988 release, *... And Justice For All*. But it was the band's 1991 self-titled release, the 'Black Album', that enshrined them as the reigning kings of metal. Ironically, while the band had achieved mass commercial success, Hammett's bluesier, wah-drenched soloing approach on this and later releases saw his stock among some in the guitar community drop. But as evident in his 2007 endorsement deal with **Randall** amplifiers and **ESP**'s limited-run twentieth anniversary **Kirk Hammett** model guitar, the Metallica guitarist maintains his relevance. In 2009, Metallica was inducted into the Rock and Roll Hall of Fame.

Tony Iommi
BLACK SABBATH'S IRON MAN

Frank Anthony Iommi (b. 1948) was born in Birmingham, England. Like so many other teenage boys in 1960s Britain, he was inspired to pick up the guitar upon hearing Hank Marvin and the Shadows. In 1967, after playing in various local acts, Iommi hooked up with three former school mates – Bill Ward (drums), Terry 'Geezer' Butler (bass) and John 'Ozzy' Osbourne – to form the blues-rock outfit Earth. But just as Iommi was set to begin a full-time music career, he suffered a horrific accident on the last day of his job at a sheet-metal factory, where a machine sliced the tips off his right hand's index and ring fingers. Crafting artificial fingertips from melted plastic bottle-tops covered with leather, the disciplined young guitarist persevered.

Earth later changed their name to Black Sabbath, and with it, a new, darker and heavier musical direction emerged. When the band entered the studio in 1970 to record their self-titled debut, Iommi, like his idol Marvin, was a dedicated **Fender Stratocaster** player. While recording the first track, one of his pickups blew, so he picked up a **Gibson SG** he had as a backup, and the iconic sight and sound of Iommi paired to an **SG** was born. When Sabbath released their landmark *Paranoid*, also in 1970, it was clear that heavy metal was here to stay, and the band's next three albums, *Master Of Reality* (1971), *Vol. 4* (1972) and *Sabbath Bloody Sabbath* (1973), cemented their position as the most influential heavy-metal band of all time. With such leaden yet glorious riffs as 'Black Sabbath', 'Paranoid', 'War Pigs', 'N.I.B.' and 'Iron Man', Iommi secured his place as the father of heavy-metal guitar.

Although Osbourne left the band to pursue a solo career in 1979, Iommi kept the Sabbath locomotor chugging with a rotating stable of singers. In late 1998, the original Black Sabbath line-up released *Reunion*, a live album that earned the band a second chance at the

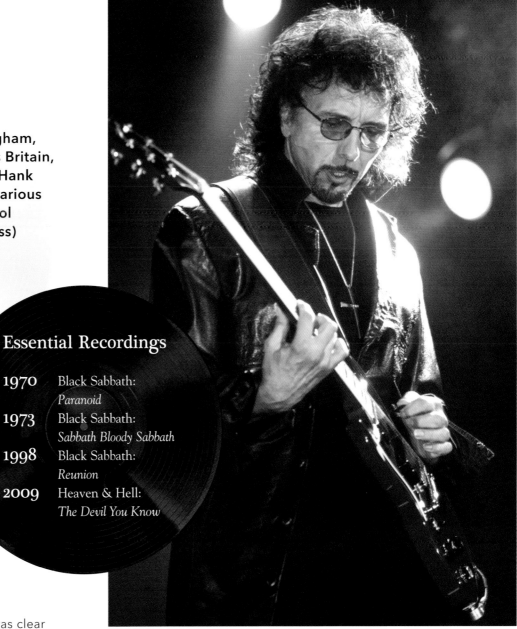

Essential Recordings

1970	Black Sabbath: *Paranoid*
1973	Black Sabbath: *Sabbath Bloody Sabbath*
1998	Black Sabbath: *Reunion*
2009	Heaven & Hell: *The Devil You Know*

spotlight. They headlined summer festivals several times in the 2000s, inspiring a new generation of metal fans and musicians to carry the heavy-metal torch.

In 2007, Iommi teamed up with Geezer Butler, Ronnie James Dio and Vinny Appice to form Heaven & Hell. They toured the US and UK in 2007 and released their first studio album, *The Devil You Know*, in 2009, but disbanded in 2010 following Dio's death. Iommi rejoined Black Sabbath in 2011.

Playlists | Links ebooks & more

FlameTreeRock.com

John 5
MODERN-DAY HERO

Guitar One magazine declared him a 'modern-day master of the Telecaster'. In the 2007 *Guitar World* readers' poll, his instrumental guitar tour de terror *The Devil Knows My Name* was named Best Shred Album of 2007. Also in 2007, he graced the covers of *Guitar Player* and *Guitarist* magazines, while in 2008, he was featured on the cover of *Guitar Edge* magazine, which proclaimed him one of the 'new guitar heroes'. Finally, it seems, guitarist John 5 (b. 1971) is shedding the cloak of 'underrated' for some hard-earned and long-overdue time in the spotlight.

Essential Recordings

1999 Marilyn Manson:
The Last Tour On Earth

2004 Solo:
Vertigo

2006 Rob Zombie:
Educated Horses

2007 Solo:
The Devil Knows My Name

John 5 was born John Lowery in July 1971 in Grosse Point, Michigan. He started playing guitar at the age of seven, inspired by the US country television show 'Hee Haw'. When he turned 18, John moved to California to pursue a career as a professional session guitarist. There, he met producer Bob Marlette and began working on a number of TV shows, commercials and film soundtracks.

After touring with Lita Ford and k.d. lang, and working on short-lived projects with drummer Randy Castillo and singer Rob Halford, John landed a gig with David Lee Roth's DLR Band. Shortly thereafter, shock-rocker Marilyn Manson invited John for lunch and hired him on the spot, christening him with his current 'John 5' moniker. John 5 would play with Manson until April 2004, at which time – at the urging of the legendary Les Paul – he set out to record his first solo album, *Vertigo* (2004).

With *Vertigo* and his subsequent release, *Songs For Sanity* (2005), John 5 revealed to his primarily metal fan base a multifaceted approach to guitar that included heavy bluegrass and country influences. That unusual musical pedigree created an underground buzz in the guitar community. Since then, a permanent gig with metal superstar Rob Zombie garnered John 5 even greater mass appeal. In 2007, John released an album of instrumental guitar music called ***The Devil Knows My Name***. Featuring guest appearances from the likes of Joe Satriani and Eric Johnson, it contains all the no-holds-barred shred essentials, but its injections of country and bluegrass phrasing, mixed with industrial and futuristic sounds, breaks the old mould and sets the twenty-first-century standard for instrumental guitar music. John 5 works on projects with various artists, including Rob Zombie, with whom he still tours. His eighth solo album, ***Season Of The Witch***, was released in 2017.

Playlists | Links ebooks & more

FlameTreeRock.com

Jake E. Lee
OZZY TO BADLANDS TO LEGEND

Jakey Lou Williams (b. 1957) was born in Norfolk, Virginia. His father was a member of the US Navy, which meant frequent relocation. Finally, however, the Williams family settled down in San Diego, California, where Jake began taking classical piano lessons. But, upon hearing his older sister's Jimi Hendrix, Led Zeppelin and Black Sabbath records, he soon turned to the guitar.

During high school, Jake formed a band called Teaser, with whom he would dominate the San Diego club scene. He next joined Stephen Pearcy's band Mickey Rat, which moved to Los Angeles and changed its name to Ratt. After developing a huge following on the LA scene, Lee decided to leave the band. After a few gigs with Rough Cutt and abbreviated writing sessions with the great metal singer Ronnie James Dio, singer Ozzy Osbourne asked him to audition for the lead guitarist spot made available by the tragic death of Randy Rhoads. Brimming with confidence, Lee gave it a shot and was chosen from 500 other guitarists to stand at Ozzy's side onstage and in the studio for the next four years.

Lee's first record with Ozzy was 1983's *Bark At The Moon*. Knowing his worthiness to fit Rhoads' sizeable shoes would be questioned, Lee ensured that his playing shone bright on the record, particularly on the title track. *The Ultimate Sin* (1986) followed and, anchored by the MTV video hit 'Shot In The Dark', peaked at No. 1 on the album charts. Despite the album's success, Osbourne was in the midst of a drug and alcohol funk, and, in one of his frequent rages, he fired Lee.

Lee hooked up with ex-Black Sabbath singer Ray Gillen in 1989 to form the blues-metal outfit Badlands. Their self-titled debut received critical acclaim but weak public support. Their follow-up, *Voodoo Highway* (1991), again earned critical raves. Since Badlands, Lee has been invited to play on several compilation and tribute albums.

He has also released solo albums *A Fine Pink Mist* (1996), *Retraced* (2005), *Guitar Warrior* (2007) and *Running With The Devil* (2008). His new band, Red Dragon Cartel, released their eponymous debut album in January 2014.

Essential Recordings

1983	Ozzy Osbourne: *Bark At The Moon*
1991	Badlands: *Voodoo Highway*
1996	Solo: *A Fine Pink Mist*
2014	Red Dragon Cartel: *Red Dragon Cartel*

Alex Lifeson
RUSH TO ROCK LEGEND

For over 30 years, guitarist Alex Lifeson has quietly served as the cohesive key to success for progressive rockers Rush – arguably the most enduring and successful hard-rock band of all time. A guitarist always more interested in finding the right chord voicing or textural effect to make a chorus work than in shredding the frets off his axe du jour, it's no wonder every one of his power trio's 20 studio albums have achieved gold sales.

Essential Recordings

1975   Rush:
          Fly By Night

1976   Rush:
          2112

1981   Rush:
          Moving Pictures

2012   Rush:
          Clockwork Angels

Born Alex Zivojinovich in Fernie, Canada, in August 1953, Lifeson grew up in Toronto and received his first guitar at the age of 13. He drew inspiration from the usual crowd of guitar heroes, like Jimi Hendrix and Eric Clapton, and in the autumn of 1968, he formed his first substantive band, teaming up with drummer John Rutsey and bassist Geddy Lee, and calling themselves Rush. After several years on the Toronto covers circuit, the trio signed a deal with Mercury Records and released their self-titled debut in 1974.

Soon after, Rutsey left the group, opening the door for virtuoso drummer and gifted lyricist Neil Peart. After two more albums in 1975, *Fly By Night* and *Caress Of Steel*, the trio broke through in 1976 with *2112*, an album of epic, complex tunes that carried the band to the top of the progressive-rock mountain.

The band's next three albums – *A Farewell To Kings* (1977), *Hemispheres* (1978) and *Permanent Waves* (1980) – burnished the trio's reputation as superior instrumentalists, while songs like 'Closer To The Heart', 'Xanadu', 'La Villa Strangiato', 'Free Will' and 'The Spirit Of Radio' established Lifeson as a bona fide guitar hero. In 1981, Rush achieved its greatest commercial success with the release of *Moving Pictures*, featuring the cult hit 'Tom Sawyer', as well as guitar extravaganzas 'Limelight', 'Red Barchetta' and 'YYZ'.

During the 1980s, Rush experimented heavily with synthesizers, crafting a more futuristic sound. But by 1993's *Counterparts*, the band had largely gone back to guitar- and riff-driven songwriting; their 2007 release *Snakes And Arrows* contained no keyboards whatsoever. In an interview with *Guitar One* magazine in 2007, when asked if keyboards would ever again be used in Rush, Lifeson replied, 'Yes – over my dead body'. Rush continued to experiment with instrumentation, however; 2012's well-received *Clockwork Angels* featured violin and cello string arrangements. In 2013 Rush were inducted into the Rock & Roll Hall of Fame.

Playlists | Links
ebooks & more

FlameTreeRock.com

George Lynch
TOP OF THE MOB

With his wide range of standard and unorthodox techniques, George Lynch (b. 1954) became a guitarist's guitarist as he cruised through the various incarnations of his bands Dokken and Lynch Mob. Born in Spokane, Washington, and raised in California, Lynch became lead guitarist of Dokken in 1980 after auditioning for Ozzy Osbourne in 1979 and losing out to Randy Rhoads.

Dokken had a string of platinum albums such as *Under Lock And Key* (1985) and *Back For The Attack* (1987), which feature Lynch's inventive lead guitar work. The instrumental track 'Mr Scary' on the latter album contributed to his popularity among guitar players. The band earned a Grammy nomination for Best Rock Instrumental in 1989. Dokken disbanded in 1989 and Lynch formed Lynch Mob, a distinct stylistic departure. In 1993, he released his first solo album, *Sacred Groove*. Dokken reunited in 1994 and released *Dysfunctional*, but the album was unsuccessful. Dokken released an unplugged concert from a 1994 show titled *One Live Night*, but three years later, the band again split up and Lynch reassembled Lynch Mob.

In 1999, Lynch Mob adopted a new sound with *Smoke This*, and in the intervening years, Lynch continued to release albums and tour with various assemblages of bandmates from the two groups. In 2003, Lynch formed the George Lynch Group. *Furious George* (2005) featured covers of classic rock tunes from ZZ Top, Jimi Hendrix and Led Zeppelin, among others. Lynch Mob released *Smoke And Mirrors* in 2009. In 2010, Lynch joined with other former members of Dokken to form T&N, releasing an album, *Slave To The Empire*, in 2012. He teamed up with Stryper frontman Michael Sweet to release *Only To Rise* (2015) and *Unified* (2017).

Lynch has been an endorser of **ESP** guitars since 1986. His famed **Skull and Bones** guitar, named 'Mom', is actually a **J Frog** guitar with a neck by **ESP**. Several **George Lynch** signature guitars have been produced by **ESP**. Common Lynch techniques include using open-string chords, root-5 power chords, tritone accents and right-hand picking techniques to create unique tones. He uses unusual scales, and employs string bends and the whammy bar to slide into pitches.

Essential Recordings

1985	Dokken: *Under Lock And Key*
1987	Dokken: *Back For The Attack*
1990	Lynch Mob: *Wicked Sensation*
1993	Solo: *Sacred Groove*

Tom Morello
A MUSICIAN WITH A MESSAGE

Driven by a fierce intelligence, a relentless pursuit of social justice and a wide-ranging taste in sounds and songs, Tom Morello (b. 1964) was the driving force behind the bands Rage Against the Machine and Audioslave. Morello has won Grammys and performed around the world inspiring and uniting people with music. Known for innovative guitar solos and varied, effects-laden tones, he was ranked number 40 on *Rolling Stone*'s list of the 100 Greatest Guitarists of All Time.

Essential Recordings

1992	Rage Against The Machine: *Rage Against The Machine*
1996	Rage Against The Machine: *Evil Empire*
2002	Audioslave: *Audioslave*
2007	The Nightwatchman: *One Man Revolution*

Morello was born to a Kenyan father and Irish-Italian mother. His mother exposed him to politics and the classics from an early age, and Morello became the first person from his Illinois town to enroll at Harvard, after graduating with honours from high school. After college, he moved to Los Angeles. Morello had studied guitar throughout high school, initially influenced by KISS, Iron Maiden and Alice Cooper, later by the Clash, the Sex Pistols and Devo. In LA, he formed a band with vocalist Zack de la Rocha, drummer Brad Wilk and childhood friend Tim Commerford on bass. After frequenting the LA club circuit, Rage Against the Machine signed to Epic Records in 1992. That same year, the band released their self-titled debut, and eventually three more studio albums.

In 2000, de la Rocha quit the band, and Morello, Wilk and Commerford formed Audioslave with ex-Soundgarden singer Chris Cornell, releasing three albums and a DVD of the band's landmark free concert in Cuba. In 2007, Rage Against the Machine reunited at the Coachella Music Festival. Though they have played for big events, RATM do not play together regularly.

In recent years, Morello has performed and recorded folk music under the alias The Nightwatchman and has toured in support of activist causes, joining like-minded musicians, including Bruce Springsteen, for a slew of projects and performances. With Boots Riley in the duo Street Sweeper Social Club, Morello released two albums in the late 2000s. He has contributed to albums by artists including Primus, Johnny Cash and the Crystal Method. Morello has appeared in movies, such as *Iron Man* (2008) in which he played a terrorist, as well as contributing to soundtracks.

Playlists | Links ebooks & more
FlameTreeRock.com

Dave Murray
IRON MAIDEN TO ICON 2

More than any other hard-rock or heavy-metal duo, Iron Maiden guitarists Adrian Smith and Dave Murray (b. 1956) set the standard for twin-guitar harmony lines and riffs. Indeed, their killer riffs and epic songs have helped to make Iron Maiden one of the most influential metal bands of all time.

Murray was born in Edmonton, England. Inspired by the early rock sounds of Jimi Hendrix, Free and Deep Purple, he got his first guitar at the age of 15 and started a band called Stone Free, which also happened to contain future Maiden guitarist Adrian Smith. In 1976, he met bassist Steve Harris, who asked him to join his fledgling metal band, Iron Maiden. Murray accepted the gig, but left almost immediately after, citing irreconcilable differences with singer Dennis Wilcock. Murray then rejoined Smith, this time in a metal band called Urchin. Together, they recorded one single, but when informed that Wilcock had left the band, Murray bolted back to Maiden.

In 1980, Iron Maiden released their eponymous debut, followed in 1981 by *Killers*. To this day, metal guitarists cite these two records as among the most influential metal albums of all time. But in terms of worldwide superstardom, it would be the arrival of singer Bruce Dickinson and Maiden's subsequent amazing string of albums from 1982 to 1984, including *Number Of The Beast* (1982), *Piece Of Mind* (1983) and *Powerslave* (1984), that would put the band on top of the world.

During this time of exploding publicity and recognition, Murray began to garner ever-increasing coverage in guitar magazines and metal-based fanzines, his black **1957 Fender Strat** ever present. Murray's legato-fuelled lines proved technically proficient yet unpretentious, presenting aspiring guitarists with a 'more metal' yet robust alternative to the emerging neoclassical stylings of Randy Rhoads and Yngwie Malmsteen.

Iron Maiden has continued to release albums regularly (2010's *The Final Frontier* is their latest), and the band's appeal as a live act has never waned. From their 1984 World Slavery Tour, which saw them play 322 gigs in 20 countries over a 14-month period, to headlining festivals like Reading, Monsters Of Rock and Rock In Rio, Iron Maiden has by unofficial count entertained more fans than any band in music history. That is their, and Murray's, greatest legacy.

Essential Recordings

1981	Iron Maiden: *Killers*
1982	Iron Maiden: *Number Of The Beast*
1983	Iron Maiden: *Piece Of Mind*
1984	Iron Maiden: *Powerslave*

Dave Mustaine
MEGADETH MAESTRO

Dave Mustaine (b. 1961) was the original lead guitarist for the heavy-metal band Metallica and the cofounder, lead guitarist and lead singer of the thrash-metal band Megadeth. He was born in La Mesa, California. Brought up as a Jehovah's Witness, by the age of 17, he was surviving financially by dealing drugs. In the 1970s, Mustaine began playing electric guitar and joined a band called Panic.

In 1981, Mustaine left Panic to join Metallica as the lead guitarist. But Mustaine's time in Metallica ended before recording *Kill 'Em All* in 1983, due to his heavy drinking and drug use. Mustaine toured with the band, cowrote four songs that appeared on *Kill 'Em All* and cowrote two songs that would eventually appear on *Ride The Lightning*. Mustaine then started a new band, Fallen Angels, connecting with neighbours Dave Ellefson and Greg Handevidt to play bass and guitar, respectively. The first of many drummers, Dijon Carruthers, joined the band. The line-up of Mustaine, Ellefson, Handevidt and Carruthers would be the first incarnation of Megadeth, with Mustaine on vocals.

Essential Recordings

1985 Megadeth: *Killing Is My Business … And Business Is Good!*.

1986 Megadeth: *Peace Sells … But Who's Buying?*

1992 Megadeth: *Countdown To Extinction*

1994 Megadeth: *Youthanasia*

In November 1984, the band signed a deal with Combat Records and began touring. In May 1985, Megadeth released their first album, *Killing Is My Business ... And Business Is Good!*. The following year, Capitol Records signed Megadeth and released *Peace Sells ... But Who's Buying?*. This album produced the notable title track as well as the thrash anthem 'Wake Up Dead'. The videos for both songs became staples on MTV's 'Headbanger's Ball'.

In the ensuing years, Megadeth became one of the iconic bands of heavy metal, and Mustaine one of heavy metal's most revered guitarists. Through countless personnel changes and erratic behaviour due to Mustaine's continued drug and alcohol abuse, he retained a firm grip on the group's development, members and projects, which encompassed

albums, videos, original music for pro wrestling events and video games, and the metal festival Gigantour.

After a freak arm injury while in rehab, Mustaine became a Christian in 2003. He was forced to stop playing and disband Megadeth, but eventually recovered fully and restarted the band. On 3 August 2010, Mustaine released his autobiography, *Mustaine: A Heavy Metal Memoir*.

Ted Nugent
MOTOR CITY MADMAN

Theodore 'Ted' Nugent (b. 1948), the Motor City Madman, first gained fame as the lead guitarist of The Amboy Dukes. With the Dukes, and later as a solo artist, Nugent's intense playing formed the backbone of songs like 'Journey To The Center Of The Mind', 'Stranglehold', 'Free For All', 'Cat Scratch Fever', 'Motor City Madhouse', 'Paralyzed', and 'Wango Tango'.

Born in Detroit, MI, Nugent picked up the guitar in his teens, inspired by British blues-rockers like the Rolling Stones and the Yardbirds. Nugent, a lifelong conservative with a taste for hunting and distaste for drugs and drinking, didn't fit the image championed by the Dukes' psychedelic material. The band issued three albums before Nugent, as the sole original member, rechristened the band Ted Nugent & The Amboy Dukes, and began conducting guitar duels on stage.

By the mid-1970s, Nugent was a solo artist with a backing band and stage show that wowed the metal crowd. With **Cat Scratch Fever** (1975), Nugent rose to the top of the charts and became one of the biggest concert draws in rock. His live set, 1978's **Double Live Gonzo!**, cemented his success, but over the course of **Weekend Warriors** (1978), **State Of Shock** (1979) and **Scream Dream** (1980), desertions by band members and bad business decisions drove Nugent into bankruptcy.

Nugent released a series of albums that failed to catch fire in the 1980s. He tried his hand at acting and became known as much for his right-wing views as for his music. At the end of the decade, he joined rock supergroup Damn Yankees, which scored a hit with 'High Enough' from their self-titled 1990 album. The band dissolved after one more release and Nugent became a solo act again, turning out the well-received **Spirit Of The Wild** (1995). The 1990s also saw re-releases of his best work: 1993's three-disc box set **Out Of Control**, **Live At Hammersmith '79** (1997), and his first three albums, remastered, in 1999. He has continued to tour and release solo

Essential Recordings

1975	Solo: *Ted Nugent*
1977	Solo: *Cat Scratch Fever*
1978	Solo: *Double Live Gonzo!*
1990	Damn Yankees: *Damn Yankees*

albums as well as several live collections, the most recent of which, **Ultralive Ballisticrock**, was released in 2013.

A well-known conservative and survivalist, Nugent played the US national anthem using alternate picking and whammy bar at the Alamo in Texas for a Tax Day Tea Party in 2009.

Playlists | Links
ebooks & more

FlameTreeRock.com

Joe Perry
GUITAR-WIELDING TOXIC TWIN

One half of the infamous 'Toxic Twins', along with vocalist Steven Tyler, Aerosmith's Joe Perry projects a swagger and ultra-cool stage presence that few guitarists can match. Fewer still possess his capacity for muscular, gritty soloing and hook-laden riffing. For over 30 years now, Perry and his stinging guitar tone, generated most often via his signature Gibson Les Paul through Marshall amps, have inspired countless aspiring guitarists to cut out the fluff and rock with soul.

Essential Recordings

1975 Aerosmith: *Toys in the Attic*

1976 Aerosmith: *Rocks*

1980 The Joe Perry Project: *Let The Music Do The Talking*

1993 Aerosmith: *Get A Grip*

Anthony Joseph 'Joe' Perry was born in Lawrence, Massachusetts, in September 1950, and by the age of six, he was turned on to the rock'n'roll sounds of Little Richard and Bill Haley & His Comets. Later, inspired by the music of the Beatles and the Rolling Stones, the teenage Perry picked up the guitar and soon discovered the playing of such British blues-rock guitar greats as Jeff Beck, Jimmy Page and Peter Green. In 1969, while playing in the Jam Band (with future Aerosmith bassist Tom Hamilton), Perry met singer Steven Tyler, and the two decided to join forces, calling themselves Aerosmith.

Combining the gritty rock of the Stones with the heavy riffing of Led Zeppelin and the boogie of American blues, Aerosmith would become the top American hard-rock band of the 1970s. Their albums **Toys In The Attic** (1975) and **Rocks** (1976) are generally recognized as two of the most important hard-rock albums of the 1970s, producing such timeless hits as 'Walk This Way', 'Sweet Emotion' and 'Back In The Saddle'. Sadly, the Toxic Twins' heavy drug and alcohol abuse would lead to the demise of Aerosmith in 1979.

In 1980, working as the Joe Perry Project, the guitarist released **Let The Music Do The Talking**, a vastly underrated album of incendiary guitar work. After two more Project albums, Perry rejoined the original Aerosmith line-up in 1984 for a reunion tour. A surprising collaboration with rap group Run-DMC on the classic hit 'Walk This Way' put the Toxic Twins back on the mainstream map. They sobered up and went on to huge success with **Permanent Vacation** (1987), **Pump** (1989) and **Get A Grip** (1993). Perry continued to work on solo projects as well, even receiving a Grammy nomination for the song 'Mercy', from his 2005 release **Joe Perry**. In late 2009, Perry released a new Joe Perry Project album, **Have Guitar, Will Travel**. Despite various in-band tensions, Aerosmith continue to tour and record, and Perry released his fourth solo album, **Sweetzerland Manifesto**, in 2018.

Chris Poland
MASTER OF MEGADETH

In the early 1980s, as the new wave of British heavy metal was taking the US by storm, an American music revolution called 'thrash metal' was brewing, combining the heavy sounds of metal with the unabashed aggression and speed of punk. At the centre of this sonic storm was a young quartet called Megadeth, which featured the lightning-fast yet fluid lead licks of guitarist Chris Poland (b. 1957).

Though best known for his work in Megadeth, Poland was drawn to the complex musical style of jazz fusion as a young man, playing in a jazz-rock band called Welkin while still at high school. Upon graduation, he moved to LA, where he played in a jazz-fusion outfit called the New Yorkers from 1977 to 1982. Their complex songs and improvisations, informed by such fusion luminaries as Mahavishnu Orchestra and Weather Report, proved fertile for Poland, who would later use these fusion roots to set himself apart from the myriad metal clones lining the Sunset Strip in the 1980s.

Poland joined Megadeth in 1984, recording the band's debut, *Killing Is My Business … And Business Is Good* (1985), and their breakthrough follow-up, *Peace Sells … But Who's Buying?* (1986), which finds the multifaceted guitarist's commanding chops on full display in both the title track and 'Wake Up Dead'. Suffering from substance abuse issues, Poland was fired from the band. He eventually kicked his habits and returned to the music scene, first as a bass player with punk band the Circle Jerks and then with his first solo album, a jazz-metal opus titled *Return To Metalopolis* (1990). He subsequently formed the progressive fusion outfit Damn The Machine, and later, Mumbo's Brain. Poland would once again play with Megadeth, recording several solos on the band's 2004 release *The System Has Failed*.

Poland's greatest labour of love in recent years has been OHM, a progressive metal-fusion project. In 2009, Poland formed OHMphrey, a side project with Robby Pagliari of OHM, and Jake Cinninger, Kris Myers and Joel Cummins of progressive rock band Umphrey's McGee. OHMphrey released an eponymous debut album in 2009 but have been largely quiet since.

Essential Recordings

1985	Megadeth: *Killing Is My Business … And Business Is Good*
1986	Megadeth: *Peace Sells … But Who's Buying?*
2005	OHM: *Amino Acid Flashback*
2009	OHMphrey: *OHMphrey*

Uli Jon Roth
SCORPIONS TO SKY GUITAR

Born in Düsseldorf, Germany, Ulrich 'Uli' Jon Roth (b. 1954) began his lifelong musical journey on the trumpet, before switching to the classical guitar at the age of 13. This training, combined with his passion for classical music, would help Roth become one of the main protagonists of the neoclassical shred guitar style, later brought to the forefront by Swedish guitarist Yngwie Malmsteen.

Essential Recordings

1975 Scorpions: *In Trance*

1978 Scorpions: *Taken by Force*

1984 Electric Sun: *Beyond The Astral Skies*

2000 Solo: *Transcendental Sky Guitar*

From 1973 until 1978, Roth was the primary songwriter and lead guitarist for legendary German rock group Scorpions, having replaced guitarist Michael Schenker, who left to form UFO in 1973. Roth recorded five albums with the band, the final one being 1978's ***Taken By Force***, which featured the Roth-penned 'Sails Of Charon'. This track, which Roth says was musically inspired by a Tchaikovsky violin concerto, is significant in that it represents arguably the first example of neoclassical shred guitar, and it would also come to be Roth's best-known song in the US.

Soon after ***Taken By Force*** was released, Roth left Scorpions, dissatisfied with the commercial turn the band's sound was taking. He next formed Electric Sun, which lasted from 1978 until 1985. It was during this time too that Roth focused more on the neoclassical aspects of his guitar playing. To execute his classically based compositional ideas, he replaced his long-beloved **Fender Strat** with a newly commissioned six-octave 32-fret guitar. The result, the **Sky Guitar**, made its debut on Electric Sun's final album, ***Beyond The Astral Skies*** (1984) and has been Roth's weapon of choice for over 20 years now.

Starting in 1985, Roth spent much of his time working in the classical music spectrum, writing four symphonies and two concertos, and playing with symphony orchestras throughout Europe. In 1998, he joined Michael Schenker and Joe Satriani on the European leg of the G3 tour. In 2000, he released the two-CD set ***Transcendental Sky Guitar***, and in 2004, the concerto ***Metamorphosis Of Vivaldi's Four Seasons***, a twenty-first-century incarnation of the spirit of Vivaldi's music. Roth's ***Under A Dark Sky*** was released in 2008. ***Scorpions Revisited*** and the tour that followed in 2015 enraptured his loyal following

Richie Sambora
A GUITAR HERO AMONG US

Though guitar playing in the 1980s was often thought of as a 'guitar Olympics' of sorts, Bon Jovi guitarist Richie Sambora typically eschewed fretboard flights of fancy in favour of melodic, tastefully arranged solos designed to serve the band's infectious hit songs. While this approach has kept him on the outside of the guitar-hero clubhouse, his impact on the greater musical community is rarely matched.

Richard Stephen Sambora was born in Perth Amboy, New Jersey, in July 1959. He began playing guitar in his early teens, inspired by Jimi Hendrix, Eric Clapton, Jeff Beck and the Beatles. In 1978, he made his recording debut with his band Shark Frenzy, but the mix tapes were damaged in a flood and thus remained unreleased. (Shark Frenzy member Bruce Foster eventually remastered the tapes, and the album was released on Sanctuary Records in 2004.) In 1983, fellow New Jerseyan Jon Bongiovi hired Sambora to replace guitarist Dave Sabo in his newly signed band Bon Jovi. The rest, as they say, is history. Over the past 25 years, Bon Jovi has released 10 studio albums that have collectively sold over 120 million copies, and the band has played over 2,500 shows in over 50 countries. Additionally, Sambora has released two critically acclaimed solo albums – *Stranger In This Town* (1991) and *Undiscovered Soul* (1998). Suffice it to say, few guitarists have spent as much time onstage as Sambora has in his remarkable career.

Through the years, Sambora – an avid guitar collector – has played just about every guitar possible. In the early years of Bon Jovi, he favoured custom **Gibson Les Pauls**, often equipped with floating tremolo systems. He then went through a period of '**super-Strats**', from such manufacturers as **Charvel**, **Jackson** and **Kramer**, which made his first signature-model guitar, in 1987. He was also one of the top endorsers of **Ovation** acoustic guitars, as featured in the video for 'Wanted Dead Or Alive' (1986).

Since then, the guitarist has continued to mix it up, using various vintage **Fenders** and **Gibsons**, as well as the '**Sambora**' guitar, made by his long-time associate and luthier **Chris Hofschneider**. In 2008, Sambora announced his new **ESP** endorsement deal. Sambora released a third solo album, *Aftermath Of The Lowdown*, in 2012 and left Bon Jovi in 2013 following the release of their twelfth studio album, *What About Now*. He was inducted into the Rock & Roll Hall of Fame as a member of Bon Jovi in 2018

Essential Recordings

1986	Bon Jovi: *Slippery When Wet*
1988	Bon Jovi: *New Jersey*
1991	Solo: *Stranger In This Town*
2005	Bon Jovi: *Have A Nice Day*

Michael
Schenker
UFO GUITAR LEGEND

Though he has been cited by countless rock guitarists as a major influence, and despite the fact that he cofounded legendary metal band Scorpions, guitarist Michael Schenker (b. 1955) remains one of the most underrated and underappreciated guitarists of all time.

Born in Sarstedt, Germany, Schenker was first turned on to the guitar when his older brother Rudolf brought home a **Gibson Flying V**. Inspired by the heavy tone of Mountain's Leslie West and the nimble fretwork of Hank Marvin, Michael taught himself to play and would then join Rudolf in forming Scorpions, recording their first album, *Lonesome Crow* (1972), when he was just 17. But even at this young age, it was clear that Michael possessed considerable talent.

Essential Recordings

1972   Scorpions:
       Lonesome Crow
1974   UFO:
       Phenomenon
1981   Michael Schenker Group:
       MSG
1993   Solo:
       Thank You

During the ensuing tour, British space-metal group UFO witnessed Schenker's formidable guitar chops at a sound check and asked him to join the band as lead guitarist. With Rudolf's blessing, Michael took the gig, and it was with UFO that Schenker's reputation as a guitarist would begin to be formed. His first album with UFO, **Phenomenon** (1974), contained such future hard-rock classics as 'Doctor Doctor' and 'Rock Bottom'. The album also contained an instrumental track titled 'Lipstick Traces', which Schenker played entirely with his *feet*! It was also around this time that he would begin playing his famous black and white **Gibson Flying V**, an instrument with which Michael would become synonymous.

After several more successful albums, Schenker's alcohol abuse led to his exit from UFO in 1979. He rejoined Scorpions later that year, staying just long enough to record **Lovedrive**, before leaving again. He next set out on his own, starting the first of many incarnations of the Michael Schenker Group (MSG). Craving commercial success, however, he steered away from his hard-rock roots, and in the mid- to late 1980s, reached the cusp with singer Robin McCauley supplying the 'M' in MSG. Since then, Schenker has focused mostly on solo albums, including three releases in 2001 alone (**MS 2000: Dreams And Expressions**, **Odd Trio** and **Be Aware Of Scorpions**). The MSG album **In The Midst Of Beauty** was released in 2008, with further solo releases from Schenker including **Temple Of Rock** (2011) and **Bridge The Gap** (2013). Schenker also received an endorsement deal with **Dean Guitars**, which makes the black and white **Michael Schenker Signature V** guitar.

Alex Skolnick
TESTAMENT TO REMEMBER

Alex Skolnick (b. 1968) is best known as a metal guitarist with thrash pioneers Testament, but metal is just one facet of the talented guitarist's abilities. Skolnick was born in Berkeley, California. At the age of nine, he discovered KISS and subsequently decided to learn guitar. He was later inspired by the highly technical work of Eddie Van Halen and Randy Rhoads. At the age of 16, he joined a band called Legacy. Two years later, the band changed their name to Testament and entered the studio to record their first album, *The Legacy*, which was released in 1987. Skolnick would go on to record five more albums with Testament before the group disbanded in 1992.

During that era, Skolnick earned well-deserved praise in the guitar community, regularly appearing at the top of readers' polls in guitar magazines as Best Thrash Guitarist or Most Underrated Guitarist. It was also during this time that Skolnick saw one of jazz legend Miles Davis's guitar-driven bands on television, sparking an intense passion for jazz music. He began to study the jazz language intently, eventually moving to New York City to attend New School University, where he earned a degree in jazz performance in 2001.

While attending New School, he founded the Alex Skolnick Trio. Their first recording, **Goodbye To Romance: Standards For A New Generation** (2002), featured jazz arrangements of classic metal songs. Subsequent releases **Transformation** (2004) and **Last Day In Paradise** (2007) featured similar arrangements of metal tunes, accompanied by original bebop compositions.

In recent years, Skolnick has toured as a member of the Trans-Siberian Orchestra, a classical-rock odyssey that performs technically demanding arrangements of Christmas songs to sold-out arenas. He is also featured in 'Jekyll & Hyde: In Concert', the touring version of the hit Broadway show 'Jekyll & Hyde', and has begun working with composer Jim Steinman on the Dream Engine project, performing new songs and classics. In 2005, Skolnick reunited with Testament for

a highly successful series of sold-out concerts in Europe and Japan. **The Formation Of Damnation** was released in 2008. It was the first studio album of all-new material for Testament in nine years and the first to feature Skolnick on guitar since 1992's **The Ritual**. A further Testament album, **Dark Roots Of Earth**, was released in 2012.

Essential Recordings

1987	Testament: *The Legacy*
2002	The Alex Skolnick Trio: *Goodbye To Romance: Standards For A New Generation*
2007	The Alex Skolnick Trio: *Last Day In Paradise*
2009	Trans-Siberian Orchestra: *Night Castle*

Playlists | Links ebooks & more
FlameTreeRock.com

Slash
APPETITE FOR BRILLIANCE

The man beneath the top hat, Saul 'Slash' Hudson (b. 1965) was born in the Hampstead area of London. When he was 11, his family moved to Los Angeles, California, where at the age of 14, he heard Aerosmith's *Rocks* for the first time and found his life's calling.

Practising guitar for hours on end, learning the licks of his heroes Joe Perry, Eric Clapton and Angus Young, among others, Slash set about forming his own band to play the famed Sunset Strip. Teaming up with friend and drummer Steven Adler, Slash formed the blues-rock act Road Crew. Soon, the two friends hooked up with singer Axl Rose, guitarist Izzy Stradlin and bassist Duff McKagan to form a new band called Guns N' Roses.

Essential Recordings

1987 Guns N' Roses:
Appetite For Destruction
1995 Slash's Snakepit
It's Five O'Clock Somewhere
2004 Velvet Revolver:
Contraband
2010 Solo:
Slash

In 1987, GN'R released their debut, **Appetite For Destruction**, an album that would go on to become one of the biggest rock'n'roll albums in history. The album would catapult the band (and its excesses) into the realms of Aerosmith and the Rolling Stones. But on an individual level, it would install Slash as the era's premier guitar antihero, a role model for aspiring guitarists uninterested in the fretboard flash of players like Steve Vai or Yngwie Malmsteen.

Slash's meteoric ascension would impact the guitar-gear world as well. With his low-slung **Les Paul** harking back to the sights and sounds of Led Zeppelin's Jimmy Page and 1970s-era Joe Perry, the once grand but then-stalled **Gibson** brand was suddenly resurrected to its prior position of esteem.

Following the demise of GN'R, Slash released two albums with Slash's Snakepit and recorded sessions with dozens of top-name artists, ranging from Michael Jackson to Alice Cooper to the Yardbirds. Then, in 2003,

he reunited with former Gunners McKagan and Matt Sorum and recruited guitarist Dave Kushner and singer Scott Weiland to form Velvet Revolver. The band's two releases, **Contraband** (2004) and **Libertad** (2007), helped to return Slash to the world's biggest stages. The band took a hiatus in 2012 to concentrate on solo projects. Following Slash's eponymous 2010 debut, he teamed up with Mike Kennedy and the Conspirators to record **Apocalyptic Love** (2012), with a follow-up album released in 2014. He succumbed to temptation and rejoined Guns N' Roses for their Not In This Lifetime tour in 2016.

Adrian Smith
IRON MAIDEN TO ICON

With the exception of Judas Priest, no metal band has been more influential than Iron Maiden. And it is no coincidence that Maiden first took flight when guitarist Adrian Smith joined the band one month into recording their second album, *Killers*, in 1981.

Adrian Frederik 'H' Smith was born in Hackney, East London, in February 1957. At school, he was drawn to the rock-guitar sounds of Jimi Hendrix and Ritchie Blackmore, and so set about learning how to play. While at school, he became friends with Dave Murray, and the two would play in Stone Free and would later form Urchin, though Murray would flit between them to form and then rejoin Iron Maiden. While Maiden rose to become one of England's most popular metal bands, Urchin fell apart, and so Smith welcomed the invitation to once again play alongside Murray in 1981. Starting with *Killers*, and continuing with *Number Of The Beast* (1982), *Piece Of Mind* (1983), *Powerslave* (1984), *Somewhere In Time* (1986) and *Seventh Son Of A Seventh Son* (1988), Smith's deceptively 'lazy' and melodic soloing approach would play perfect straight man to Murray's often fiery, scalar lines, and their harmony parts would set a metal-guitar standard adhered to even today.

Smith played a variety of guitars during this era, including an **Ibanez Destroyer**, **Gibson Les Pauls** and **SGs**, various **Dean** models, custom **Jacksons**, **Lado** models and, of course, his preferred **Fender Stratocasters**. His amplification was – and continues to be – **Marshall**.

Equally important to Maiden's sound and success during this era were Smith's songwriting sensibilities. He wrote or cowrote such classic FM radio hits as 'Flight Of Icarus', '2 Minutes To Midnight', 'Wasted Years' and 'Can I Play With Madness', and helped steer the band into ever more progressive waters. This direction, however, collided with bassist Steve Harris's musical vision, which was to return to a more straightforward metal sound. Thus, Smith left Iron Maiden to pursue solo ambitions.

Essential Recordings

1982	Iron Maiden: *Number Of The Beast*
1988	Iron Maiden: *Seventh Son Of A Seventh Son*
1997	Psycho Motel: *Welcome To The World*
2010	Iron Maiden: *The Final Frontier*

Recording under the acronym A.S.A.P. (Adrian Smith And Project), he released *Silver And Gold* in 1989, and later formed the alternative rock-influenced Psycho Motel, releasing *State Of Mind* (1996) and *Welcome To The World* (1997). Smith then rejoined Maiden in 1999 for the Ed Hunter tour and continues to record and tour with them now.

Glenn Tipton
JUDAS PRIEST
TO ROCK GOD

Clad head to toe in studded black leather and featuring a thundering rhythm section, a dynamic twin-guitar assault and one of the purest rock vocalists in music history, it simply doesn't get any more 'metal' than Judas Priest. And the man behind many of the band's greatest riffs and solos is guitarist Glenn Tipton (b. 1947, pictured below, centre).

Essential Recordings

1978   Judas Priest:
        Stained Class

1980   Judas Priest:
        British Steel

1982   Judas Priest:
        Screaming For Vengeance

1997   Solo:
        Baptizm Of Fire

Born in Blackheath, England, Tipton was a latecomer to the guitar, first picking it up at the age of 21. By the early 1970s, he was making a name for himself on the Birmingham club circuit in the Flying Hat Band, an early metal outfit in the vein of Black Sabbath. In 1974, guitarist K.K. Downing asked Tipton to join his own burgeoning metal band, Judas Priest. The partnership, with Tipton's classically influenced style

contrasting with Downing's more straight-ahead, heavy blues-rock approach, proved a winning formula. Priest became one of the most influential heavy-metal acts of the 1970s, and the two guitarists spearheaded the twin-guitar harmony approach that ruled the new wave of British heavy metal.

In those formative years, Tipton maintained a primarily blues-influenced approach to his metal noodlings, occasionally adding neoclassical phrasing. An early example of his affinity for more complex harmony is heard in his solo in 'Beyond The Realms Of Death', from *Stained Class* (1978). Sonically, Tipton favoured a **Fender Stratocaster**, later switching to a modified **Strat**, swapping its standard single-coil pickup for a fatter-sounding humbucking pickup. As Priest's sound began to modernize, with the mainstream success of *British Steel* (1980), *Point Of Entry* (1981) and *Screaming For Vengeance* (1982), so did Tipton's sound and approach. During the World Vengeance Tour, he switched to the metal-approved **Gibson SG**, before getting an endorsement deal with **Hamer Guitars**, which crafted Tipton's signature-model **Phantom GT**, a guitar he still uses today.

After a lull through the 1990s, which saw singer Rob Halford replaced by Tim 'Ripper' Owens, Judas Priest reunited with Halford and revived their career. In 2009, they released *A Touch Of Evil: Live*, featuring previously unreleased live tracks. 'Dissident Aggressor' won the 2010 Grammy Award for Best Metal Performance. Their Epitaph World Tour took place in 2011–12.

Mark Tremonti
A STORY OF SUCCESS

Mark Tremonti (b. 1974) rose to fame as the lead guitarist of Creed, enjoying enormous success at the turn of the twenty-first century with metal-influenced songs that crossed over to the pop charts. Tremonti's tasteful power has garnered him many fans. His instructional DVD *The Sound and the Story* adds tips from several guitarists, including Michael Angelo Batio, Rusty Cooley, Troy Stetina, Bill Peck and Myles Kennedy.

Tremonti was born and grew up near Detroit, Michigan. He got his first guitar at age 11 for about $25. Tremonti learned guitar by ear and with the help of books and videos. At 16, Tremonti and his family moved to Florida, where he met future Creed singer Scott Stapp in high school. Although the two were not friends at the time, Tremonti encountered Stapp again at Florida State University. They formed Creed with guitarist Brian Brasher, bassist Scott Phillips and drummer Brian Marshall.

Creed's debut album, *My Own Prison*, was released independently in 1997. After Wind-Up Records picked up the group and re-released the album, it became a surprise success, spinning off several hit singles, including 'My Own Prison'. When Creed's second album, *Human Clay*, was released in 1999, 'Higher' and 'With Arms Wide Open' hit No. 1. Overall, the band had seven consecutive hits on rock radio and sold over 30 million records worldwide in seven years. Internal squabbles led to Creed's splitting and Tremonti's forming Alter Bridge in 2004. The band has released four studio albums: *One Day Remains* (2004), *Blackbird* (2007), *AB III* (2010) and *Fortress* (2013). After ten years apart, Creed reunited in 2009 with a tour and the album *Full Circle*.

Tremonti has contributed to many artists' records over the years, including Sevendust's *Hope & Sorrow*, and Fozzy's *All That Remains*. He also played on the cover of Deep Purple's 'Burn' from Michael

Essential Recordings

1997	Creed: *My Own Prison*
1999	Creed: *Human Clay*
2004	Alter Bridge *One Day Remains*
2010	Alter Bridge: *AB III*

Angelo Batio's *Hands Without Shadows*. Mark Tremonti plays several of his signature-model **Paul Reed Smith** guitars, with **Fender** and **Bogner** amps and **Mesa/Boogie** heads and cabinets. He also uses a **Taylor 614CE** acoustic.

Playlists | Links ebooks & more
FlameTreeRock.com

Leslie West
MOUNTAIN MAESTRO

A pioneering hard-rock guitarist with a tone as big as his waistline, Leslie West (b. 1945) is one of the most underrated guitar heroes in rock history. Best known as the leader of the hard-rock trio Mountain, which was named by VH1 as one of the Top 100 Hard Rock Bands of All Time, West's monster guitar sound was made immortal on the group's timeless hit 'Mississippi Queen'.

Essential Recordings

1969	Solo: *Mountain*
1970	Mountain: *Climbing*
1971	Mountain: *Nantucket Sleighride*
1972	West, Bruce & Laing: *Why Dontcha*

Born in New York City, West first made a name for himself in the mid-1960s with the Vagrants, an East-Coast powerhouse band that had a minor hit with a cover of Otis Redding's 'Respect' in 1967. After leaving the Vagrants, West teamed up with bassist Felix Pappalardi, who also produced the Vagrants and Cream, and his debut album, *Mountain*, was released in 1969. Soon after, they recruited drummer Corky Laing to complete the band and called themselves Mountain, a name reportedly referring to West's rather rotund figure. The group debuted at the Fillmore in 1969 and went on to play at the Woodstock festival. Although Mountain's existence was relatively brief, the band racked up two gold albums and a handful of hit singles, including 'Never In My Life', 'Theme From An Imaginary Western' and, of course, 'Mississippi Queen'.

It's rare that a single song can launch an enduring legacy, but that's exactly what the giant riff and fat intro solo to 'Mississippi Queen' did for West. He possessed a rare gift of a signature guitar sound that would influence a new generation of rock guitar icons, including Michael Schenker, Richie Sambora and even tone-god Eddie Van Halen. Key to his monster tone, aside from his special touch, was the **Gibson Les Paul Jr**, which he paired with **Sunn** amplifiers. Though West these days favours his **Dean Soltero** signature-model guitar along with **Marshall** amplifiers to churn out fat blues lines for his solo

works (***Got Blooze***, 2005; ***Blue Me***, 2006; ***Unusual Suspects***, 2011; ***Still Climbing***, 2013), his greatest legacy is that magical guitar tone of 1970 that set the standard for hard rock and heavy metal to come.

Playlists | Links
ebooks & more
FlameTreeRock.com

Zakk Wylde
THE LAST TRUE HERO

Though he maintains a gruff, beer-drinking, hell-raising public persona, guitarist Zakk Wylde (b. 1967) is one of the most talented, dedicated and hard-working guitarists of the past 20 years and, as some in the guitar community have speculated, the last true guitar hero.

Wylde was born Jeffrey Phillip Wiedlandt in Bayonne, New Jersey. He started playing guitar at the age of 15, drawing influence from such guitar legends as Jimmy Page, Eddie Van Halen and Randy Rhoads. He soon started a band called Stone Henge, playing *Animal House*-style house parties in central New Jersey. A few years later, while playing a gig in Sayreville, New Jersey, a photographer offered to get his press kit into the hands of Ozzy Osbourne, who was looking for a new guitarist. A short while later, Wylde was making his debut with the Prince of Darkness at Wormwood Scrubs prison, in London, England.

Wylde's first album with Ozzy was *No Rest For The Wicked* (1988), featuring the hits 'Miracle Man' and 'Crazy Babies'. From the start, Wylde's minor pentatonic-based lines, aggressive vibrato and screaming pinch harmonics proved a perfect fit for the Osbourne sound. Their next studio record, *No More Tears* (1991), which produced the hits 'No More Tears' and 'Mama I'm Coming Home', solidified Wylde's reputation as a guitarist who's here to stay. Indeed, since that time, Wylde has recorded three more studio records with the madman, including 2007's *Black Rain*.

In addition to his Ozzy gig, Wylde has worked on several side projects, such as *Pride And Glory* (1994) and a solo album titled *Book Of Shadows* (1996). But Wylde's most prolific work has been with his own Black Label Society, formed in 1999. BLS has released 14 studio records, along with live albums and DVDs. Additionally, Wylde has several signature-model **Gibson Les Paul Customs** – the most famous being his black and antique-white bulls-eye design – and a signature-model **Marshall** head.

Essential Recordings

1988	Ozzy Osbourne: *No Rest For The Wicked*
1991	Ozzy Osbourne: *No More Tears*
1996	Solo: *Book Of Shadows*
1999	Black Label Society: *Sonic Brew*

Angus Young
ON A HIGHWAY TO HERO

AC/DC guitarist Angus Young – all five feet two inches of him – is a larger-than-life figure. Rising up from working-class Scottish roots to become the heart and soul of one of the greatest rock'n'roll bands of all time, Young, with his schoolboy outfit and Gibson SG in hand, has become the definitive rock-guitar icon.

Born in Glasgow, Scotland, in March 1955, Young moved to Australia with his family in the 1960s. Inspired by their big brother George (guitarist in the Easybeats) as well as by Chuck Berry, Muddy Waters and the Rolling Stones, the brothers Young teamed up to form AC/DC in 1973. After a couple of years, the brothers hooked up with singer Bon Scott and subsequently signed a deal with Atlantic Records, releasing their debut, **High Voltage**, in 1975.

Essential Recordings

1979 AC/DC: *Highway To Hell*

1980 AC/DC: *Back In Black*

1981 AC/DC: *For Those About To Rock (We Salute You)*

2008 AC/DC: *Black Ice*

In contrast to the glam-rock and disco sounds that were popular in the mid-1970s, AC/DC pounded out no-nonsense three-chord rock with a good-time message, thus setting the band apart from the crowd. Although there were countless rock guitarists playing power chords and minor pentatonic licks on **Gibson SGs** through **Marshall** amps, *nobody* sounded like Angus Young. His singular tone and vibrato, in addition to his wild stage antics not only made Young a rising guitar hero but also turned AC/DC into a must-see live act.

After several more highly successful albums, including 1979's **Highway To Hell**, tragedy struck AC/DC, when singer Scott died of acute alcohol poisoning after a night of heavy partying. Downhearted, the band nearly called it quits, until they met British singer Brian Johnson. The fit was perfect, and AC/DC rebounded with one of the top five albums in rock history, **Back In Black** (1980). Songs like the

title track, 'Hells Bells', and 'You Shook Me All Night Long' helped enshrine AC/DC as the world's greatest rock'n'roll band.

Forty-odd years and millions of albums later AC/DC has survived the departure of singer Brian Johnson and the death of Angus' brother Malcolm. Younghas never strayed from his **SG-Marshall** sound or from his schoolboy uniform and high-voltage stage act, remains a bona fide hard-rock guitar hero.

Malcolm Young
POWER BEHIND THE THRONE

Hailed as one of hard rock's greatest rhythm guitarists, Malcolm Young (1953–2017) was born in Glasgow, Scotland. When he was 10, the family emmigrated to Sydney, Australia, where Malcolm and younger brother Angus were taught to play guitar by elder sibling George, a member of the Easybeats. Malcolm founded AC/DC with Angus in 1973. The recruitment of vocalist Bon Scott the following year provided the catalyst for the band's unstoppable rise from their early Australian-only albums to international stardom with *Highway To Hell* (1979). AC/DC survived Scott's death from acute alcohol poisoning in 1980, bouncing back to even greater success (and excess) with new frontman Brian Johnson.

Essential Recordings

1979   AC/DC:
Highway To Hell

1980   AC/DC:
Back In Black

1981   AC/DC:
For Those About To Rock (We Salute You)

2008   AC/DC:
Black Ice

Although less visible than the band's charismatic singers and ostentatious lead guitarist Angus, Malcolm Young was the power behind the throne of AC/DC; he was chief decision-maker and co-songwriter. Providing the foundation for his younger brother's guitar heroics, Malcolm nailed down the rhythm on his **1963 Gretsch Jet Firebird**, although for the tours in support of *Back In Black* (1980) and *For Those About To Rock (We Salute You)* (1981), he played a **Gretsch White Falcon**. His long association with **Gretsch** guitars was recognized by the introduction of the **Malcolm Young signature model**, based on the **Firebird**.

His style was simple, direct and brutal; he plugged straight into the amps and shunned the use of effects. AC/DC standards like 'Highway To Hell' and 'Problem Child' were built on his insistent three-chord riffs, creating a powered-up version of Chuck Berry's rock'n'roll blueprint. AC/DC's guitar sound influenced the new wave of British heavy metal that arose in the late 1970s; bands like Saxon and Iron Maiden have acknowledged their debt to the expatriate Scots, while Malcolm Young's riffs have inspired speed metal, thrash and grunge.

The rock'n'roll lifestyle caught up with Malcolm when he was forced to miss the band's 1988 tour because of problems with alcohol. Lookalike nephew Stevie Young substituted until Malcolm resumed his rightful place as the unassuming general in AC/DC's engine room. In 2014, he was diagnosed with dementia and retired from the band. He died of the disease in November 2017, aged 64

Playlists | Links ebooks & more

FlameTreeRock.com

I had no ambition when I was a kid other than to play guitar and get in a rock'n'roll band.

George Harrison

Soft Rock & Pop

The Edge
SEARCHING FOR SONIC MEANING

A master of texture and sonic architecture based on a minimalist style of playing, as opposed to contemporaries who sought impenetrable technique and unrestrained speed, Dave Evans (b. 1961) created a signature sound for a signature band, U2, just as surely as he created for himself a new identity – the Edge.

The Edge grew up in Dublin. He took piano and guitar lessons and often performed with his brother Dick while attending St. Andrew's National School. Later, at Mount Temple Comprehensive School, they answered an advertisement posted by drummer Larry Mullen, Jr., seeking musicians to form a band. At the initial practice in Mullen's kitchen, the group featured Mullen on drums, Paul Hewson (Bono) on lead vocals, Dave and Dick Evans on guitar and Adam Clayton, a friend of the Evans brothers, on bass. Soon after, the group chose the name Feedback. Mostly, they covered versions of songs they knew.

Essential Recordings

1987 U2:
The Joshua Tree

1991 U2:
Achtung Baby

1993 U2:
Zooropa

1997 U2:
Pop

Along the way, Dave Evans became the Edge. Exactly how this happened has taken on the mythic proportions of John Lennon's vision of a man on a flaming pie. At various times, the moniker was said to have been inspired by the Evans nose, his overall angular features or his propensity to show off his fearlessness of high places by walking close to the edge of precarious perches. Whatever the source, it was not yet clear that U2 had an edge that would carry them to stratospheric heights.

Feedback became the Hype and then U2, a name they 'disliked least' among several possibilities, and became a four-piece with Dick Evans' departure. After winning a talent show in Limerick and landing manager Paul McGuiness, U2 released a pair of Ireland-only singles before signing with Island Records. The band's initial release *Boy* (1980), produced by Steve Lillywhite, won positive reviews, but the follow-up, *October* (1981),

reflecting an immersion in spiritual themes, was a misfire. Then in 1984, the band released *War*, which contained 'Sunday Bloody Sunday' and 'New Year's Day'. Soon, U2 were gaining international attention for their striking sound, passionate lyrics and charismatic frontman, Bono.

U2 were looking for a new sound, however, and the Edge's interest in the unconventional work of Brian Eno and his engineer Daniel Lanois led to the pair's involvement with the band's biggest album to date. *The Unforgettable Fire* (1984) spawned the hit 'Pride (In The Name Of Love)' and, helped by MTV, solidified U2's following in the US. The band's riveting performance at Live Aid in 1985 further expanded their worldwide audience. On tour in

Playlists | Links
ebooks & more
FlameTreeRock.com

1986, U2 developed songs for an album that would confront America's place, for better or worse, in the world. *The Joshua Tree* (1987) became the fastest-selling album in British chart history, and was No. 1 for nine weeks in the United States, winning the band their first two Grammy Awards. The ensuing tour spawned the film and album *Rattle And Hum* (1988), which wowed fans and divided critics.

Throughout the 1990s and into the twenty-first century, U2 continued a phenomenal pattern of releasing albums – *Achtung Baby* (1991), *Zooropa* (1993), *Pop* (1997) – that were accompanied by critical praise and followed by tours that grew ever more elaborate in an attempt to comment on the superficiality of modern life, art and media. After each cycle, the band would attempt to reinvent itself or its sound. It is in part this obsession with freshness, along with a commitment to social justice and the core talents of the band, that established U2 as one of the greatest bands in rock history as they soldiered on with *All That You Can't Leave Behind* (2000) and *How To Dismantle An Atomic Bomb* (2004). The band released *No Line On The Horizon* in 2009, launching the U2 360° Tour the same year. In 2014, their song 'Ordinary Love', composed for the 2013 film *Mandela: Long Walk To Freedom*, won the Golden Globe Award for Best Original Song.

Crucial to U2's achievement has been the Edge's search for sonic meaning as he crafted a guitar sound with delays, reverbs and a minimalist approach to playing that complemented the passion, pain and joy embedded in U2's music. Just as he salvaged the sessions for *Achtung Baby* when he came up with the chord progression for the song 'One', throughout U2's career, it has been his dedication to artistic growth that has pushed the band to new sonic destinations.

Trey Anastasio
STAR OF THE JAM SCENE

Princeton, New Jersey native Trey Anastasio (b. 1964) became the star of the jam-band resurgence through his prolific work both with his band Phish and a multitude of side projects. Phish's initial touring and recording life spanned from 1983 to 2000, experienced a hiatus from 2000 to 2003 and dissolved in 2004, before regrouping in 2009. Inheriting the mantle and rabid following of the Grateful Dead and its departed guitar hero Jerry Garcia while attracting new fans to Phish's more complex, improvisatory works, Anastasio displayed a deep knowledge of rock, blues, jazz and country guitar styles.

Essential Recordings

1993 Phish:
Rift

1997 Phish:
The Story Of The Ghost

1998 Phish:
The Siket Disc

2005 Solo:
Shine

As a boy, Anastasio attended Princeton Day School, where he met future songwriting partner Tom Marshall. As a teenager, he helped his mother Dina write songs for children's records. At the University of Vermont, he teamed up with bassist Mike Gordon, drummer Jon Fishman and guitarist Jeff Holdsworth (later replaced by keyboardist Page McConnell) to form Phish. Anastasio was suspended for a year after breaking into the school's science building and stealing body parts for a prank. Transferring to Goddard College, he studied composition while he and the band developed Phish's early material.

Phish developed its loyal following by combining progressive rock-influenced compositions with a genial, inventive stage show that encouraged trading taped copies of performances and included crowd-pleasing departures such as covers of Beatles and Queen tunes and a much-discussed detour into bluegrass. Constant touring helped the band's sound develop into highly focused works like *Rift* (1993) and on to more improvisational works such as *The Story Of The Ghost* (1997) and *The Siket Disc* (1998), both developed from hours of recordings of the band jamming.

Anastasio has always played hollow-body electrics built by his friend and former audio technician **Paul Languedoc**. Since the dissolution of Phish, he has appeared onstage with many artists, including Phil Lesh and Friends, reaffirming Anastasio's allegiance to the legacy of the Grateful Dead and cofounder and guitarist Jerry Garcia. Anastasio ran afoul of the law as a result of drug use in 2007, and was sidelined for part of 2008. But the ever-expanding community of Phish fans that he helped create thrives online. Phish reunited in 2009 with shows in the US, and the band toured throughout the year, also releasing the new album *Joy*.

Playlists | Links
ebooks & more

FlameTreeRock.com

James Burton
PICKIN' MASTER

Louisiana native James Burton (b. 1939) is one of several guitarists weaned on country music who parlayed his unique talent into session and tour work with rock musicians while maintaining his ties to the country community.

Burton first achieved local fame as a backing musician on the popular 'Louisiana Hayride' radio show, which spotlighted a young Elvis and rivalled the 'Grand Ole Opry' as a radio institution in 1950s America. In Louisiana, Burton got his first significant exposure with his guitar solo on the 1957 Dale Hawkins hit 'Suzie Q'. Soon, Burton was in California, and his talents were deemed perfect for the sound of the emerging teen idol Ricky Nelson, whose family television show, 'The Adventures Of Ozzie And Harriet', was another American pop culture icon. Burton spent six years recording and touring with Ricky, even appearing on the TV show himself while establishing Nelson as a pop presence with distinctive guitar riffs on hits like 'Hello Mary Lou', 'Lonesome Town' and 'Teenage Idol'.

Burton's 'chicken pickin'' mastery on **Dobro** and guitar landed him studio gigs with artists as diverse as Joni Mitchell, the Monkees and Merle Haggard, as part of the legendary LA studio band known as the Wrecking Crew. Burton soon began an eight-year stint with Elvis's TCB band, which lasted until the singer's death in 1977. Almost immediately thereafter, Burton began a 16-year musical relationship with John Denver, again recording and touring with the singer up to his untimely death in 1997. Burton is unrivalled in his melding of country and rock guitar idioms and in his association with pop superstars (Nelson, Presley and Denver) whose lives ended tragically.

Burton was also part of the acclaimed Cinemax special, 'Roy Orbison And Friends, A Black And White Night'. Beginning with *King Of America* (1987), Burton also recorded and toured with Elvis Costello for about a decade. Burton was elected to the Rock and Roll Hall of

Fame in 2001. He was elected to the Musicians Hall of Fame in November 2007 as a member of the Wrecking Crew and has since collaborated with musicians including Brad Paisley and Jerry Lee Lewis.

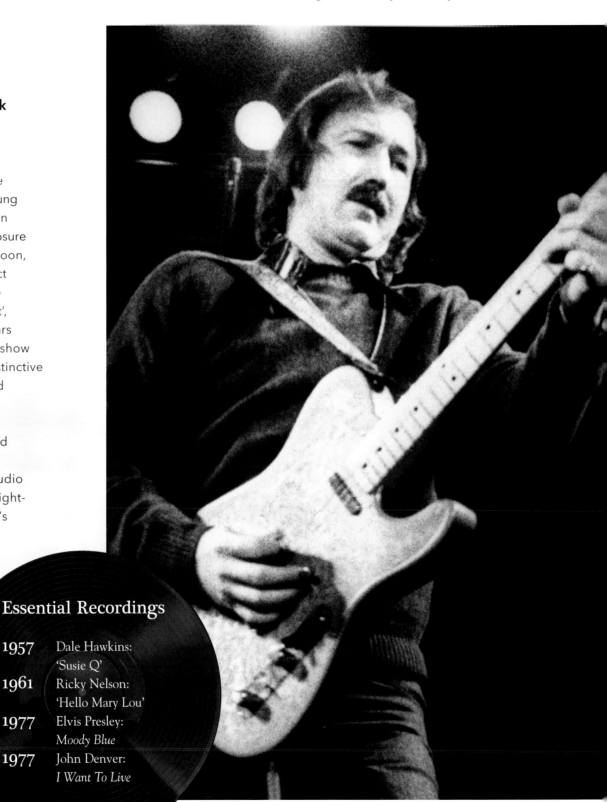

Essential Recordings

1957	Dale Hawkins: 'Susie Q'
1961	Ricky Nelson: 'Hello Mary Lou'
1977	Elvis Presley: *Moody Blue*
1977	John Denver: *I Want To Live*

Peter Frampton
LEGEND COMES ALIVE

Peter Frampton (b. 1950) rode a slow-developing wave of popularity that transported him from British teen idol to international pop megastar, only to see the wave crash in a show-business wipeout of legendary proportions. In the ensuing 30 years, Frampton has managed to mix a fair number of successes with disappointments while navigating much calmer musical seas.

Essential Recordings

1969   Humble Pie:
As Safe As Yesterday Is

1976   Solo:
Frampton Comes Alive!

1977   Solo:
I'm In You

2006   Solo:
Fingerprints

Frampton got his first guitar at the age of eight and took classical lessons. But by the age of 10, he was playing rock'n'roll and by his mid-teens, was in the Preachers, who were produced and managed by Bill Wyman. By 1966, he was lead singer and guitarist in the Herd, with whom he scored a handful of British hits. In early 1969, at 18, he cofounded Humble Pie. In two years, Frampton recorded five albums with Humble Pie, leaving to concentrate on a solo career just as the band's *Rockin' The Fillmore* (1971) ascended the American charts.

Guesting on George Harrison's *All Things Must Pass* (1970), Frampton encountered an effects device, the talk box, for the first time. He released four solo albums between 1972 and 1975, and his buzz began to build through nonstop touring. His show, as recorded at San Francisco's Winterland in 1975, was released in February 1976 as *Frampton Comes Alive!*. Within months, Peter Frampton was the biggest pop-rock star in the world.

The album became the biggest-selling live LP of all time. But Frampton was pressured to record a follow-up quickly. The result, *I'm In You* (1977), was deemed a disappointment in the wake of *FCA!*.

Then, the film *Sergeant Pepper's Lonely Hearts Club Band* (1978), in which Frampton starred, flopped. The crash was complete when Frampton suffered a near-fatal car accident in the Bahamas and an ensuing bout with drug dependency. Frampton was never able to regain the popularity that attended *Frampton Comes Alive!*, though he would continue to record and tour, sometimes in support of pals like David Bowie and Ringo Starr. Frampton, however, never lost his dedication to guitar. In 2006, he released an all-instrumental work, *Fingerprints*. In 2007, it won the Grammy for Best Pop Instrumental Album. A new album titled *Thank You Mr Churchill* was released in 2010, and in 2011, Frampton toured the US with the Frampton Comes Alive 35th Anniversary Tour.

George Harrison
BEATLEMANIA

Pigeonholed as the 'quiet one', misunderstood as an adopter of Eastern religion and music, and overshadowed (sometimes maligned) by his prolific, trail-blazing bandmates Lennon and McCartney, George Harrison (1943-2001) might have become a footnote in musical history. But as a member of the Beatles, Harrison made the words 'lead guitar' a household term and steadily developed as a songwriter and player to the point of equal artistic footing with his mates, as evidenced by his contributions to the band's penultimate album *Abbey Road* (1969) and the abundant creativity of his early solo career. He demonstrated amply that there was life (and love and peace) after the Beatles.

Essential Recordings

1969	The Beatles: *Abbey Road*
1970	Solo: *All Things Must Pass*
1971	with Friends: *The Concert For Bangladesh*
1988	Traveling Wilburys: *Traveling Wilburys Vol. 1*

Influenced by the British skiffle star Lonnie Donegan, American rockabilly guitarist Carl Perkins and Nashville stalwart Chet Atkins, Harrison was already developing a unique style when, at the invitation of schoolmate Paul McCartney, he joined John Lennon's Quarrymen and became part of rock history. Harrison would endure the mayhem of Beatlemania and find solace in the music and faith he encountered in India. As a songwriter, he would grow slowly from the telling solitude of 'Don't Bother Me' to the universality of 'Something' and 'Here Comes The Sun'. As a guitarist, he would often defer to the wishes of McCartney and producer George Martin on solos (and to the talents of Eric Clapton on 'While My Guitar Gently Weeps'). But his carefully crafted solos and phenomenal exposure with the band inspired millions to take up the guitar, while making the **Gretsch Country Gentleman** and **Rickenbacker 360** 12-string two of the world's most recognized instruments.

Embracing Indian music (along with the Hare Krishna faith), Harrison exposed the Western world to the sitar and brought exotic sounds to the Beatles' records as they shifted their focus from live performing to studio work. As a solo artist, Harrison was the first ex-Beatle to score a major hit with his three-disc **All Things Must Pass**. He adopted a signature slide-guitar sound and branched out with historic work as a humanitarian (**The Concert For Bangladesh**), film-maker (Handmade Films) and bandmate (the Traveling Wilburys). When he died of brain cancer in 2001, he left a legacy of guitar music and influence that justified his 2004 entry as a solo artist into the Rock and Roll Hall of Fame. Martin Scorsese's documentary film **George Harrison: Living In The Material World** was released in 2011.

Playlists | Links ebooks & more
FlameTreeRock.com

Davey Johnstone
VERSATILITY AND COMMAND

Davey Johnstone (b. 1951) rocketed to fame with the Rocket Man himself, Elton John, as the former Reg Dwight exploded on to the music scene in the early 1970s, rising from thoughtful love balladeer to raucous glam rocker/showman to international pop-music institution and legend. Except for a short period from the late 1970s to the early 1980s, Johnstone always occupied the nucleus of John's band, along with drummer Nigel Olsson and bassist Dee Murray, who died in 1992.

Essential Recordings

1972   Elton John:
        Honky Chateau
1973   Elton John:
        Goodbye Yellow Brick Road
1973   Solo:
        Smiling Face
1998   with John Jorgenson:
        Crop Circles

Johnstone was a busy studio acoustic guitarist when he was asked to join the British folk group Magna Carta. Johnstone was part of the band for three albums, during the recording of which he played a wide variety of instruments, including guitar, mandolin, sitar and dulcimer. Magna Carta producer Gus Dudgeon asked Johnstone to play on a self-titled 1970 solo album by a new artist, Bernie Taupin. Taupin's collaborator, John, then invited Johnstone to play on his 1971 album *Madman Across The Water*. Johnstone found a sonic niche for himself on the prolific John's piano-based arrangements, ranging from *Madman*'s moody atmospherics to the spacey effects of 'Rocket Man', on 1972's *Honky Chateau*, to his signature crunch on 'Saturday Night's Alright For Fighting' (*Goodbye Yellow Brick Road*, 1973).

Johnstone did work with other acts occasionally, including future wife Kiki Dee, Joan Armatrading, Leo Sayer, Alice Cooper, the Who, Meat Loaf, Stevie Nicks, Yvonne Elliman, Bob Seger, Rod Stewart, George Jones, Belinda Carlisle and Vonda Shepherd. The who's who list is a testament to Johnstone's versatility and command of genre.

Johnstone also released a solo album, 1973's *Smiling Face*, and has created the *Warpipes* project with other John alumni and a well-received album of acoustic instrumentation, 1998's *Crop Circles*, with ex-John and Hellecasters guitarist John Jorgenson. In 1996, Johnstone released a video of instructional guitar called *Davey Johnstone: Starlicks Master Sessions*, on which he plays a wide variety of Elton John classics, joined by Billy Trudel on vocals and Bob Birch on bass. In 2009, Johnstone played his 2,000th show as a member of the Elton John band.

Playlists | Links ebooks & more

FlameTreeRock.com

Terry Kath
CHICAGO'S PARAGON

Terry Kath (1946–78) was the guitarist and a founding member of the jazz-rock ensemble Chicago Transit Authority (soon shortened to Chicago), which, like their contemporaries Blood, Sweat & Tears, brought a jazzy, horn-based sound to hard rock with their early albums, before settling into a superstardom built around anthemic pop ballads. Early on, however, it was the virtuoso playing and guttural blues singing of Kath that helped define the band's unique sound.

Kath grew up in Chicago, playing bass and guitar in local bands in the early and mid-1960s. Towards the end of the decade, he joined his pal, saxophonist Walter Parazaider, and two other horn players in a big band of serious songwriter/instrumentalists, including keyboardist Robert Lamm and bassist Peter Cetera. The Chicago Transit Authority's first (eponymous) album from 1969 was a smash, driven by Kath's self-styled masterpiece 'Introduction', his rhythmic acoustic strumming on 'Beginnings', his inspired wailing on the cover of 'I'm A Man' and his Hendrix-like adventurousness on 'Free Form Guitar'. (Kath knew and admired Hendrix, who famously told Parazaider, 'Your guitar player is better than me'.) The follow-up *Chicago II* (1970) was an even bigger smash, with Kath blazing a fiery solo on the hit '25 or 6 to 4', and perhaps initiating the group's appeal as a ballad band with his vocals on the popular make-out classic 'Colour My World'.

Kath most often played a **Gibson SG** or a **Fender Strat** and used multiple effects boxes, including a wah-wah pedal that he used to great effect, along with his vocals, on the *Chicago III* (1971) social commentary 'Dialogue'. Kath was a major part of the first seven Chicago albums, but was known to be unhappy in 1978 and working on a solo album. He would not live to see its release, however. At a party in January 1978, Kath, a gun aficionado, was pointing a handgun to his head and pulling the trigger, reassuring friends, 'Don't worry, it's not loaded'. But Kath was mistaken, and he died from a self-inflicted head wound a week shy of his thirty-second birthday.

Essential Recordings

1969 The Chicago Transit Authority: *The Chicago Transit Authority*
1970 Chicago: *Chicago II*
1971 Chicago: *Chicago III*
1976 Chicago: *Chicago X*

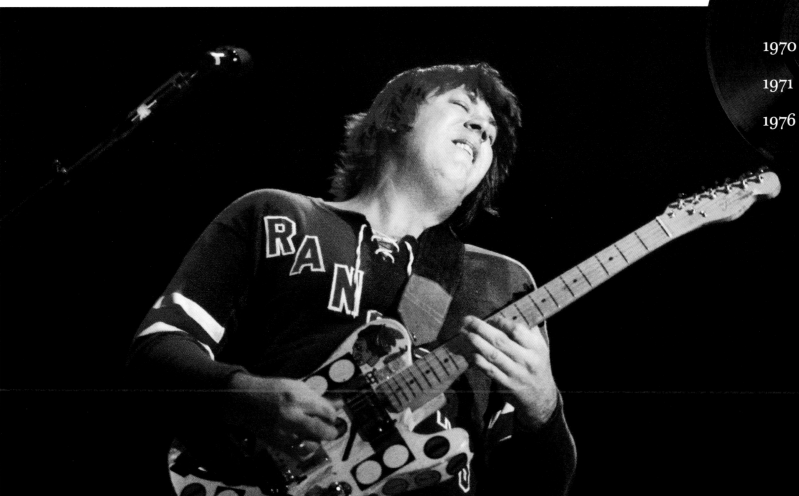

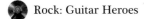

Lenny Kravitz
RETRO ROCKER AND TRENDSETTER

Producer-performer Lenny Kravitz (b. 1964) has explored multiple genres during his 25-year career as a music star, but has often been thought of as married to retro styles. Born in New York, Kravitz was raised in Los Angeles. His parents, a television producer and an actress, were well connected in show business. Kravitz decided to pursue rock'n'roll while in high school. Heavily influenced by Prince, Kravitz at first patterned his style and approach directly after Prince and became known as Romeo Blue.

Essential Recordings

1991   Solo:
Mama Said

1993   Solo:
Are You Gonna Go My Way

1998   Solo:
5

2001   Solo:
Lenny

In the late 1980s, Kravitz moved back to New York and began looking to classic rockers for inspiration. Kravitz inked a recording deal and issued his debut release, *Let Love Rule* (1989). The title track became a hit single and video, and Kravitz gained a reputation as a trendsetter. He began to compose for other artists, writing Madonna's 'Justify My Love'.

Kravitz's work in the 1990s included: *Mama Said* (1991), which featured the funk rocker 'Always On The Run' (a collaboration with Guns N' Roses guitarist Slash) and the soul ballad 'It Ain't Over 'Til It's Over'; 1993's *Are You Gonna Go My Way*, which made Kravitz an arena headliner and media star; and 1998's *5*, which included the biggest hit of his career, 'Fly Away'.

In the twenty-first century, Kravitz continued to record, and branched out with his own design company. He recorded a funky version of John Lennon's 'Cold Turkey' for Amnesty International's 2007 benefit compilation *Instant Karma*. Kravitz returned in 2008 with *It Is Time For A Love Revolution*. In 2011, he released the album *Black And White America*, opened for U2 on a handful of tour dates and was honoured in Paris by being made an Officer of the Ordre

des Arts et des Lettres – a prestigious cultural award. In 2018 he released his 11th studio album, *Raise Vibration*.

Kravitz's first guitar was a **Fender Jazzmaster**. 'I'd always wanted a **Les Paul**', he said in 2002. 'And then my dad got me the **Jazzmaster**, which was cool, but I always wanted a **Les Paul**. And so I traded it in when I had some money, a couple years later, and got my first **Les Paul**'. He has also used a **Les Paul Goldtop** with a **Park** amplifier, a **Flying V** that he designed and had built at **Gibson**, and a **Les Paul Custom SG** with three pickups, as well as an **Epiphone Sorrento**.

Steve Lukather
TOTO TO COOL LICKS

Although his band of high-school buddies achieved international fame under the name Toto, Steve Lukather (b. 1957), session guitarist extraordinaire, has had to struggle under the same suspicion under which his bandmates have toiled: that the whole may add up to less than the sum of its parts. For Toto, despite achieving worldwide fame with singles like 'Rosanna' and 'Africa' in the early 1980s, was first and foremost a band of extraordinarily talented and seasoned studio players who emerged in the Los Angeles recording scene of the 1970s.

Lukather, a native of LA, first played drums and keyboards, but switched to guitar when he discovered the Beatles as a boy. In high school, he met drummer Jeff Porcaro and keyboardist Steve Porcaro, as well as keyboardist/singer David Paich, son of veteran film and TV arranger/conductor Marty Paich. All were becoming active in the burgeoning LA studio scene, and the Porcaro brothers were crucial to Lukather's obtaining session work and burnishing his reputation as a multi-style studio guitarist. By the time he was asked to join the Porcaros, Paich, bassist David Hungate and singer Bobby Kimball in Toto, Lukather had already recorded and toured with Boz Skaggs. In the coming years, he would play on hundreds of hit records, including releases by Leo Sayer, Boz Scaggs, Alice Cooper, Barbra Streisand, the Pointer Sisters, Cher and Cheap Trick – in the 1970s alone.

Toto garnered a lot of buzz with their debut album, and exploded two years later with *Toto IV* (1982), but after that, the band settled into a long run with a mostly international cult following. With a breakout performance on Michael Jackson's *Thriller* (1982), Lukather became a superstar guitarist and took on a larger role with Toto, cowriting most of the group's songs and taking over lead vocals. He launched a solo career in the late 1980s and won a Grammy for his collaboration with Larry Carlton, *No Substitutions* (2001). Toto continued to tour internationally, but the band couldn't regain its early popularity in the US. In 2008, Lukather left Toto and the band

Essential Recordings

1978	Toto: *Toto*
1982	Toto: *Toto IV*
1982	Michael Jackson: *Thriller*
2001	with Larry Carlton: *No Substitutions*

dissolved, although they later reformed to tour again in support of bassist Mike Porcaro after he was diagnosed with Lou Gehrig's disease. Lukather continues to work on solo projects – his most recent release being 2013's *Transition* – and perform on other artists' recordings. Lukather plays his own **MusicMan** signature model 'Luke', which incorporates his signature **EMG** pickup system.

Playlists | Links ebooks & more
FlameTreeRock.com

Roger
McGuinn
SIGNATURE SOUNDS

James Joseph McGuinn (b. 1942) was raised in Chicago and became a fan of folk music as a teenager. He asked for and received a guitar from his parents after hearing Elvis's 'Heartbreak Hotel'. In 1957, McGuinn entered Chicago's Old Town School of Folk Music, where he studied five-string banjo and guitar.

Essential Recordings

1965   The Byrds:
       Mr. Tambourine Man

1965   The Byrds:
       Turn! Turn! Turn!

1968   The Byrds:
       Sweetheart Of The Rodeo

1975   Solo:
       Roger McGuinn & Band

McGuinn's skills and solo performances attracted the attention of recording artists in the burgeoning folk-music craze, and by 1964, he had been a member of the Limeliters, the Chad Mitchell Trio and Bobby Darin's band. As a session musician for Darin's New York publishing company, he recorded with Hoyt Axton, Judy Collins and a young duo named Tom & Jerry, soon to become Simon & Garfunkel. Relocating to Los Angeles in 1964 was the move that would initiate the making of McGuinn's legend.

In LA, McGuinn met singer-guitarist David Crosby and singer-songwriter Gene Clark, with whom McGuinn released a failed single as the Beefeaters before adding bassist Chris Hillman and drummer Michael Clarke to form the Byrds. The goal was to bring elements of the British invasion sound to the folk-influenced modern songs of Bob Dylan and the band's writers. The first single, Dylan's 'Mr. Tambourine Man', featured McGuinn's new, revolutionary guitar sound: a **Rickenbacker** 12-string heavily compressed in the studio to create a jingly sustain that would influence guitarists for decades. McGuinn would later adapt the sound for the spacey ambience of the Byrds' psychedelic hit 'Eight Miles High' (1966).

Along the way, Chicago's Jim McGuinn was renamed Roger by the founder of the Subud spiritual group. The original Byrds would enjoy enormous success, but would soon split, reform and spawn solo careers.

McGuinn has continued to tour and record solo albums, his latest release being 2011's sea shanty-inspired *CCD*. He has also become an internet pioneer artist, covering classic songs on his Folk Den website. In November 2005, McGuinn released a four-CD box set containing 100 of his favourite songs from the Folk Den. But he will for ever be remembered as the guitarist who melded folk, country, rock and psychedelia into a signature guitar sound.

Joni Mitchell
CREATIVE TUNER

Joni Mitchell (b. 1943) evolved from a traditional folk singer in the 1960s to a world-class singer, composer and innovator whose unique guitar tunings and jazz explorations in the 1970s and 1980s are still widely influential.

Mitchell began singing in small nightclubs in Canada. In 1965, she moved to the United States and began touring. Some of her original songs were covered by notable folk singers, which led to her debut album in 1968. Popular songs like 'Big Yellow Taxi' and 'Woodstock' expanded her popularity, and her 1971 album *Blue* received wide critical and popular acclaim. Mitchell began exploring jazz rhythms on 1974's *Court And Spark*, her bestselling LP, which featured the radio hits 'Help Me' and 'Free Man In Paris'.

Her gymnastic vocals and distinctive open-tuned guitar and piano compositions grew more complex as she explored jazz, melding it with influences of rock'n'roll, R&B, classical music and non-Western rhythms. In the late 1970s, she began working closely with noted jazz musicians, among them Jaco Pastorius, Herbie Hancock, Pat Metheny and Charles Mingus, who asked her to collaborate on his final recordings. She is the sole record producer credited on most of her albums, including all her work in the 1970s. She has designed her own album artwork throughout her career.

Mitchell initially learned guitar from a folk songbook, but polio in childhood had weakened her left hand, and some fingerings were difficult for her to execute. As she added new folk songs to her repertoire, she began to devise alternative tunings that allowed her to play each song. Later, she said, this improvised approach would be 'a tool to break free of standard approaches to harmony and structure' in her own songwriting.

Almost every song Mitchell composes on the guitar uses a non-standard open tuning, and she has written songs in some 50 tunings. In 1995, Mitchell began using a **Roland VG** system that could reproduce her numerous tunings electronically without the need to

physically change the tuning of the guitar. Mitchell's longtime archivist, the San Francisco-based Joel Bernstein, maintains a detailed list of all her tunings at jonimitchell.com, and has assisted her in relearning the tunings for several older songs.

Essential Recordings

1970	Solo: *Ladies Of The Canyon*
1971	Solo: *Blue*
1974	Solo: *Court And Spark*
2000	Solo: *Both Sides Now*

Rick Nielsen
NO CHEAP TRICKS

As lead guitarist and primary songwriter of the rock band Cheap Trick, Rick Nielsen fired the band's melting pot of pop melodies and punk energy. Nielsen also became a highly coveted session player in the 1970s. With his legendary guitar collection (numbering over 250) and a unique stage wardrobe featuring bow ties and baseball caps, Nielsen's style made him one of the true rock iconoclasts.

Richard Nielsen was born in December 1946 in Rockford, Illinois. He took up the guitar in the wake of the British invasion, and had a short-lived record deal in the late 1960s with his band Fuse. Later, Nielsen and bassist Tom Petersson started Cheap Trick with drummer Bun E. Carlos and vocalist Randy 'Xeno' Hogan. In 1974, Hogan left the band and was replaced by Robin Zander.

Essential Recordings

1978 Cheap Trick: *Heaven Tonight*

1978 Cheap Trick: *At Budokan*

1979 Cheap Trick: *Dream Police*

1988 Cheap Trick: *Lap Of Luxury*

Epic signed the group in 1976, and released its self-titled album in February 1977. Neither the debut nor their next two albums, *In Color* (1977) and *Heaven Tonight* (1978), were well received at the time, although *Heaven Tonight*, with its teen anthem 'Surrender', is now considered by many to be the group's best album. But Cheap Trick's real strength was their live show, and on tour in Japan in 1978, they recorded the breakthrough live album *At Budokan*. By the spring of 1979, it was No. 4 on the US Top 40 album charts, fuelled by the single 'I Want You To Want Me' (originally on *In Color*), which was written by Nielsen.

Cheap Trick would endure many ups and downs, but Nielsen's reputation would continue to build. He performed on Alice Cooper's *From The Inside* (1978), Hall & Oates' *Along The Red Ledge* (1978) and, along with Carlos, the sessions for John Lennon's *Double Fantasy* (1980). His work has turned up frequently on American TV shows such as 'That 70's Show'. Nielsen also wrote, and performed with Cheap Trick, the theme for the comedy news show 'The Colbert Report'. Cheap Trick have continued to tour and record, their most recent studio release being *The Latest* (2009).

Nielsen's unique guitars, including a five-necked monster, have been stars of the band's shows. Nielsen has collaborated with guitar manufacturer **Hamer** on several 'themed' guitars, including the **Rockford** and **Doctor** models.

Orianthi
SANTANA'S APPOINTED SUCCESSOR

Orianthi Panagaris (b. 1985) was born in Adelaide, South Australia, to Greek and Australian parents. She began playing piano at age three, switched to acoustic guitar at six, and to electric at 11. After listening to a lot of Whitesnake, Van Halen and Def Leppard, she was wowed by Carlos Santana at a concert in Adelaide. By the time she was 15, she had performed in her first stage show for Steve Vai. When she was 18, Orianthi met her hero Santana, who invited her join him onstage to jam at a return concert in 2003. Santana has said that if he were to 'pass the torch' to another guitarist, it would be Orianthi.

After releasing her debut studio album *Violet Journey* in 2005, Orianthi relocated to Los Angeles, signed with Geffen Records in late 2006, and opened for Steve Vai in the US. An appearance with Carrie Underwood at the fifty-first annual Grammy Awards led to Orianthi's becoming a member of the singer's band. As a result, she was hired to become Michael Jackson's guitarist for the This Is It tour, which was in rehearsal at the time of Jackson's death. Orianthi appears in the film of the rehearsals, *This Is It* (2009), with Jackson onstage. Later, she played guitar on the song 'Monster' by Michael Jackson featuring 50 Cent, which was released posthumously in 2010. Since then, she has toured or performed with multiple artists, including Alice Cooper, Kid Rock, Adam Lambert and Chris Brown, and has performed on several editions of 'American Idol'.

Orianthi's major label debut *Believe* was released in 2009. It contained the hit 'According To You'. In 2011, she released the five-track EP 'Fire', produced by Dave Stewart. Her third studio album, *Heaven In This Hell*, was released in 2013. In December 2013, she paid tribute to Carlos Santana, performing in the Kennedy Center Honors Gala. In 2014, she toured and recorded an album with Bon Jovi guitarist Richie Sambora. They later teamed up to form RSO and released an album, *Radio Free America*, in 2018.

Essential Recordings

2005	Solo: *Violet Journey*
2009	Solo: *Believe*
2010	Michael Jackson feat. 50 Cent: 'Monster'
2013	Solo: *Heaven In This Hell*

Mick Ronson
BOWIE'S BACKING

In the 25 years before cancer ended his life at the age of 46, Mick Ronson (1946–93) became a guitar icon through his seminal work as part of David Bowie's Spiders From Mars band, work that would lead to production and performance assignments with artists such as Ian Hunter, Lou Reed and Morrissey, as well as American roots rockers such as Bob Dylan and John Mellencamp.

Ronson played in local bands throughout the mid-1960s in his native Hull and endured a failed stint trying to establish himself in London before returning to Hull and joining the Rats. In 1970, former Rat John Cambridge came back to Hull to recruit Ronson as guitarist in David Bowie's backing band. The band, originally called the Hype, at points included producer Tony Visconti and keyboardist Rick Wakeman. Ronson's flair for arranging and playing grounded Bowie as he developed his outsized persona on the early albums *The Man Who Sold The World* (1970), *Hunky Dory* (1971) and *The Rise And Fall Of Ziggy Stardust And The Spiders From Mars* (1972).

Essential Recordings

1970   David Bowie:
The Man Who Sold The World

1971   David Bowie:
Hunky Dory

1972   David Bowie:
The Rise And Fall Of Ziggy Stardust And The Spiders From Mars

1974   Solo:
Slaughter On 10th Avenue

Ronson's playing and arranging brought him the producer's hat in 1972 for Lou Reed's *Transformer* with Bowie, as well as the unlikely leap to work on American country-rock group Pure Prairie League's *Bustin' Out* (1972), on which Ronson contributed string-ensemble arrangements along with guitar and vocals. Ronson played on Bowie's *Aladdin Sane* and *Pin Ups* (both 1973), but left Bowie after the 'Farewell Concert' in 1973. In the ensuing years, Ronson released three solo albums. The first, *Slaughter On 10th Avenue* (1974), featured Ronson's best-known solo piece, 'Only After Dark'.

After a brief stint with Mott The Hoople, Ronson worked steadily with former Hoople singer Ian Hunter. Ronson was also part of Dylan's Rolling Thunder Revue and worked on records by Elton John, T-Bone Burnett and Roger McGuinn. His last high-profile live performance was his appearance at the Freddie Mercury Tribute Concert in 1992.

For his work with Bowie, Ronson favoured a stripped-paint **Gibson Les Paul** and **Marshall** amp. Thereafter, he often used a **Fender Telecaster**. Ronson died from liver cancer in April 1993.

Todd Rundgren
FROM ECLECTIC TO ICONIC

Perhaps no other artist has forged so eclectic a career as guitarist-singer-songwriter-producer-technologist-experimenter Todd Rundgren (b. 1948). In his 40 years on the rock scene, Rundgren has pursued interests ranging from pop songcraft to experimental composition with his band Utopia, and from innovative record production to nostalgic reinvention tours with Ringo Starr's All-Starr Band and the New Cars.

Rundgren's guitar playing took a backseat to his far-reaching production concepts while shining brightly within its designated assignment. The harmonized slide solos on the hit 'I Saw The Light' and his playing on extended-instrumental albums like 1974's *Todd* and the same-year debut *Todd Rundgren's Utopia* define guitar as a support instrument, as did his sound-for-sound remake of the Beach Boys' 'Good Vibrations'.

Rundgren began playing guitar as a child in Philadelphia and was influenced in his teens by Motown and the British invasion. He played in bar bands, culminating in Woody's Truck Stop, a blues band. In 1967, he left the group to form the Nazz, which landed a record deal in 1968. The debut album's first single was a slow version of Rundgren's later hit, 'Hello, It's Me'. He left to record as Runt, which served as a front for his expanding solo producing and performing skills. The first album generated a buzz in 1971 with the Top 40 hit 'We Gotta Get You A Woman'. At the same time, Rundgren became an in-demand producer, helming the Band's *Stage Fright* and Badfinger's *Straight Up*. Rundgren's *Something/Anything?* (1972) became a smash due to the Carole King tribute, 'I Saw The Light', and the reworked 'Hello, It's Me'. But Rundgren, proclaiming his disinterest in being a pop star, followed up in 1973 with *A Wizard, A True Star*, a sonic collage of genres that

turned off his mainstream audience and cemented his cult following. In the years that followed, Rundgren expanded his production skills into computer-based, commercial video operations while occasionally touring with performers including Ringo Starr.

In 2009, he produced a theatrical concert version of *A Wizard, A True Star*, with costumes and props to accent the songs. In 2017 he released *White Knight*, featuring collaborations with Trent Reznor, Joe Walsh and Donald Fagen among others.

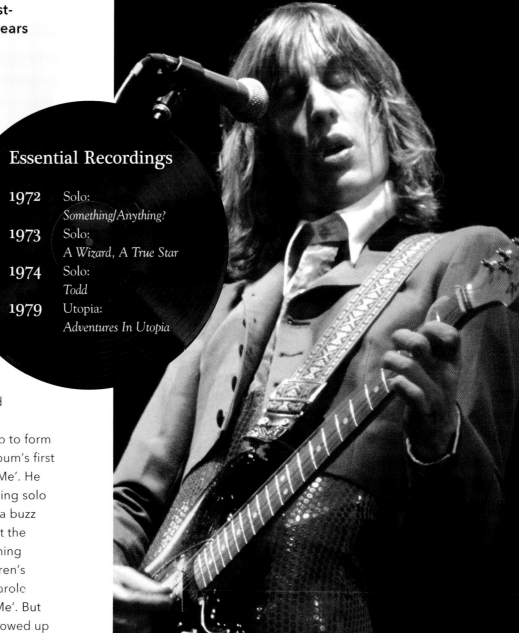

Essential Recordings

1972	Solo: *Something/Anything?*
1973	Solo: *A Wizard, A True Star*
1974	Solo: *Todd*
1979	Utopia: *Adventures In Utopia*

Steve Stevens
BILLY IDOL TO GUITAR IDOL

Brooklyn's Steve Stevens (b. 1959) grew up as a fan of progressive rock and honed his chops by studying guitar at Manhattan's LaGuardia High School of Performing Arts. He worked the Long Island and Manhattan club scenes with bands and eventually was hired for session work, including tracks for ex-KISS drummer Peter Criss. But Stevens' star really began to shine when he met former Generation X frontman Billy Idol in the early 1980s.

Essential Recordings

1983 Billy Idol: *Rebel Yell*

1986 Billy Idol: *Whiplash Smile*

1993 Vince Neil: *Exposed*

1997 Bozzio Levin Stevens: *Black Light Syndrome*

With Stevens' flamboyant shredding jumping out of his songs and videos, Idol's new solo works became smashes, as albums such as 1982's *Billy Idol* and 1983's *Rebel Yell* drove the new music channel MTV. Idol and Stevens collaborated on a third album, 1986's *Whiplash Smile*, another big hit, after which Stevens embarked on a solo career.

Stevens' work with Idol led to work with Michael Jackson (*Bad*), Ric Ocasek (*This Side Of Paradise*), Thompson Twins (*Here's To Future Days*) and Robert Palmer (*Don't Explain*), and he won a Grammy for work with keyboardist Harold Faltermeyer on 'Top Gun Anthem' from the Tom Cruise film. From 1992 to 1994, Stevens worked with ex-Mötley Crüe singer Vince Neil on the album *Exposed*, which featured the cuts 'Sister Of Pain', 'Can't Have Your Cake' and 'You're Invited But Your Friend Can't Come'.

Stevens eventually got back to his prog-rock roots, working with bassist Tony Levin and drummer Terry Bozzio in the Bozzio Levin Stevens group, recording 1997's *Black Light Syndrome* and 2000's *Situation Dangerous*. Stevens reunited with Idol in 1999 for a series of tours across the USA and in Australia. They appeared in 2002 in an episode of 'VH1 Storytellers', which was subsequently released on CD

and DVD. Stevens also appeared in the Billy Idol episode of VH1's 'Behind The Music'. Stevens, influenced by the great flamenco guitarist Paco de Lucía, also recorded a solo release, *Flamenco A Go-Go*, which he recorded in his home studio.

Stevens' renewed collaboration with Idol also resulted in Billy Idol's *Devil's Playground* (2005) with keyboardist Derek Sherinian. This was the first album to feature the trio since *Whiplash Smile*. Stevens recorded his latest album, *Memory Crash*, for Magna Carta Records in 2008.

Stephen Stills
CROSBY, STAR AND NASH

Stephen Stills (b. 1945) turned acoustic guitar into a fiery blues instrument as a solo artist and performer. That alone might have made him a rock icon, but of course Stills was also busy producing, composing and singing with the most popular rock vocal group of all time, creating hit singles on his own, teaming up with individual members of his band and forming new groups for successful albums, and enjoying a 40-year career in the rock spotlight.

An oft-travelled military child, Stills gravitated to California in 1965 after stints with New York-based groups the Au Go Go Singers, which included a young singer named Richie Furay, and the Company, a folk-rock group that toured Canada, where Stills met Squires guitarist Neil Young. In California, Stills recruited the relocated Furay and Young to form Buffalo Springfield and make his first international splash as the composer, singer and guitarist of the socially conscious 'For What It's Worth' (1967). But the Springfield dissolved after two years.

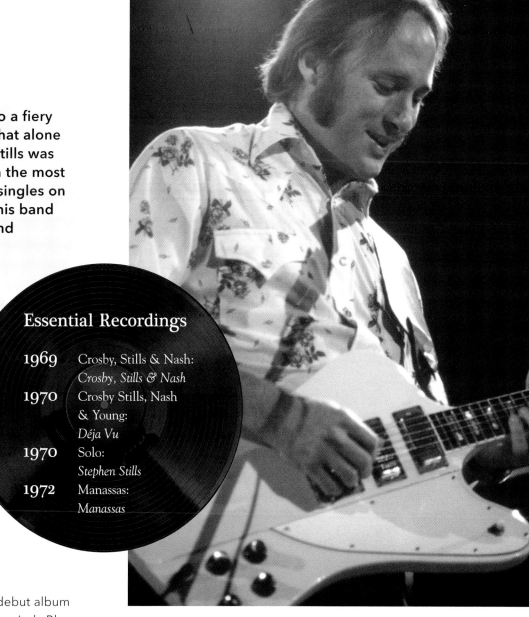

Essential Recordings

1969	Crosby, Stills & Nash: *Crosby, Stills & Nash*
1970	Crosby Stills, Nash & Young: *Déja Vu*
1970	Solo: *Stephen Stills*
1972	Manassas: *Manassas*

A jam session at the home of Joni Mitchell united Stills and former Byrd David Crosby with Hollies singer Graham Nash. As Crosby, Stills & Nash, the trio made a landmark appearance at Woodstock in 1969, and their eponymous debut album from the same year, featuring 'Marakesh Express' and 'Suite: Judy Blue Eyes', became an international smash. The band added Neil Young for the second album **Déjà Vu** (1970), and have continued to perform together in various combinations into the twenty-first century.

Along the way, Stills branched off with projects such as Manassas, a collaboration with another former Byrd, Chris Hillman. The Manassas albums allowed Stills to show his songwriting mastery in hard rock and Latin genres as well as acoustic and country rock. Stills' first two solo albums spawned the hits 'Love The One You're With' and 'Change Partners' (both 1970). As a guitarist, Stills was famous for wild experimentation, and CSNY's sound is identifiable for the rich acoustic guitars utilizing D5 (D-A-D-D-A-D) and Drop D tunings, as well as the iconic 'Suite: Judy Blue Eyes' with its E-E-E-E-B-E tuning. Stills' solos on songs like the CSNY hit 'Woodstock' (1970) and the bluesy solo turn 'Black Queen' (1970) show the fire in the playing of this soft-rock superstar. Stills continues to tour and record sporadically as a solo artist, to mixed reviews. His new blues band, the Rides, released an album, **Can't Get Enough**, in 2013.

Joe Walsh
THE OUTRAGEOUS EAGLE

Joe Walsh (b. 1947) was born in Kansas and spent his childhood in Ohio and his high-school years in New Jersey before returning to Ohio to attend college at Kent State. He played bass in various bands before adopting guitar for a stint in the local group the Measles from 1965 to 1969. That led to a spot with Cleveland-based trio the James Gang, with whom Walsh appeared on the band's debut *Yer' Album* (1969). The follow-up *James Gang Rides Again* produced the rock-radio staple 'Funk #49' (1970).

Essential Recordings

1973	Solo: *The Smoker You Drink, The Player You Get*
1976	Eagles: *Hotel California*
1978	Solo: *But Seriously, Folks …*
1994	Eagles *Hell Freezes Over*

Walsh found the James Gang confining and relocated to Colorado, forming the group Barnstorm and hitting big with the solo follow-up **The Smoker You Drink, The Player You Get** (1973) and its smash hit 'Rocky Mountain Way'. In the wake of expanding solo success, Walsh adopted an even bigger profile in 1976 as the new guitarist in the Eagles, replacing Bernie Leadon and helping change the band's sound from mellow West-Coast country to the harder rock of **Hotel California** (1976).

Walsh continued to impact the Eagles until their breakup in 1980, all the while releasing his own solo material, including **But Seriously, Folks …** (1978), which featured his brilliant comic statement on the rock life, 'Life's Been Good'. In the 1980s, Walsh maintained a lower profile, dealing with alcohol addiction, and returned to touring with Ringo Starr in 1989. With the Eagles' reunion in 1994, Walsh returned to the road and the studio for the band's live **Hell Freezes Over** set and 2007 studio album **Long Road Out Of Eden**. His most recent solo album, **Analog Man**, was released in 2012.

Walsh's rhythm-guitar playing defines classic funk-rock and his fluid lead lines on tracks like 'Life In The Fast Lane' and 'Hotel California' are

textbook meldings of rock and soul. Combined with an outrageous personality that has made him a staple on American comedy radio and TV shows, his considerable talents helped Walsh forge one of the best-known and most endearing characters in rock. But his comic freewheeling nature belies his skills as one of the most tasteful, precise and accomplished guitarists in rock.

Playlists | Links
ebooks & more

FlameTreeRock.com

Clarence White
INNOVATOR OF COUNTRY ROCK

In his short life, California guitarist-mandolinist Clarence White (1944–73) conceived innovations that would inspire country and rock guitarists from both a stylistic and technical perspective long after his death. He brought bluegrass picking to the forefront of rock, turning acoustic guitar into a solo instrument. He developed a device for electric guitar that let traditional guitarists sound like pedal-steel players. As a member of the Byrds from 1968 to 1973, he brought a new level of musicianship to a band that, with the exception of Roger McGuinn, didn't even play on their first hit single.

Born into a family of musicians, White played with his brothers in the Country Boys, which became the Kentucky Colonels. His skills led to session work on many mid-1960s pop and rock albums, as well as live gigs alongside Gene Parsons, Gib Gilbeau and former Byrd Gene Clark. White joined Parsons and Gilbeau in the band Nashville West and was invited to record with the Byrds as the band was leaving behind their British invasion bent for a tighter focus on the marriage of country and rock. White's innovative string bending and solos on the group's seminal *Sweetheart Of The Rodeo* (1968) enlivened tracks like 'The Christian Life' and 'One Hundred Years From Now'. In 1968, he joined the band and toured with them until their final split in 1973. He had continued studio work during his tenure, alternating with Ry Cooder as guitarist on Randy Newman's *12 Songs* (1970) and collaborating with Jackson Browne on his albums.

With fellow Byrd Gene Parsons, White developed a device, the B-Bender, that would allow guitarists to bend strings independently of their fretting hands, giving six-string guitarists the mournful sound of a pedal steel with less work. The sound is perhaps most familiar from Bernie Leadon's solo on the Eagles' 'Peaceful Easy Feeling' (1972), but has been used on records by artists as diverse as Led Zeppelin and Donna Summer. White, however, wouldn't live to see his invention gain its following. He was killed by a drunk driver while loading gear into his car after a performance with the Kentucky Colonels in 1973.

Essential Recordings

1964   The Kentucky Colonels
            Appalachian Swing!
1968   The Byrds:
            Sweetheart Of The Rodeo
1969   The Byrds:
            Ballad Of Easy Rider
1970   Randy Newman:
            12 Songs

I can't play [guitar] like Segovia. … [but] Segovia could probably never have played like me.

Kurt Cobain

Alternative
& Indie

Matthew Bellamy
RULER OF THE RIFF

Twenty-first-century guitar hero Matthew Bellamy (b. 1978) was born in Cambridge, England. His father George was rhythm guitarist in the Tornadoes, who scored a massive transatlantic hit with the Joe Meek-produced 'Telstar'. Before learning guitar, Bellamy took piano lessons as a boy, equally inspired by Ray Charles and classical music. In the mid-1980s, the family moved to Teignmouth, Devon, where Bellamy formed Muse with Chris Wolstenholme (bass) and Dominic Howard (drums).

Essential Recordings

2001   Muse:
            Origin Of Symmetry
2003   Muse:
            Absolution
2006   Muse:
            Black Holes And Revelations
2009   Muse:
            The Resistance

The band served their apprenticeship through constant gigging while soaking up more influences, notably Jeff Buckley and Radiohead, to whom they would often be compared,

much to Bellamy's irritation. After an independently released limited edition EP, Muse signed a major deal in 1998. Debut album *Showbiz* (1999) marked them as a band with the potential for crossover appeal to fans of indie, metal and prog rock. With the guitarist emerging as an energetic frontman, *Origin Of Symmetry* (2001) was a more expansive collection, featuring Bellamy's untamed riffing and drawing on influences as diverse as Rage Against The Machine, Ned's Atomic Dustbin, Rachmaninov and Philip Glass. As remarkable as his guitar style was, Bellamy's soaring voice added emotion to the bombast. His riff from the single 'Plug In Baby' has been hailed as one of the greatest of all time.

Absolution (2003) developed the classical influences as Muse's popularity began to grow. Bellamy's lyrical themes of Armageddon, global conspiracy theories and corruption were explored further on *Black Holes And Revelations* (2006), with its political subtext expressed through a series of linked songs. Shortly after its release, Muse became the first group to play the rebuilt Wembley Stadium, confirming their status as one of the biggest bands in Britain. Muse released the live *HAARP* in 2008, *The Resistance* in 2009, *The 2nd Law* in 2012, *Drones* in 2015 and *Simulation Theory* in 2018. Bellamy uses guitars made by **Mansons** of Exeter, principally a silver model that he helped design. Among its customized features is a built-in fuzzbox, through which Bellamy achieves his unique sound and which also allows him to control feedback. He has also played a **Fender Stratocaster**, a **Gibson SG**, a **Les Paul** and a **Yamaha Pacifica**.

Kurt Cobain
LEADING A GENERATION

Arguably the most important alternative guitarist of the 1990s, Kurt Cobain (1967–94) was born in Aberdeen, Washington. His parents divorced when he was seven, which had a traumatic effect on Cobain, tainting the remainder of his life. From an early age, he showed a keen interest in music, singing along to Beatles' songs on the radio. Given a guitar for his fourteenth birthday, he taught himself to play along to AC/DC and the Cars.

Cobain was influenced equally by hard rock, punk and pop, admiring Aerosmith, Black Sabbath, Led Zeppelin, Cheap Trick, Boston, Sex Pistols, Sonic Youth, the Pixies and, he claimed, the Bay City Rollers. He formed Nirvana with bassist and fellow punk-rock fan Krist Novoselic, and with drummer Chad Channing, they formed part of the burgeoning Seattle scene, which would later be termed 'grunge'. The band recorded an album, **Bleach** (1989), for the local Sub Pop label.

Essential Recordings

1989   Nirvana: *Bleach*

1991   Nirvana: *Nevermind*

1993   Nirvana: *In Utero*

1994   Nirvana: *Unplugged In New York*

Soon afterwards, Channing was fired and replaced by powerhouse Dave Grohl. In 1990, Nirvana signed to DGC Records and recorded the crossover smash **Nevermind** (1991) with producer Butch Vig. Trailed by the classic single 'Smells Like Teen Spirit' with its genre-defining quiet verse/loud chorus structure, **Nevermind** mixed abrasive guitar with pop melodies. Cobain felt that Vig had smoothed out the rough edges of the band's live sound and was determined that the follow-up would capture the real Nirvana; the booming, rumbling **In Utero** (1993) did just that. Best known for his raw, angry style, Cobain was also adept at acoustic work as **Unplugged In New York** (1994) demonstrates. A notorious destroyer of guitars, Kurt favoured the **Fender Mustang**. He also used **Stratocasters**, **Jaguars** and occasionally a **Telecaster**, plus his beloved 1960s **Mosrite Gospel**.

The defiantly anti-Establishment Cobain did not cope well with his newfound celebrity, and his life degenerated into a tabloid soap opera after his marriage to fellow rocker Courtney Love. Struggling with heroin addiction, and stomach pains which had plagued him since childhood, he tried to commit suicide in Rome while on tour in March 1994. A month later, he shot and killed himself at his home in Seattle. Nirvana was inducted into the Rock and Roll Hall of Fame in April 2014.

Playlists | Links ebooks & more

FlameTreeRock.com

Billy Corgan
PUMPKINS' PERFECTIONIST

Alternative-rock guitarist Billy Corgan (b. 1967) was born in Chicago, Illinois. Shortly after starting high school, Corgan began to learn guitar on an imitation Gibson Les Paul. His father, a musician, suggested that Billy listen to Jeff Beck and Jimi Hendrix but refused to teach him to play; consequently, Corgan was self-taught. His early influences were the mainstream rock of Queen, Boston, ELO and Cheap Trick, along with heavier outfits like Black Sabbath and Led Zeppelin. Later, he discovered the alternative scene via Bauhaus, the Cure and the Smiths.

Essential Recordings

1991	The Smashing Pumpkins: *Gish*
1993	The Smashing Pumpkins: *Siamese Dream*
1995	The Smashing Pumpkins: *Mellon Collie And The Infinite Sadness*
2005	Solo: *TheFutureEmbrace*

Corgan formed The Smashing Pumpkins in Chicago in 1988 with James Iha (guitar) and D'arcy Wretzky (bass). The addition of drummer Jimmy Chamberlain pumped up the band's intensity. The Pumpkins' debut album **Gish** (1991) combined hard rock and psychedelia and was recorded under difficult circumstances resulting from tensions within the band (Corgan is believed to have replaced Wretzky's bass and Iha's guitar parts with his own). The recording of **Siamese Dream** (1993) was similarly fraught, with Corgan's control-freak tendencies again dominating the sessions, but it provided a breakthrough success for the Pumpkins. **Siamese Dream** was characterized by multiple layers of guitar that created a distinctive buzzing effect. 'Soma' incorporated Corgan's quieter side before shifting dynamically into a wall of 40 overdubs. Other songs were reputed to contain up to 100 guitar tracks. Corgan's squalling solos were prominent on 'Cherub Rock' and 'Quiet'. **Mellon Collie And The Infinite Sadness** (1995) was an ambitious double CD based around the loose concept of the cycle of life and death. The guitars were often tuned down a half tone as Corgan tried for a greater variety of overdubs. Its success (nine million sold) proved hard to follow and, after two more albums, Smashing Pumpkins disbanded in 2000.

In 2006, the Pumpkins reformed with Corgan and Chamberlain as the only original members, releasing the album **Oceania** in 2012 as part of the wider **Teargarden By Kaleidyscope** project. Iha rejoined in 2018 and the Pumpkins released an album, **Shiny And Oh So Bright, Vol 1/LP: No Past No Future No Sun** later that year after celebrating their 30th anniversary with a show in Holmdel, New Jersey. Corgan's favourite guitar is a **1957 Fender Stratocaster**, although he has used a variety of instruments, including a **Gibson 335**, a **Les Paul** and an **Epiphone SG**.

Graham Coxon
BRINGING GUITAR INTO FOCUS

Indie guitarist Graham Coxon (b. 1969) was born in West Berlin, the son of an army bandsman. His early years were characterized by the itinerant army life until the family settled in Colchester in the late 1970s. The young Coxon was a Beatles fan and possessed a talent for art. He began to learn saxophone and then at 12, obtained his first guitar, which he taught himself to play, inspired by the Jam and the Specials. At secondary school, he made the acquaintance of Damon Albarn.

In 1989, Coxon was studying for a degree in Fine Arts at Goldsmiths College, London, where he met bassist Alex James, and which singer Albarn also attended. Together with drummer Dave Rowntree, they formed Seymour, renamed Blur on signing to indie label Food in 1990. Their first album *Leisure* (1990) was derivative of both the Madchester and shoe-gazing scenes. *Modern Life Is Rubbish* (1993) reacted against grunge and American culture by celebrating Englishness. The two-million-selling *Parklife* (1994) helped to popularize what was soon dubbed 'Britpop'. The theme continued on the oddly lacklustre *The Great Escape* (1995). Coxon's guitar added bite and aggression to Blur's early albums. Their fifth album, *Blur* (1997), represented a radical change in direction influenced by American indie-guitar bands, particularly Pavement. In this environment, Coxon's angular guitar work thrived. On *13* (1999), gospel and electronica were added to the blend.

Early in the sessions for Blur's seventh album, *Think Tank* (2003), Coxon's increasing distance from his bandmates led to his departure. Having already released four solo albums, his first post-Blur work and most successful solo venture was *Happiness In Magazines* (2004). Coxon plays most of the instruments on his albums and supplies the artwork for the covers. His differences with Blur were resolved in 2008 and they have since toured together again, as well as releasing the single 'Fool's Day' in 2010.

Coxon's seventh studio album, *The Spinning Top* (2009), garnered critical raves, and *A+E* followed in 2012. Coxon is an idiosyncratic guitarist, much admired by his peers; Radiohead's Jonny Greenwood is an avowed fan. From early in his career, he has used the **Fender Telecaster** almost exclusively, although more recently, he has started to diversify by playing a **Gibson SG** and a **Les Paul**.

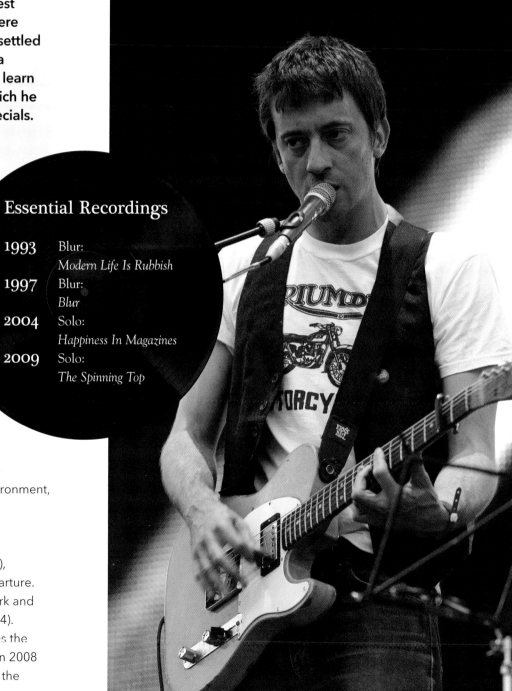

Essential Recordings

1993	Blur: *Modern Life Is Rubbish*
1997	Blur: *Blur*
2004	Solo: *Happiness In Magazines*
2009	Solo: *The Spinning Top*

John
Frusciante
MELODIC MAESTRO

Alt-rock guitarist John Frusciante (b. 1970) was born into a musical family in Queens, New York. While living in Los Angeles after his parents' divorce, Frusciante became involved with the city's punk-rock scene and was particularly inspired by the Germs, teaching himself to play the songs on their first album before taking guitar lessons. He studied Jeff Beck, Jimmy Page and Jimi Hendrix; mastered the blues scale; and then became obsessed with Frank Zappa.

Essential Recordings

1991   Red Hot Chili Peppers:
Blood Sugar Sex Magik

1999   Red Hot Chili Peppers:
Californication

2005   Red Hot Chili Peppers:
Stadium Arcadium

2009   Solo:
The Empyrean

On seeing the Red Hot Chili Peppers at age 15, he became a devotee, learning the guitar parts from their first three albums, as performed by the band's lead guitarist Hillel Slovak. When Slovak died from a heroin overdose in 1988, Frusciante successfully auditioned to replace his role model. His second album with the Chili Peppers, ***Blood Sugar Sex Magik*** (1991), turned the band into stars, but Frusciante was unable to handle the newfound success and quit in May 1992. Struggling with depression, he became addicted to heroin, crack cocaine and alcohol for more than five years, once nearly dying from a blood infection, although he did manage to record and release two solo albums in that period.

By 1998, he had been through rehab and cleaned up. He rejoined the Chili Peppers when his replacement Dave Navarro was fired. The band has since gone on to even greater worldwide success and acclaim. Frusciante's guitar is particularly upfront on ***Stadium Arcadium*** (2005), which saw his playing receive belated recognition from critics and musicians. Following the Stadium Arcadium tour, the Red Hot Chili Peppers agreed to a hiatus of indefinite length. During this period, Frusciante released his tenth solo album, ***The Empyrean***

(2009), with contributions from Flea, Josh Klinghoffer and Johnny Marr. Since leaving the Chili Peppers, he has explored electronica, releasing two further solo albums to a mixed critical reception.

Frusciante is an emotional and melodic guitarist who possesses great technical ability, and many of his live solos are improvised. He is a fan of guitarists with a melody-driven style, such as Bernard Sumner, John McGeoch (Siouxsie and the Banshees) and XTC's Andy Partridge. He prefers pre-1970 guitars for their sonic qualities and selects the most appropriate instrument for the song. Following his 1998 return to the Chili Peppers, he used a **1962 Sunburst Fender Stratocaster**.

Playlists | Links ebooks & more

FlameTreeRock.com

Noel Gallagher
BRITPOP'S TRAIL-BLAZER

Britpop guitarist Noel Gallagher (b. 1967) was born in Manchester, England. He began teaching himself guitar at the age of 13, later adopting Johnny Marr as his role model. His other inspirations were primarily British guitar bands: the Kinks, the Who, Slade, the Jam and the Stone Roses.

After unsuccessfully auditioning for the role of lead singer with Manchester indie group Inspiral Carpets, Gallagher became their roadie. Returning home in 1992 from an American tour, he discovered younger brother Liam singing in a band, Rain, with Paul 'Bonehead' Arthurs (guitar), Paul McGuigan (bass) and Tony McCarroll (drums). Noel allowed himself to be persuaded to join, on the condition that he take creative control. Renamed Oasis, their rise was swift, as the band graduated to stadium gigs within two years of the release of their debut single 'Supersonic' in 1994.

Oasis's first album, *Definitely Maybe* (1994), was steeped in rock classicism, recalling the Sex Pistols with the bass buried beneath multiple layers of guitars. Further homage to his influences was evident in Gallagher's appropriation of T. Rex's 'Get It On' riff for 'Cigarettes And Alcohol'. New drummer Alan White joined for *(What's The Story) Morning Glory?* (1995), and his skills enabled Oasis to craft a more varied, Beatles-influenced collection. Noel's strident lead on the title track and adroit acoustic work on 'Wonderwall' stood out, but he is dismissive of his abilities: 'I'm more of a strummer than a lead guitarist.' Gallagher favours **Epiphone Sheratons** and has a signature blue 'Supernova' model. Carefully matching guitar to song, he also uses a **Fender Stratocaster**, **Telecaster** and **Gibson Les Paul**. Although naturally left-handed, he plays right-handed. Oasis spearheaded a revival in British guitar bands like Cast and Ocean Colour Scene, and later, Travis and Coldplay, who took their lead from the band's quieter side. The Gallagher brothers' pursuit of the rock'n'roll lifestyle resulted in an overproduced third album, *Be Here Now* (1997). Oasis subsequently recovered some of

their early form. Further line-up changes fostered a more flexible musical approach, while the Gallaghers' often combative relationship remained the core dynamic of the band. In 2009, however, the relationship between the two brothers reached breaking point, with Noel confirming on his blog that he had left Oasis to 'seek pastures new'. He has since worked on collaborative projects, as well as fronting new band Noel Gallagher's High Flying Birds, who have released three albums.

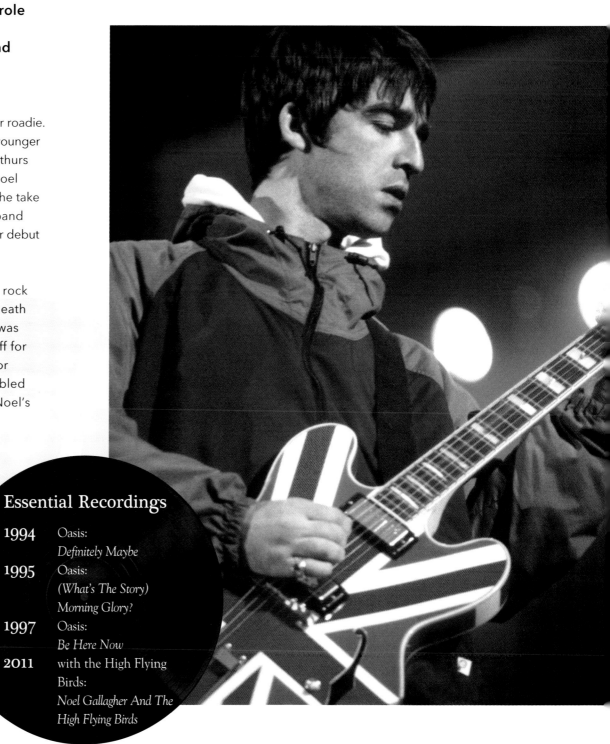

Essential Recordings

1994	Oasis: *Definitely Maybe*
1995	Oasis: *(What's The Story) Morning Glory?*
1997	Oasis: *Be Here Now*
2011	with the High Flying Birds: *Noel Gallagher And The High Flying Birds*

Adam Jones
ALTERNATIVE ALL THE WAY

Alternative-metal guitarist Adam Jones (b. 1965) was born in Park Ridge, Illinois. He learned violin in elementary school, continuing with the instrument in high school, before playing acoustic bass for three years in an orchestra and later teaching himself guitar by ear. Jones studied art and sculpture in Los Angeles before working in a Hollywood character shop sculpting models. His work appeared in several movies, including *Ghostbusters 2* and *Predator 2*. He also worked on set design for various films.

Essential Recordings

1993 Tool: *Undertow*

1996 Tool: *Ænima*

2001 Tool: *Lateralus*

2006 Tool: *10,000 Days*

In 1990, Jones formed Tool with Danny Carey (drums), Maynard James Keenan (vocals) and Paul D'Amour (bass), who was replaced in 1995 by Justin Chancellor. The band's recorded debut, the EP 'Opiate' (1992), was firmly in heavy-metal mode, but *Undertow* (1993), *Ænima* (1996), *Lateralus* (2001) and *10,000 Days* (2006) took the band in not so easily classifiable directions that have been described as art rock, alternative metal, progressive metal and psychedelic metal. The use of unpredictable time signatures, of which 'Schism' from *Lateralus* is a prime example, and their commitment to experimentation, have resulted in Tool being hailed as standard-bearers for the new prog rock. King Crimson, with whom the band has toured, were a major inspiration for Jones, along with Yes. Tool in turn have influenced alternative metal outfits System Of A Down, Breaking Benjamin and Deftones.

Jones employs multiple techniques: power chords, arpeggios, offbeat rhythms and minimalism. On 'Jambi', from *10,000 Days*, he played the solo on a talk box. Although wary of the overuse of effects, he has employed several, in particular the wah-wah, plus a flanger, digital delay and volume pedal. He uses an electric hair remover in

preference to an E-bow, claiming it produces a better sound. He favours **Gibson Silverburst Les Paul Customs** made between 1978 and 1985; he has also used a **Gibson SG** and is rumoured to have played a **Fender Telecaster** on *10,000 Days*. Jones utilizes his background in visual arts and film to create most of Tool's striking artwork and videos. Tool toured in 2009, headlining at Lollapalooza, and again in 2012. The band has been working on a new album for the past five years but for numerous reasons they have been unable to complete it.

Johnny Marr
BONA FIDE
BRITISH LEGEND

Indie guitar legend Johnny Marr (b. 1963) was born John Maher in Manchester, England. He grew up in a household where music was a constant fixture, and he recalled: 'I always had guitars, for as long as I could remember.' Guitar technique came easily to young Johnny, and he quickly mastered chord structures and progressions along with picking and fingering techniques.

As a teenager, he fell under the spell of Marc Bolan and T. Rex, and went on to soak up an extensive range of influences, including Television, Thin Lizzy, Bert Jansch, Howlin' Wolf and Rory Gallagher.

Marr played in various teenage bands before teaming up with singer and lyricist Steven Morrissey in 1982 to form the Smiths. In little more than a year, they were in the charts with their second single, 'This Charming Man', ignited by Marr's exuberant riff played on a **Fender Telecaster**.

Marr employed a diverse range of techniques in the Smiths, including the shimmering effect on 'How Soon Is Now?'; the jangly opening of 'The Headmaster Ritual' from **Meat Is Murder** (1985); the dynamic riffing of 'Bigmouth Strikes Again'; and the wah-wah attack of 'The Queen Is Dead'. Marr took only two solos in the Smiths, on 'Shoplifters Of The World Unite' and 'Paint A Vulgar Picture'.

Marr left the Smiths in 1987, frustrated with the direction of the group and exhausted by the demands of being the de facto manager. He went on to work with many artists, including Billy Bragg, the Pet Shop Boys, Talking Heads, Beck and Bert Jansch.

In 1991, he formed Electronic with Bernard Sumner, which produced three albums, and in 2001, Marr put together his own band, the Healers. He became a member of US indie band Modest Mouse in 2006, and in 2009, began performing and recording with the Cribs,

Essential Recordings

1985	The Smiths: *Meat Is Murder*
1987	The Smiths: *Strangeways, Here We Come*
2003	with the Healers: *Boomslang*
2013	Solo: *The Messenger*

but left the band in 2011. His debut solo album, **The Messenger**, was released in 2013. His second, Playland, came out in 2014.

Johnny Marr has acquired numerous guitars over the years; his 12-string **Rickenbacker 330** once belonged to Pete Townshend. His other favourites are a **1959 Gibson ES-355**, frequently heard on Smiths records, and a **1959 Sunburst Les Paul**.

Playlists | Links ebooks & more

FlameTreeRock.com

Mike McCready
PEARL JAMMER

Alternative-rock guitarist Mike McCready (b. 1966) was born in Pensacola, Florida. His family moved to Seattle soon afterwards. He was 11 when he bought his first guitar and began to take lessons. In high school, McCready formed a band that disintegrated after they were unsuccessful in obtaining a record contract in Los Angeles. Disillusioned, he did not pick up a guitar again for several months until inspired to resume playing by Stevie Ray Vaughan.

Essential Recordings

1991	Temple Of The Dog: *Temple Of The Dog*
1991	Pearl Jam: *Ten*
1993	Pearl Jam: *Vs.*
2000	The Rockfords: *The Rockfords*

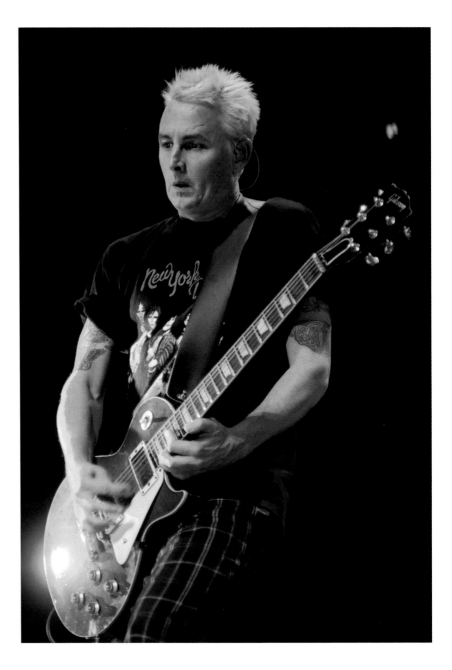

McCready was working with old friend and rhythm guitarist Stone Gossard when the pair were invited to participate in recording *Temple Of The Dog* (1991), a one-off project founded by Soundgarden singer Chris Cornell. McCready's four-minute-plus solo on 'Reach Down' remains one of his proudest achievements. Shortly after recording *Temple Of The Dog*, McCready and Gossard formed Pearl Jam with Eddie Vedder (lead vocals, guitar) and Jeff Ament (bass). Their debut, *Ten* (1991), was lyrically dark, combining classic rock with an anthemic feel, informed by McCready's love of the blues in his prominent solos. *Ten* sold in excess of 15 million copies, establishing Pearl Jam as one of America's biggest rock acts.

Pearl Jam were associated with the Seattle grunge scene, which the band comfortably outlived, but were accused by their contemporaries of cashing in on the alternative rock boom. The band seemed uneasy with their own success and rebelled against music industry practices, refusing to appear in music videos and boycotting the booking agency Ticketmaster. McCready fought his own battles against drug and alcohol addiction. He has participated in various side projects, including Mad Season, the Rockfords, Walking Papers and UFO-

tribute act Flight To Mars. Pearl Jam's eponymous eighth studio album was released in 2006, followed by *Backspacer* in 2009 and *Lightning Bolt* in 2013.

Influenced by Neil Young, Jeff Beck, George Harrison, Jimmy Page, Joe Perry and Jimi Hendrix, Mike McCready has a reputation as a forceful blues guitarist. In live work, he hates to repeat himself, refusing to play the same solo twice and relishing improv. He is an energetic performer, sometimes soloing behind his head, Hendrix-style. He has used the **Fender Stratocaster** extensively, along with the **Gibson SG**, **Les Paul**, **Hummingbird** acoustic and **Flying V**.

Thurston Moore
SONIC YOUTH'S GROUNDBREAKER

Alternative experimental guitarist Thurston Moore (b. 1958) was born in Coral Gables, Florida. Inspired by New York's punk and new-wave scene, Moore moved to the city in 1977. While playing in a band called the Coachmen, he met Lee Ranaldo, an art student and member of Glenn Branca's avant-garde guitar orchestra. Moore assembled a band with bassist and future wife Kim Gordon, and along with Ranaldo, they played on Branca's *Symphony No. 3* **(1983).**

The trio formed the core of Sonic Youth, which became part of New York's No Wave experimental scene. The band's early work was released on a variety of independent labels. *Bad Moon Rising* (1985) was their first album to be distributed widely in America, where it was largely ignored, and in the UK, where it received critical acclaim and encouraging sales. Switching to the influential independent label STT, Sonic Youth produced what is arguably their masterpiece, *Daydream Nation* (1988), before moving to Geffen.

Sonic Youth are one of the most original guitar bands of all time due to the twin guitars of Moore and Ranaldo, which characterized their sound. In addition to Glenn Branca, they were influenced by Can, the Velvet Underground, the Patti Group and the Stooges, as well as the speed and intensity of early 1980s hardcore punk bands Bad Brains, Minor Threat and Black Flag.

Moore relies on alternative tunings as part of his quest for new sounds. He and Ranaldo also make extensive use of prepared guitar – one that has had its timbre altered by placing objects, such as a drumstick, under the strings. In this way, cheap instruments like the Japanese **Stratocasters**, can produce amazing sounds. This experimentation resulted in their taking numerous instruments on tour, some of which have been specially prepared. Moore has used numerous guitars, favouring **Fender**, but also playing **Gibson** and **Ibanez** models.

In 2007, Moore joined Original Silence for live-recorded *The First Original Silence*, followed by *The Second Original Silence* (2008). In 2012, along with Samara Lubelski, John Moloney and Keith Wood, Moore formed Chelsea Light Moving; their eponymous debut album was released the following year. He released a solo album, *The Best Day*, in 2014 and premiered a piece for an experimental guitar ensemble titled 'Galaxies' at London's Barbican Centre in 2018.

Essential Recordings

1985 Sonic Youth: *Bad Moon Rising*

1988 Sonic Youth: *Daydream Nation*

2007 Original Silence: *The First Original Silence*

2013 Chelsea Light Moving: *Chelsea Light Moving*

Bob Mould
GODFATHER OF GRUNGE

Alternative guitarist Bob Mould (b. 1960) was born in Malone, New York. Mould was 16 when, inspired by the Ramones, he took up the guitar. While attending college in Minnesota in 1979, he founded Hüsker Dü, originally a hardcore punk/thrash band, with drummer Grant Hart and bassist Greg Norton.

Essential Recordings

1984 Hüsker Dü: *Zen Arcade*

1989 Solo: *Workbook*

1991 Solo: *Black Sheets Of Rain*

1992 Sugar: *Copper Blue*

The band's third album, *Zen Arcade* (1984), was a double album that broadened the noisy, guitar-driven style to embrace jazz, psychedelia, acoustic folk and pop. Hüsker Dü were instrumental in establishing alternative rock in America, making them one of the 1980s' most influential acts. Signing to major label Warner Brothers in 1986, they made *Candy Apple Grey* (1986) and another double set, *Warehouse: Songs And Stories* (1987), which, although popular on college radio, failed to bring them to a wider audience. The band split in 1988 because of drug problems and the ongoing tensions between Mould and Hart, the group's other songwriter and vocalist.

Mould launched a solo career with *Workbook* (1989), which surprised many. His characteristic wall-of-guitars sound, which was to see him hailed as the godfather of grunge, was largely replaced by a more reflective, acoustic ambience. *Black Sheets Of Rain* (1991) returned him to familiar guitar-heavy terrain, which continued in Mould's new band Sugar, whose debut *Copper Blue* (1992) received widespread acclaim. Another power trio, Sugar were more accessible and melodic yet louder and angrier than Hüsker Dü, and Mould's guitars were very much to the fore. The mini-album *Beaster* (1993) was notable for the angst-ridden 'JC Auto', on which Mould's powerful playing achieved climactic momentum. For Sugar and his solo work, Mould favoured a 1980s **Fender Stratocaster**. After *File Under: Easy Listening* (1994), he

disbanded Sugar and resumed his solo career. He worked briefly as a pro-wrestling scriptwriter, before returning to music as a performer and remixer. *Modulate* (2002) and *Body Of Song* (2005) added electronica to his rock template, while *Long Playing Grooves* (2002) was a full-on dance album released under the pseudonym LoudBomb. *District Line* was released in 2008, *Life And Times* the following year and *Silver Age* in 2012. His most recent album is 2019's *Sunshine Rock*.

Dave Navarro
MASTER OF ADDICTION

Alternative-rock guitarist Dave Navarro (b. 1967) was born in Santa Monica, California. After hearing Jimi Hendrix, Navarro began playing guitar at the age of seven and was in various bands in school. In 1986, he joined Jane's Addiction on the recommendation of drummer Stephen Perkins, a childhood friend. Inspired by the Velvet Underground, Joy Division, the Doors, PiL and Faith No More, the band quickly gained a following in Los Angeles and released their first album, *Jane's Addiction* (1987), independently.

A live set with copious studio overdubs, the album was an unpredictable mix of folk, rock, funk and new wave, punctuated by Navarro's unusual, angular guitar. Their second album for Warner Brothers, *Ritual De Lo Habitual* (1990), provided their breakthrough and is regarded as the band's masterpiece. It extends Jane's Addiction's musical palette to progressive rock with Eastern influences creeping in. Navarro's solo on 'Three Days' is one of his finest. After the trail-blazing Lollapalooza tour in 1991, which was organized by singer Perry Farrell and put alternative rock into large arenas for the first time, Jane's Addiction split up.

Navarro formed Deconstruction, whose sole album *Deconstruction* (1994) is now considered a cult classic, before joining the Red Hot Chili Peppers, making his live debut at the 1994 Woodstock Festival. After one album, *One Hot Minute* (1995), Navarro was dismissed in 1998 due to creative differences, as he was uneasy with the band's improvisational style. Navarro participated in a Jane's Addiction reunion tour in 1997, and the band reunited again in 2001 for an album and tour, disbanding again in 2004. In between, Navarro worked with artists as diverse as Marilyn Manson and Christina Aguilera. Following the demise of Jane's Addiction, he was cohost of MTV's reality show 'Rock Star' and put together a new band, the Panic Channel. In recent years, Navarro has worked on many projects with

artists such as DJ Skribble and Billy Corgan, as well as the reformed Jane's Addiction, who released a new album, *The Great Escape Artist*, in 2011. Navarro also broadcasts an internet radio show called Dark Matter.

From Jane's Addiction days, Navarro has played **PRS** guitars, notably his signature model. While a member of the Chili Peppers, he used **Fender Stratocasters** and has also played **Telecasters** and a **Gibson Les Paul**.

Essential Recordings

1987	Jane's Addiction *Jane's Addiction*
1990	Jane's Addiction *Ritual De Lo Habitual*
1994	Deconstruction: *Deconstruction*
1995	Red Hot Chili Peppers *One Hot Minute*

Johnny Ramone
DOYEN OF THE DOWNSTROKE

Johnny Ramone (1948–2004) was born John Cummings in Long Island, New York. As a teenager, Johnny played in a band called the Tangerine Puppets alongside future Ramones drummer Tamás Erdélyi (better known as Tommy Ramone). Johnny worked as a plumber with his father before the Ramones became successful. He also attended military school and briefly attended college in Florida.

Essential Recordings

1976 Ramones:
Ramones

1978 Ramones:
Road To Ruin

1980 Ramones:
End Of The Century

1989 Ramones:
Brain Drain

He met future bandmate Douglas Colvin, later to become Dee Dee Ramone, in the early 1970s. Together, they went in January 1974 to Manny's Music in New York City, where Johnny bought a used blue **Mosrite** guitar and Dee Dee bought a **Danelectro** bass. They collaborated with future bandmate Jeffry Hyman, later to become Joey Ramone, and formed the Ramones. Erdélyi joined the band in the summer of that year. Although Johnny Ramone wasn't as prolific a songwriter as his bandmates, his guitar style was a key part of the Ramones' sound and would become a major punk rock influence.

Ramone was known for his fast, high-energy guitar playing. His style almost exclusively consisted of rapid downstrokes and barre chord shapes. This unique playing style, combined with heavy gain on his amp, created the bright, buzzsaw-like sound his guitar parts were known for, and it was highly influential on many early punk-rock guitarists. This technique was also very influential on the new wave of British heavy-metal bands such as Iron Maiden. His style has also been an influence on many alternative-rock bands, as well as on thrash-metal performers such as Kirk Hammett of Metallica and Dave

Mustaine of Megadeth. Guitar virtuoso Paul Gilbert has cited Johnny Ramone as one of his influences.

It has been suggested that Jimmy Page's fast downstroke guitar riff in Led Zeppelin's 'Communication Breakdown' was an inspiration for Ramone's guitar style. Ramone, who described Page as 'probably the greatest guitarist who ever lived', stated in the documentary *Ramones: The True Story* that he improved at his picking style by playing the song over and over again for the bulk of his early career. 'I guess that before me,' he said, 'people played downstrokes for brief periods in a song, rather than the whole song through. It was just a timing mechanism for me.'

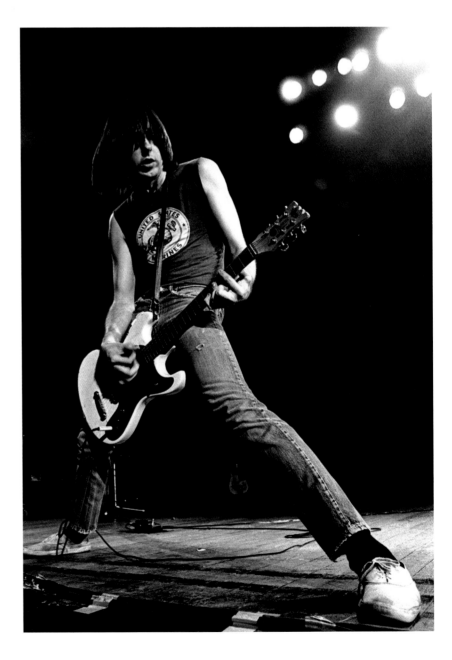

Kevin Shields
MY BLOODY GENIUS

Alternative-rock guitarist Kevin Shields (b. 1963) was born in Queens, New York. When he was 10, the family relocated to Dublin, where he learned guitar as a teenager with Johnny Ramone as his role model. My Bloody Valentine came together in 1984. The band moved to Holland and then Berlin, where they recorded the mini-album *This Is Your Bloody Valentine* (1985). They reconvened in London the following year, going on to make three EPs, influenced by the Cramps and the Birthday Party. With Bilinda Butcher recruited as main vocalist, they made other recordings, but it was not until My Bloody Valentine signed to Creation Records in 1988 that they were allowed sufficient studio time to realize their vision.

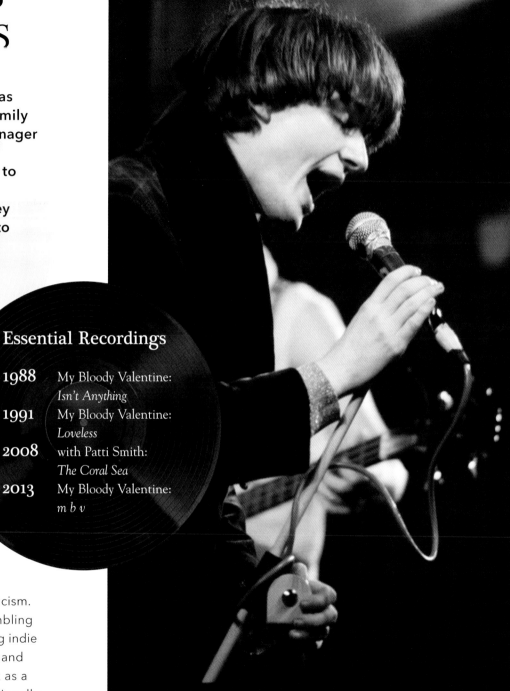

Essential Recordings

1988 My Bloody Valentine:
Isn't Anything
1991 My Bloody Valentine:
Loveless
2008 with Patti Smith:
The Coral Sea
2013 My Bloody Valentine:
m b v

After eight months of recording, the band produced 'You Made Me Realise', an EP that brought them to wider attention and acclaim. The band followed up with **Isn't Anything** (1988). Influenced by the Jesus and Mary Chain, Dinosaur Jr. and the Cocteau Twins, the album defined My Bloody Valentine's idiosyncratic approach and established them as a major force in the British indie scene. Shields' onslaught of meticulously layered guitars was demonstrated on the single 'Feed Me With Your Kiss'. The band's wall of noise was complemented by a dreamy melodicism. Shields was a perfectionist in the studio, painstakingly assembling **Loveless** (1991), which consolidated their position as a leading indie band and inspired outfits like Ride, Chapterhouse, Slowdive and the short-lived shoe-gazing trend. Shields continued to work as a producer, remixer and composer, as well as recording occasionally, until My Bloody Valentine reformed in 2007. A new album, **m b v**, was released in 2013.

Shields has customized the tremolo arms of his **Fender Jaguar** and **Jazzmaster** guitars to achieve his trademark sound. The process involves extending the tremolo arm, so that it sits high on the guitar for ease of operation and to allow for chord bending. This produces a warping effect, which initially caused some buyers of **Loveless** to return their vinyl copies. The thickness of his sound is achieved by using a reverse reverb effect. He plays at extremely high volume, but does not make extensive use of effects pedals.

Playlists | Links ebooks & more
FlameTreeRock.com

Kim Thayil
A GRUNGE GREAT

Grunge guitarist Kim Thayil (b. 1960) was born in Seattle, Washington. He was inspired to play guitar by KISS, subsequently backtracking to the music which inspired them – the New York Dolls, MC5, the Stooges and Velvet Underground. He bought his first guitar, a Guild S-100, which he would use throughout his career, and formed his first band in high school. While studying philosophy at the University of Washington, he became a member of Soundgarden in 1984.

Essential Recordings

1991	Soundgarden: *Badmotorfinger*
1994	Soundgarden: *Superunknown*
1996	Soundgarden: *Down On The Upside*
2000	No WTO Combo: *Live From The Battle In Seattle*

With a sound influenced equally by heavy metal and punk, Soundgarden were crucial to the development of the Seattle movement that was dubbed 'grunge'. Their first album, *Ultramega OK* (1988), was released on independent label SST, before they became the first band from the Seattle scene to sign with a major label, although they only found commercial success in the wake of Nirvana and Pearl Jam. They released four albums, *Louder Than Love* (1989), *Badmotorfinger* (1991), *Superunknown* (1994) and *Down On The Upside* (1996). Their breakthrough came with *Superunknown*, which featured the singles 'Spoonman' and 'Black Hole Sun', and added a radio-friendly sheen to their trademark heaviness. The final album, *Down On The Upside*, represented a departure from their grunge roots, and creative tensions between Thayil and singer Chris Cornell led to the band splitting up in 1997. Thayil has since collaborated with former Nirvana bassist Krist Novoselic, the Dead Kennedys' Jello Biafra, Presidents of the United States of America and Johnny Cash. Thayil went on to play with Greg Gilmore and Danny Kelly in the group Set and Setting, then again with Soundgarden when they reformed in 2010. A new Soundgarden album, *King Animal*, was released in 2012, but they disbanded again after Chris Cornell's death in 2017. Best known for his hard-edged riffing, Thayil has said of his own style, 'I play guitar because I like to make loud noises. And the

guitar is the coolest way to make a loud noise.' He is disparaging about guitar solos: 'Most are annoying, self-indulgent.' In addition to his ever-present **Guild S-100**, Thayil has also used **Gibson Les Paul** models, the **Gibson Firebird** and the **Fender Telecaster** and **Jazzmaster**. Thayil often employs alternative and unorthodox tunings.

Playlists | Links ebooks & more
FlameTreeRock.com

Tom Verlaine
EXPERIMENTER EXTRAORDINAIRE

A crucial figure in New York's late 1970s new-wave scene, Tom Verlaine (b. 1949) was born Thomas Miller in New Jersey. At an early age, he learned piano before switching to saxophone, inspired by John Coltrane. He took up the guitar in his teens and began forging his own style, searching for new ways of expressing himself on the instrument.

At boarding school, Verlaine met kindred spirit Richard Hell, and in 1973, they formed the short-lived Neon Boys. The band became Television a few months later, when Verlaine found second guitarist Richard Lloyd. Due to friction with Verlaine, Hell left to found the Heartbreakers. In 1975, Television began playing legendary New York venues Max's Kansas City and CBGB's, where the city's new-wave movement began to ferment. Verlaine briefly dated punk poetess Patti Smith. The band released their first single, 'Little Johnny Jewel', a tribute to Iggy Pop, independently in 1975. For the

recording, Verlaine plugged his guitar straight into the mixing desk. Television's debut album, *Marquee Moon* (1977), was hailed as a masterpiece. After a disappointing follow-up, *Adventure* (1978), the band split up amidst musical and personal differences. Television's sound was characterized by dual interlocking guitars, heard to stunning effect on the epic 'Marquee Moon'. The nominal roles of rhythm (Lloyd) and lead (Verlaine) were largely equivalent, with the backing as vital as the solo instrument. Influences came from twin-guitar bands Love, Quicksilver Messenger Service, Buffalo Springfield and the Rolling Stones.

Verlaine launched a solo career with *Tom Verlaine* (1979), and has continued to release regular solo albums since. Later albums showcased his sparkling guitar work, highlighted by a fine solo on 'Ancient Egypt' from *The Wonder* (1990) and the all-instrumental *Warm And Cool* (1992). Television reformed for a third, eponymous album in 1992 and have performed together occasionally since.

Verlaine has consistently sought unconventional guitar sounds. He favours **Fender** guitars and his use of the company's **Jazzmaster** and **Jaguar** models in Television's early days inspired Thurston Moore, Kevin Shields and John Frusciante to do likewise.

Essential Recordings

1977	Television: *Marquee Moon*
1979	Solo: *Tom Verlaine*
1990	Solo: *The Wonder*
1992	Television: *Television*

Paul Weller
THE MODFATHER

The enduring and iconic guitarist and songwriter Paul Weller (b. 1958) was born John William Weller in Woking, Surrey. He was a boyhood Beatles fanatic before discovering the Who and, through them, the mod movement. His father, who managed him for the majority of his career, bought his 12-year-old son an electric guitar for Christmas; at first, neither realized that an amplifier was necessary too.

Essential Recordings

1978 The Jam:
All Mod Cons

1986 The Style Council:
The Cost Of Loving

1995 Solo:
Stanley Road

2008 Solo:
22 Dreams

The Jam was formed at secondary school, and Weller played bass in early incarnations of the band. With Rick Buckler on drums and Bruce Foxton on bass, the Jam learned their trade by constant gigging. The band's arrival in London coincided with the burgeoning punk scene, and seeing the Sex Pistols live was a pivotal moment for Weller. While adopting punk's energy, the Jam remained distinct from the movement, not least because of the band's musical ability.

Weller's first role models on guitar were Pete Townshend and Dr. Feelgood's Wilko Johnson, whose dynamic rhythm-lead style impressed Weller. The Jam's arguably best album, ***All Mod Cons*** (1978), showcases Weller's maturing style and use of techniques ranging from power chords ('Billy Hunt') to acoustic-electric work ('Fly') and backwards masking ('In The Crowd'). With the Jam at the height of their popularity in 1982, Weller disbanded the outfit, citing frustration with the limitations of the three-piece format. His next project, the Style Council, a loose confederation of musicians based around Weller and keyboardist Mick Talbot, enabled him to explore more diverse musical areas, adding Latin and jazz to his repertoire. The Style Council folded in 1989, leaving Weller out of favour and without a recording contract.

Influenced by the classic rock of Traffic, Free and Neil Young, Weller returned to basics by playing live and mounted an impressive

comeback, beginning with his self-titled solo debut in 1992 and culminating in the million-selling ***Stanley Road*** (1995). Weller's influence was a rare point of unity between rivals Blur and Oasis. Weller's 2005 album ***As Is Now*** was a critical hit, and he released his 15th studio album, ***True Meanings***, in 2018 and played two live shows at London's Royal Festival Hall with an orchestra.

Playlists | Links ebooks & more
FlameTreeRock.com

Jack White
REVIVING THE BLUES

Modern blues guitarist Jack White (b. 1975) was born John Gillis in Detroit, Michigan. He taught himself to play drums, starting at the age of five. On leaving school, he played in various Detroit bands. In 1996, he married Meg White and, reversing normal practice, took her surname. The White Stripes were born when Meg, with no previous experience on the drum kit, started bashing along to his guitar, and he realized that her primitive beat was exactly the accompaniment he needed.

After two independent albums, the White Stripes' breakthrough came with the release of **White Blood Cells** (2001), when DJ John Peel enthused about the band, and the excitement surrounding them in the UK transferred back to America. White was hailed as the most explosive rock performer in the world and credited with returning the blues to the forefront of modern rock. This was achieved with the setup of just guitar (occasionally piano) and drums. As White explained, 'All you need is two people. The music is from the guitar or piano and the rhythm is Meg's accompaniment. There is nothing else that needs to be there.' During downtime from the White Stripes in 2005, White formed the Raconteurs, a more conventional 1960s-influenced outfit. In 2009, he formed a new group called the Dead Weather with the Kills frontwoman Alison Mosshart. The White Stripes announced that they were splitting in 2011, and White released his debut solo album, **Blunderbuss**, the following year. Since then he has released **Lazaretto** (2014) and **Boarding House Reach** (2018), both highly acclaimed.

In addition to blues masters Son House and Robert Johnson, White was equally inspired by Captain Beefheart, Dylan and obscure US garage bands. White's most famous guitar is a red and white **Airline**, a cheap 1960s department-store model. For the White Stripes, he also used a **Harmony Rocket**, a **Crestwood Astral** and a **Gretsch White Penguin**. In the Raconteurs, he favoured **Gretsch** guitars. To achieve the White Stripes' powerful live sound, he made extensive use of effects, mainly a **DigiTech Whammy** to shift the

pitch down and compensate for the absence of bass. When playing barre and power chords, he uses the little finger on his left hand, partly because of an injury to his index finger sustained in a car accident in 2003.

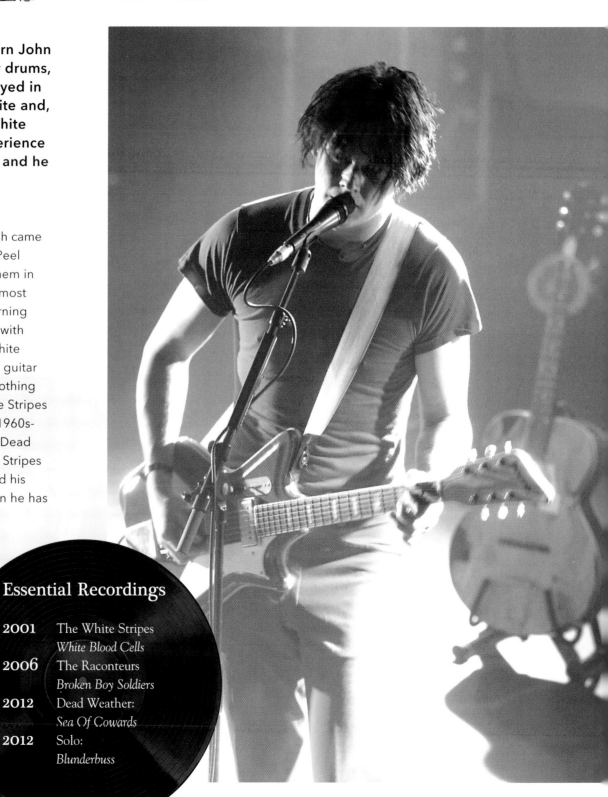

Essential Recordings

2001	The White Stripes
	White Blood Cells
2006	The Raconteurs
	Broken Boy Soldiers
2012	Dead Weather:
	Sea Of Cowards
2012	Solo:
	Blunderbuss

I don't play a lot of fancy guitar. […] The kind of guitar I want to play is mean, mean, mean licks.

John Lee Hooker

Pioneers & Influences

Chet Atkins
MR GUITAR

As the first superstar instrumentalist to emerge from the modern Nashville recording scene, Chet Atkins (1924–2001) was a living legend for most of his life, but the Nashville-based guitarist was also a producer, engineer, label executive and A&R man without peer.

Chester Burton 'Chet' Atkins was born in June, in Luttrell, Tennessee. Self-taught, he developed his right-hand fingerpicking style – using his thumb for bass notes and three fingers for melody and harmonies – after hearing Merle Travis on the radio.

Essential Recordings

1965   Solo:
'Yakety Axe'

1967   Solo:
Picks The Best

1976   with Les Paul:
Chester & Lester

1981   Solo:
Country After All These Years

After dropping out of high school in 1942, Atkins performed on radio and toured with regional stars. He made his first appearance at the Grand Ole Opry in 1946 and was signed by RCA in 1947, enjoying his first hit single in 1954 with 'Mr. Sandman'. He became a design consultant for **Gretsch**, who manufactured **Chet Atkins** guitars from 1955 to 1980.

In 1957, Atkins was put in charge of RCA's Nashville division. With country music record sales slumping, he eliminated fiddles and steel guitar in an attempt to appeal to pop fans. The result became known as the Nashville Sound, and Atkins' arrangements produced crossover hits for artists including Jim Reeves and Don Gibson.

Atkins' records and television appearances earned him the moniker Mister Guitar, and by 1968, he was vice president of RCA's country division. Among others, he brought Waylon Jennings, Willie Nelson and Dolly Parton to the label. He also signed country music's first African-American singer, Charley Pride.

Atkins' own biggest hit single came in 1965 with 'Yakety Axe', an adaptation of Boots Randolph's 'Yakety Sax'. In the 1970s, he recorded extensively with Jerry Reed and Les Paul, with whom he won one of his many Grammies for the album *Chester & Lester* (1976). At the end of the 1970s, Atkins left RCA and **Gretsch**, signing instead with Columbia Records and designing guitars for **Gibson**.

In the 1990s, he continued to release albums and performed with orchestras and with friends. Ultimately, he suffered a recurrence of colon cancer and died in June 2001. Atkins was posthumously inducted into the Rock and Roll Hall of Fame in 2002.

Playlists | Links
ebooks & more

FlameTreeRock.com

Robert Fripp
CRIMSON'S KING

Progressive-rock pioneers King Crimson have seen a revolving door of band members through its almost 40-year existence, including such highly respected musicians as bassists Greg Lake, John Wetton and Tony Levin, drummer Bill Bruford and guitarist Adrian Belew. But one figure has remained steadfast, and that is guitarist Robert Fripp (b. 1946).

Born in Wimborne Minster, Dorset, England, Robert Fripp faced enormous obstacles on his way to becoming one of the greatest guitarists of all time. Despite being tone-deaf, left-handed and possessing a poor sense of rhythm, the 11-year-old Fripp picked up the guitar and never looked back. In 1967, Fripp teamed up with brothers Peter (bass) and Michael Giles (drums) to form Giles, Giles & Fripp. A year later, Fripp and Michael Giles formed the first version of King Crimson. Their debut album, *In The Court Of The Crimson King* (1969), was – and still is – enormously influential, inspiring such prog-rock luminaries as Yes and Genesis. Indeed, throughout the band's on-and-off existence, albums such as *Larks' Tongues In Aspic* (1973), *Red* (1974), *Discipline* (1981) and *The Power To Believe* (2003) demonstrate Fripp's groundbreaking 'anything goes' playing style, as well as his ability to create ambitious and innovative music.

Though King Crimson has been his most high-profile gig, Fripp has worked with an impressive array of artists both as sideman and collaborator through the years, including Brian Eno, David Bowie, Talking Heads, Andy Summers and Peter Gabriel. His work with Eno was particularly rewarding, as Fripp developed his famous 'Frippertronics' – a sound-on-sound live tape-looping process that enables him to become his own backing track – from Eno's tape-delay system. Fripp introduced his 'soundscapes' approach to legions of new fans when he and his **Gibson Les Paul Custom** accompanied guitarists Steve Vai and Joe Satriani on the 2004 G3 tour.

Various collaborative recording projects have followed, including 2011's *A Scarcity Of Miracles: A King Crimson ProjeKct*, featuring other Crimson alumni. It was the prelude to

another King Crimson reunion – a seven-piece with three drummers – that undertook a world tour in 2014/2015.

In addition to his acclaimed recording career, Fripp launched Guitar Craft in 1985, a guitar seminar programme that to this day holds ongoing instructional courses all over the world.

Essential Recordings

1969	King Crimson: *In The Court Of The Crimson King*
1973	King Crimson: *Larks' Tongues In Aspic*
1975	with Brian Eno: *Evening Star*
1984	with Andy Summers: *Bewitched*

Buddy Guy
LEGEND OF LIVE LICKS

One of the young gunslingers who invigorated the blues in the 1960s, Buddy Guy (b. 1936) wowed audiences with high-octane guitar histrionics and energy that were matched by a tortured vocal manner. He is a master of dynamics, allowing a song to drift towards oblivion before suddenly bringing it back to a crescendo of intensity. Notable fans have included Jimi Hendrix, Eric Clapton and Jeff Beck. Guy is essentially a live performer who has found it hard to channel his unpredictable virtuosity into the confines of a recording studio.

Essential Recordings

1972   with Junior Wells:
          Play The Blues

1991   Solo:
          Damn Right I've Got
          The Blues

1993   Solo:
          Feels Like Rain

1995   Solo:
          Slippin' In

George Guy was born into a sharecropping family in Lettsworth, Louisiana, and started playing in and around Baton Rouge in his teens. It wasn't until 1957 that he moved north to Chicago, where he was encouraged by his idol, Muddy Waters, and developed his own style, a mixture of the showmanship of Guitar Slim and the rapid-fire phrasing of B.B. King.

He signed with Chess, Chicago's premier label, in 1960, and his first session produced the harrowing 'First Time I Met The Blues'. He scored a rhythm and blues hit with 'Stone Crazy' in 1962, but most of his own recordings remained unreleased (possibly due to internecine politics), although he appeared on countless records by Muddy Waters, Willie Dixon, Little Walter, Sonny Boy Williamson II and Koko Taylor. His first British visit in 1965 with the American Folk Blues Festival launched his prestigious fan club. He also started a long-lasting and fruitful relationship with harmonica player and singer Junior Wells. The duo played together on *Hoodoo Man Blues* (1965), *It's My Life Baby!* (1966), *Play The Blues* (1972) and *Drinkin' TNT 'N' Smokin' Dynamite* (1982), recorded at the 1974 Montreux Jazz Festival.

The 1970s and 1980s were a lean period for Buddy Guy recordings, and it wasn't until *Damn Right I've Got The Blues* (1991), which featured Clapton, Beck and Mark Knopfler, followed by Grammy-winning *Feels*

Like Rain (1993) and *Slippin' In* (1995), that he started achieving commercial success. In 2003, Guy was awarded the National Medal of Arts. He was inducted into the Rock and Roll Hall of Fame in 2005 and continues to tour. In February 2012, he performed at the White House for US President Barack Obama.

Guy has had a long relationship with **Fender**, preferring to play a **Stratocaster** through a **Fender Tweed Bassman (4 x 10)**.

Playlists | Links
ebooks & more
FlameTreeRock.com

John
Lee Hooker
THE BOOGIE MAN

The original boogie man, John Lee Hooker (1917–2001) sustained a career of more than 50 years with his incessant one-chord stomp and half-spoken vocal style. But behind the captivating, hypnotic rhythm, Hooker found his own deep blues - one with dark tones and mysterious flurries of notes - as he groped to express, often with a wicked irony, his own feelings of pain and desire. His style was particularly infectious among British blues bands of the 1960s, notably the Animals. In America, Canned Heat built a multi-platinum career out of Hooker's boogie.

The youngest of 11 children, Hooker was born in Clarksdale, Mississippi, to a family of sharecroppers. After his parents separated, he learned guitar from his stepfather before leaving home for Memphis, followed by Cincinnati and Detroit, where he made his first recordings in 1948. 'Boogie Chillen' contained all the basic elements of his style and was a No. 1 rhythm and blues hit. Hooker immediately cashed in, recording for several different labels under a variety of pseudonyms (a laughable ploy, given his distinctive style), and had more hits with 'Hobo Blues', 'Crawling Kingsnake' (1949) and 'I'm In The Mood' (1951).

In the mid-1950s, Hooker started recording with an electric band, heightening the rhythmic emphasis of his boogie with songs like 'Dimples' and 'Boom Boom'. When these records became successful in Britain in the 1960s, he toured the UK and Europe regularly. Meanwhile, he was enjoying a parallel career as a solo folk/blues artist in America, although by the end of the decade, he was back in the rock fold, thanks to the success of his disciples Canned Heat, who repaid their debt by recruiting him for *Hooker 'N' Heat* (1970).

Further collaborations with Van Morrison and guitarist Elvin Bishop maintained Hooker's profile in the 1970s, but his career sagged in the

1980s, before a sudden and unlikely revival in 1989 with *The Healer*, which featured duets with Carlos Santana, Bonnie Raitt, George Thorogood, Los Lobos and the remnants of Canned Heat. The album's success set Hooker up for the 1990s, as Van Morrison, Keith Richards, Ry Cooder, Robert Cray and Albert Collins queued up to appear on subsequent albums, including *Mr Lucky* (1991), *Boom Boom* (1992) and *Don't Look Back* (1997). Hooker died in 2001 at the age of 83.

Essential Recordings

1948	Solo: 'Boogie Chillen'
1956	Solo: 'Dimples'
1970	with Canned Heat: Hooker 'N' Heat
1989	Solo: The Healer

Elmore James
THE BOTTLENECK ELECTRIFIED

The swooping, full-octave slide-guitar riff that opened Elmore James's (1918–63) first record, 'Dust My Broom', in 1951 not only electrified the legacy of Robert Johnson, it also established one of the basic riffs of post-war blues. Bottleneck guitar had always been part of the blues, but James was the first to use it in a hard rocking electric-blues context. The fat, distorted sound he got for his primal riff was no accident either; in his day-job, James repaired radios, and he customized the components and configurations of his amplifier to get a dirty, sustained tone. These modifications are now a standard option on any modern amplifier.

Essential Recordings

1951 Solo:
'Dust My Broom'

1957 Solo:
'It Hurts Me Too'

1960 Solo:
'The Sky Is Crying'

1969 Solo:
'Shake Your Moneymaker'

James cut several versions of 'Dust My Broom', recording a new one every time he switched record labels, which was often. And many of his other songs were close copies, such as 'Dust My Blues', 'I Believe' and 'Wild About You Baby'. But James was no one-trick pony. His version of Tampa Red's 'It Hurts Me Too' and his own interchangeable 'The Sun Is Shining' and 'The Sky Is Crying' each have a slow-burning intensity and desperation that threaten to implode before the song ends.

Born Elmore Brooks in Richland, Mississippi, James started learning guitar in his teens and hung out with Sonny Boy Williamson II and Robert Johnson, from whom he learned 'I Believe I'll Dust My Broom'. He played regularly with Williamson and began playing electric guitar when he formed a band in the early 1940s. His first version of 'Dust My Broom' featured Williamson on harmonica. In 1952, he moved to Chicago, where his primal riffs were an instant success. He formed the Broomdusters and soon became one of the most popular attractions on the live scene.

James had always suffered from heart problems that were not helped by his excessive drinking and asthma. There is no evidence of any frailties on his final recordings made in New Orleans in 1961, featuring the frisky 'Look On Yonder Wall' and 'Shake Your Moneymaker', but in 1963, he died from a heart attack in Chicago. His legacy lived on among British blues bands like John Mayall's Bluesbreakers and Fleetwood Mac, and American bands like the Paul Butterfield Blues Band and the Allman Brothers.

Blind Lemon Jefferson
A COUNTRY BLUESMAN

Blind Lemon Jefferson (c. 1893–1929) opened up the market for blues records in 1926 when 'Got The Blues', backed with 'Long Lonesome Blues', became the biggest-selling record by a black male artist. It brought him the trappings of success, including a car and chauffeur, and he released nearly 100 songs over the next four years, before his death.

Jefferson played country blues, a style he customized by listening to the flamenco intonations of local Mexican guitarists in Texas, where he grew up, as well as cotton-field songs. He developed a fast, complex guitar technique that, unlike that of most blues legends, has never been duplicated. He was a direct influence on Leadbelly, Lightnin' Hopkins and T-Bone Walker, all of whom played and travelled with him. The full range of his shifting rhythms, boogie-woogie bass runs and rippling tremolos can be heard on 'Match Box Blues', a song that had a major impact on the rock'n'roll scene in the 1950s after Carl Perkins recorded it.

Little is known about Jefferson before 1926. He was reportedly born blind (although the only known photograph shows him wearing glasses), probably in 1893. He was playing house parties, brothels and drinking dens around Wortham, Texas, in his late teens, before travelling widely around Oklahoma, Louisiana, Mississippi, Alabama and Virginia. He was eventually contacted by Paramount Records, who recorded him in Chicago. He would make most of his records there, although he remained settled in Dallas. Songs like 'Black Snake Moan', one of his biggest 'hits', had a blatant sexual theme, albeit couched in humour and double entendre. Cheating women were also a concern on 'Eagle Eyed Mama', but titles like 'One Dime Blues', 'Prison Cell Blues' and 'See That My Grave Is Kept Clean' (which Bob

Dylan recorded on his first album) hint at deeper fears. He could cut a desolate sound, and while his instrumental style was hard to copy, his lyrics were widely appropriated by other performers for their own songs.

Confusion even surrounds Jefferson's death in Chicago in 1929. It was said that he froze to death, but a heart attack in the back of his car seems more likely.

Essential Recordings

1926	Solo: 'Got The Blues'
1927	Solo: 'Match Box Blues'
1927	Solo: 'Black Snake Moan'
1927	Solo: 'See That My Grave Is Kept Clean'

Robert Johnson
BLUES MYTH MAKER

The hold that the legend of Robert Johnson (1911-38, on the left in the picture) exerts on the blues is out of all proportion to his career and output. He died relatively unknown at the age of 27 and recorded just 29 songs. But those songs of dreams and nightmares, crossroads and hellhounds revealed a darkness at the heart of Johnson's blues, expressed with a chilling eloquence that has never been matched.

The legend was fostered by the 1960s generation of British blues guitarists, led by Eric Clapton and Keith Richards, who were in thrall to *King Of The Delta Blues Singers* (1962), a collection of Johnson's songs that personified the iconic image of a blues singer. The fact that there were more myths than facts about Johnson's life – no picture was known of at that time – only intensified the iconography. Clapton recorded 'Rambling On My Mind' with John Mayall and merged 'Cross Road Blues' and 'Travelling Riverside Blues' into 'Crossroads', a cornerstone of Cream's career, while the Rolling Stones' version of 'Love In Vain' was a crucial part of their late 1960s reinvention.

Essential Recordings

1936   Solo:
         'Cross Road Blues'
1936   Solo:
         'Come On In My Kitchen'
1937   Solo:
         'Love In Vain'
1937   Solo:
         'Stones In My Passway'

In fact, the legend – and myths – had started before Johnson even made a record. Born in Hazlehurst, Mississippi, he moved north to Robinsonville as a teenager and learned guitar and harmonica, hanging around with Charley Patton, Son House and Willie Brown. He disappeared for two years, and when he returned, the dramatic improvement in his playing led to speculation that he had sold his soul to the devil. Songs like 'Cross Road Blues', 'Preaching Blues (Up Jumped The Devil)', 'Stones In My Passway', 'Hellhound On My Trail' and 'Me And The Devil Blues' did nothing to dispel those notions. Even today, guitarists struggle to master Johnson's technique. The two photographs of Johnson since discovered show he had particularly long fingers, but this doesn't explain where the inspiration came from.

Johnson recorded twice, in 1936 and 1937, and had 11 records released, the most popular of which was the bawdy 'Terraplane Blues'. He was famously poisoned by a jealous husband while playing a juke joint near Greenwood, Mississippi, in 1938. As befits his legend, he has three marked burial sites. While his ardent disciples have left some of his most haunting songs alone, others like 'I Believe I'll Dust My Broom', 'Sweet Home Chicago', 'Come On In My Kitchen' and 'Walking Blues' have become a standard part of the blues repertoire.

Playlists | Links
ebooks & more

FlameTreeRock.com

Albert King
GOT BLUES AND SOUL

Few blues guitarists had more style and presence than Albert King (1923–92). At 6ft 4in (1.93m) and 250lbs (113kg), he cut an imposing figure onstage. Equally distinctive was his Gibson Flying V guitar, a right-handed instrument that King played left-handed and upside down. This gave him an unusual, tormented sound when he bent the strings on his fretboard. He also used his thumb rather than a pick. The master of the single-string solo, King was one of the earliest bluesmen to cross over to soul with his Stax recordings in the 1960s.

Born Albert Nelson in Indianola, Mississippi, the same town as B.B. King, Albert changed his name to King after B.B.'s initial success in the early 1950s. He had grown up in Arkansas, playing guitar from the age of 16. But he didn't make his first record, 'Be On Your Merry Way', until 1953, after he had moved to Gary, Indiana. His progress remained slow, and it wasn't until 1964 that he scored a minor hit with 'Don't Throw Your Love On Me So Strong'.

His fortunes changed when he signed to Memphis rhythm and blues-soul label Stax in 1966 and was paired with Booker T & the MGs, whose soulful grooves transformed King's blues in the studio. Their first session produced 'Laundromat Blues', which put the blues into a modern context. His second hit, 'Crosscut Saw', added the Memphis Horns and emphasized how far King had travelled from the Delta. *Born Under A Bad Sign* (1967), with its magnificent title track, was acclaimed as one of the most stirring blues albums of the late 1960s. Its influence on Eric Clapton and Jimi Hendrix was soon evident.

King was the first blues artist to play San Francisco's famed Fillmore, opening up a new audience, and the resulting album, *Live Wire/Blues Power* (1968), was a template for a new generation of blues bands in the American South. In the 1970s, King added funk to his

bluesy soul on *I'll Play The Blues For You* (1973), and in later years, he took to smoking a pipe and wearing a hat onstage. By the late 1980s, he was planning to retire, but died of a heart attack in 1992, just two days after another farewell performance.

Essential Recordings

1962 Solo: *The Big Blues*

1967 Solo: *Born Under A Bad Sign*

1968 Solo: *Live Wire/Blues Power*

1973 Solo: *I'll Play The Blues For You*

B.B. King
AMBASSADOR OF BLUES

The bluesman who took the blues into the mainstream, B.B. King (1925–2015) was also its ambassador to the world. His solid, seasoned style was heard internationally. His style drew on the Mississippi blues of Elmore James and Muddy Waters, the Chicago blues of Buddy Guy and Magic Sam, and the West-Coast blues of T-Bone Walker and Lowell Fulsom, all filtered through his distinctive vibrato and the phrases that flowed out of his beloved Gibson ES-355, named Lucille. His feel for the blues was consummate and instinctive, his licks coming seamlessly out of vocal lines or horn riffs, always with room to breathe within the song.

Essential Recordings

1956 Solo:
Singin' The Blues

1965 Solo:
Live At The Regal

1970 Solo:
Indianola Mississippi Seeds

2000 with Eric Clapton:
Riding With The King

Born in Itta Bena, Mississippi, King was raised in a farming family and found his voice in a gospel choir. He started playing the guitar in his teens and moved to Memphis in his early twenties, securing a sponsored radio spot. Recruiting a band, he embarked on the chitlin' touring circuit around the American South, honing his style and arrangements.

King scored a No. 1 rhythm and blues record with 'Three O'Clock Blues' in 1951, and followed it with a string of hits: 'You Know I Love You' (1952), Please Love Me' (1953), 'You Upset Me Baby' (1954), 'Sweet Little Angel' (1956) and 'Sweet Sixteen' (1960). In the 1960s, as his blues waned in favour of soul and Motown, King signed to major label MCA to broaden his audience. **Live At The Regal** (1965) failed in that respect, although it has been acclaimed as one of the greatest blues albums ever recorded. But later in the 1960s, he found an appreciative audience in the rock scene, scoring a Top 20 hit with 'The Thrill Is Gone' in 1970.

In subsequent decades, King regularly toured the world, taking on the ambassadorial role that enabled him to survive passing fashions and occasionally hitting the spotlight, as with his collaboration with U2 in 1988 on 'When Love Comes To Town'. In 2006, he undertook a farewell world tour, but after that, the performances, and awards and accolades, mounted. In 2006, President George W. Bush awarded King the Presidential Medal of Freedom. In 2007, King was awarded an honorary doctorate in music by Brown University. In 2009, *Time* named B.B. King third on its list of the 10 best electric guitarists of all time. He died, aged 89, of complications from his diabetes in 2015.

Playlists | Links ebooks & more

FlameTreeRock.com

Freddie King
BRINGING BLUES TO ROCK

Freddie (sometimes spelled Freddy) King (1934–76) revitalized the Chicago blues scene in the 1960s. His aggressive playing and piercing solos helped to set up the blues-rock movement, and he was a major influence on 1960s British guitarists like Eric Clapton, Peter Green and Mick Taylor.

King's mother taught him to play guitar as a child in Gilmer, Texas, where he was born. In 1950, the family moved to Chicago, and he was soon immersing himself in the thriving blues scene. From guitarist Jimmy Rogers, he learned a thumb-and-index-finger picking technique that he modified by using a plastic thumb pick and a steel fingerpick that added to his keening technique. He also incorporated the country blues stylings he had grown up with, along with a Texas swagger that gave his playing a raucous edge.

But it was hard for King and other young radicals like Buddy Guy and Otis Rush to break into a blues scene dominated by Muddy Waters and Howlin' Wolf, and harder still to get a record deal. When he finally landed one in 1960, he had a stack of material ready, and at his first session, he cut 'Have You Ever Loved A Woman' and the instrumental 'Hideaway', which was a Top 5 rhythm and blues hit and even made the pop Top 30. Both songs would be recorded by Eric Clapton (with Derek and the Dominos) and John Mayall's Bluesbreakers.

King's albums of snazzy, catchy instrumentals, *Let's Hide Away And Dance Away With Freddy King* (1961) and *Freddy King Gives You A Bonanza Of Instrumentals* (1965), were highly prized items among British guitarists in search of covers. Clapton's successor in the Bluesbreakers, Peter Green, picked 'The Stumble', and his successor, Mick Taylor, opted for 'Remington Ride', while Chicken Shack's Stan Webb picked 'San-Ho-Zay'.

Not surprisingly, King started making regular tours of Britain, where his disciples were happy to sing his praises, and though the hit records had dried up by the mid-1960s, his guitar prowess continued to develop, courtesy of his stinging vibrato, lyrical lines and astute phrasing, and he remained a top live attraction on both sides of the Atlantic. Clapton produced *Burglar* (1974), but King was suffering health problems, and in 1976, at the age of 42, he suffered a fatal heart attack, brought on by bleeding ulcers.

Essential Recordings

1961	Solo: *Let's Hide Away And Dance Away With Freddy King*
1965	Solo: *Freddy King Gives You A Bonanza Of Instrumentals*
1971	Solo: *Getting Ready*
1974	Solo: *Burglar*

John McLaughlin
INSPIRATION AND DEVOTION

John McLaughlin (b. 1942) led the Mahavishnu Orchestra and other bands that stretched the boundaries of jazz-rock fusion and world music. He inspired guitarists worldwide with his inventiveness, exotic sounds and spirituality.

Initially inspired by blues and swing, McLaughlin worked with Alexis Korner, Graham Bond and Ginger Baker in the 1960s, as well as playing free jazz with Gunter Hampel.

Essential Recordings

1969   Miles Davis: *Bitches Brew*

1970   Solo: *My Goals Beyond*

1971   The Mahavishnu Orchestra: *The Inner Mounting Flame*

1976   Shakti: *A Handful Of Beauty*

In 1969, he moved to New York to play with Tony Williams' Lifetime and became a member of Miles Davis's band, appearing on five albums, including *Bitches Brew* (1970) and *A Tribute To Jack Johnson* (1971). Davis paid tribute to McLaughlin in the liner notes to *Jack Johnson*, calling his playing 'far in'.

In 1970, McLaughlin recorded *My Goals Beyond* (1970), inspired by the Indian spiritual leader Sri Chinmoy. The album was dedicated to Chinmoy and included one of the guru's poems in the liner notes.

In 1971, he formed the Mahavishnu Orchestra, a group with a rock image but with the sophisticated vocabulary of jazz. After three influential albums, *The Inner Mounting Flame* (1971), *Birds Of Fire* and *Between Nothingness And Eternity* (both 1973), the group disbanded. A new Mahavishnu Orchestra, put together in 1974, broke up the following year.

McLaughlin then switched to Indian music with Shakti. He played a custom steel-string acoustic guitar that featured two tiers of strings over the soundhole: a conventional six-string configuration with an additional seven strings strung underneath at a 45-degree angle. The two string groups were independently tunable and were played as sympathetic strings, much like a sitar.

McLaughlin then alternated between electric- and acoustic-guitar projects. He led the One Truth Band; played in trios with Al Di Meola and Paco de Lucía; popped up on some mid-1980s Miles Davis records; and formed a short-lived third version of the Mahavishnu Orchestra. His ballet score 'Thieves And Poets' was released in 2003. In 2007, McLaughlin left Universal Records and joined the Abstract Logix label, on which he records with his jazz-fusion quartet 4th Dimension, releasing *To The One* (2010), *Now Here This* (2012) and live album *The Boston Record* (2014).

Les Paul
INNOVATOR AND ICON

Les Paul (1915–2009) developed a reputation in modern music beyond his status as a successful performer and guitar innovator through his pioneering work with multitrack recording. Born Lester Polsfuss in Waukesha, Wisconsin, the nine-year-old Paul first picked up the harmonica from a street musician. Soon, he was playing for money in the streets. He was attracted to electronics, and about the same time, began conducting his own experiments with sound. He started playing guitar at the age of 11 and, by the time he was 18, played country music under the name Rhubarb Red. After hearing Django Reinhardt, he switched over to jazz and changed his name to Les Paul.

Essential Recordings

1951   with Mary Ford:
'How High The Moon'

1953   with Mary Ford:
'Via Con Dios'

1976   with Chet Atkins:
Chester & Lester

2006   with Various Artists:
Les Paul & Friends:
American Made
World Played

In 1943, after a successful stint on New York radio, Paul moved to Hollywood, formed a trio, and soon was appearing with stars like Nat 'King' Cole and Bing Crosby, with whom he recorded a hit version of 'It's Been A Long, Long Time'. Crosby would help finance Paul's experiments, which resulted in the Gibson Guitar Company adopting Paul's suggestions for a guitar that, in the 1950s, became the Les Paul model. But Paul almost had to leave the guitar behind for ever. His right arm was shattered in a car crash in 1948. The doctors could not restore mobility to the arm, but set it at a right angle so that Paul could continue to play.

In 1947, Capitol Records released a recording that had begun as an experiment in Paul's garage. It featured Paul playing eight different parts on electric guitar. His experiments initiated the process of multitrack recording, which he used to successful effect when he teamed up with singer Mary Ford for a string of 1950s hits like 'How High The Moon', which featured overdubbed guitars playing in harmony. Paul's fame helped his namesake guitar gain fans, ultimately exploding in popularity in the rock era. When **Gibson** changed the design without telling him, he demanded his name be removed from the headstock. That guitar, renamed the **SG**, also became a popular guitar with rockers. Paul continued to innovate and perform, and in the twenty-first century, he still held down a long-running weekly gig at New York's Iridium Jazz Club. Les Paul succumbed to complications from pneumonia in 2009.

Playlists | Links
ebooks & more

FlameTreeRock.com

Prince
A TALENTED SHOWMAN

Prince (1958-2016) used the guitar as a stage prop, exuding flash on a par with his wardrobe and overall showmanship, but his talent on the instrument was a crucial element in bringing his unique blend of rock and soul to a worldwide audience.

Prince Rogers Nelson was born in Minneapolis, Minnesota. After playing in amateur bands, he did studio work for local musicians and producers. A demo tape made in 1976 led to a contract with Warner Bros.

Essential Recordings

1982	Solo: *1999*
1987	Solo: *Sign O' The Times*
1991	with the New Power Generation: *Diamonds And Pearls*
2003	Solo: *Musicology*

Prince's first two albums were standard late-1970s funk-pop, but the more musically versatile *Dirty Mind* (1980) made a splash, as did its follow-up, *Controversy* (1981). Then came *1999* (1982), a monster hit that sold over three million copies.

Prince became a movie star with 1985's *Purple Rain*. The soundtrack sold over ten million copies in the US and spent 24 weeks at No. 1. He experimented with psycho-psychedelia on *Around The World In A Day* (1985), and in 1986, released *Parade*, which served as the soundtrack to his second film, *Under The Cherry Moon*. In 1987, Prince continued his roll with *Sign O' The Times*.

Prince released *Lovesexy*, a commercial disaster, in 1988, but with the soundtrack to 1989's *Batman*, he returned to the top of the charts. In 1991, he formed the New Power Generation. With their first album, *Diamonds And Pearls* (1991), Prince had his biggest hit since 1985.

The following year, Prince released an album titled with a cryptic, unpronounceable symbol (later copyrighted as 'Love Symbol #2'). In 1993, he changed his stage name to the Love Symbol and was referred to as Symbol, the Artist Formerly Known As Prince, or simply the Artist.

In 1994, he released the single 'The Most Beautiful Girl In The World', his biggest hit in years. Prince then set up his own label and released jazzy albums to a mixed reception. He resurged with *Musicology* (2003), garnering a Grammy nomination, and was inducted into the Rock and Roll Hall of Fame in 2004. Prince released 39 studio albums before he died of an accidental overdose of the painkiller fentanyl at his Paisley Park complex in 2016.

Playlists | Links ebooks & more
FlameTreeRock.com

Django
Reinhardt
GYPSY GUITAR GIANT

Django Reinhardt (1910–53) overcame physical disabilities to create a unique playing style and one of the most highly influential sounds in jazz. He was born in Belgium to gypsy parents.

When he was 12, he received his first banjo-guitar from a neighbour. He learned to play by mimicking other musicians, and was soon impressing adults with his ability. Before he was 13, he began his musical career playing in dance halls.

When he was 18, Reinhardt suffered injuries to his left hand in a caravan fire. He had to create a whole new fingering system built around the two fingers that still had full mobility. Amazingly, his virtuosic soloing was accomplished with only the index and middle fingers.

Reinhardt was influenced by jazz recordings of guitarist Eddie Lang and violinist Joe Venuti, and by Louis Armstrong and Duke Ellington. In 1934, the Quintette du Hot Club de France was formed by a chance meeting of Django and violinist Stéphane Grappelli.

The small record company Ultraphone recorded the Hot Club's first tracks, 'Dinah', 'Tiger Rag', 'Oh Lady Be Good' and 'I Saw Stars'. These made a big impression, and the Quintette went on to record hundreds of tracks, building a following on both sides of the ocean. The concept of 'lead guitar' and backing 'rhythm guitar' was born, and they also used their guitars for percussive sounds.

Reinhardt played and recorded with many American jazz legends such as Coleman Hawkins, Benny Carter, Rex Stewart and Louis Armstrong. He could neither read nor write music, and was barely literate.

In 1939, the Quintette was touring in England when war broke out. Reinhardt returned to Paris while Grappelli remained in England. He played

Essential Recordings

1935	with the Quintette du Hot Club de France: 'Djangology'
1937	with the Quintette du Hot Club de France: 'Minor Swing'
1940	with the Quintette du Hot Club de France: 'Nuages'
1942	with the Quintette du Hot Club de France: 'Belleville'

and recorded throughout the war years, with Hubert Rostaing on clarinet. After the war, he rejoined Grappelli. He toured briefly with Duke Ellington in America and returned to Paris, continuing his career until 1951, when he retired to the small village of Samois sur Seine. In May 1953, Reinhardt died following a massive brain haemorrhage.

Andy Summers
AUTHORITY OF THE POLICE

One of the greatest achievements any guitar player can attain is an immediately recognizable tone and style, and few have done this as emphatically as the Police's Andy Summers (b. 1942). From the chord stabs of 'Roxanne' to the arpeggios of 'Every Breath You Take', Summers' chiming, shimmering Telecaster tones are like no other.

Essential Recordings

1978   The Police:
        Outlandos D'Amour

1983   The Police:
        Synchronicity

1984   with Robert Fripp:
        Bewitched

1989   Solo:
        The Golden Wire

Andrew James Somers was born in Lancashire, England. His family later moved to Bournemouth, where Summers took up the guitar at the age of 14. In the 1960s, he played with Zoot Money's Big Roll Band, as well as Soft Machine and a revamped version of the Animals. He then worked as a session guitarist before landing a job as sideman for Neil Sedaka.

In 1977, Summers had a chance meeting with drummer Stewart Copeland and joined the short-lived Strontium 90 with Copeland, Mike Howlett and Sting. Copeland and Sting then invited Summers to join the Police. Their debut album *Outlandos D'Amour* (1978) soon brought the band's unique brand of jazz- and reggae-influenced punk-pop to worldwide prominence.

Over the next three albums, the Police amassed numerous hit singles and two Grammy Awards. In 1983, they released *Synchronicity*, which topped the *Billboard* album charts and spawned the No. 1 smash 'Every Breath You Take'. But then the band imploded.

With the Police, Summers developed an enduring signature guitar tone. Relying most frequently on his treasured **1963 Fender Telecaster** modified with a **Gibson** PAF pickup in the neck position, Summers used

an arsenal of analogue chorus and delay effects to craft texturally rich and sophisticated rhythm parts.

After the breakup of the Police, Summers embarked on a solo career, including 1989's Grammy-nominated *The Golden Wire* and 1997's acclaimed *The Last Dance Of Mr. X*. Additionally, Summers worked on film scores, including *Down And Out In Beverly Hills* and *Weekend At Bernie's*.

In 2003, the Police were inducted into the Rock and Roll Hall of Fame, resulting in a 2007–08 reunion tour that became the third-biggest money-making tour of all time. Summers' new band, Circa Zero, released their debut album *Circus Hero* in 2014.

Richard Thompson
LAUDED BY THE CRITICS

In his 40-year career as an award-winning songwriter and guitarist, Richard Thompson (b. 1949) has won fans for his work as an original member of Fairport Convention, as part of a duo with former wife Linda Thompson and as a solo artist. His songs have been recorded by Bonnie Raitt, Elvis Costello, Emmylou Harris, the Blind Boys Of Alabama and many others.

Thompson was born in London, England. By the age of 18, he was playing with the newly formed Fairport Convention. Thompson's guitar playing caught the ear of American producer Joe Boyd, who signed them to his management company.

Soon, Thompson developed a reputation as an outstanding guitar player and began writing more songs. By the time of Fairport Convention's first album in 1968, Thompson was already crafting thoughtful songs with unconventional lyrics like 'Meet On The Ledge', 'Genesis Hall' and 'Crazy Man Michael'.

In January 1971, Thompson left Fairport Convention and released his first solo album, **Henry The Human Fly** (1972), which was not well received. Thompson began a relationship with one of the album's singers, Linda Peters, and they were married in October 1972. The first Richard and Linda Thompson album was released in April 1974; it impressed critics, but did not sell well. The Thompsons continued to release albums, slowly building their fan base, until finally **Shoot Out The Lights** (1982) was lauded by critics and sold well in the UK and in the US. The Thompsons, however, were by now finished as a couple.

With solo album **Hand Of Kindness** (1983), Thompson traded darkness and angst for outright swagger. He began to perform regularly, and in 1983 and 1984, toured the US and Europe with the Richard Thompson Big Band. In 1985, Thompson signed with Polygram, and **Across A**

Essential Recordings

1969	Fairport Convention: *Unhalfbricking*
1982	with Linda Thompson: *Shoot Out The Lights*
1985	Solo: *Across A Crowded Room*
1990	Solo: *Rumor And Sigh*

Crowded Room (1985) was released. In 1990, Thompson released his most popular album, **Rumor And Sigh**, which reached No. 32 on the UK charts and earned a Grammy nomination in the US.

In the ensuing years, Thompson continued to record unique albums, including **Mock Tudor** (1999), **Front Parlour Ballads** (2005), **Sweet Warrior** (2007) and **Electric** (2013).

Playlists | Links ebooks & more

FlameTreeRock.com

T-Bone Walker
TURNING BLUES ELECTRIC

The first bluesman to record with an electric guitar, T-Bone Walker (1910–75) shaped the course of post-war blues, influencing everyone from B.B. King and Chuck Berry to Jimi Hendrix and beyond. B.B. King acknowledges that the first time he heard Walker, he knew he had to get an electric guitar, and Berry and Hendrix took as much notice of Walker's showmanship – playing his guitar behind his head and generally thrilling the ladies – as his soulful playing. Even today, Walker's style remains an essential element of lead-guitar playing.

Essential Recordings

1942　Solo:
'Mean Old World'

1946　Solo:
'Bobby Sox Blues'

1947　Solo:
'Call It Stormy Monday'

1948　Solo:
'West Side Baby'

Born in Linden, Texas, Walker grew up in a musical household in Dallas, learning guitar, ukulele, banjo, violin and piano. Blind Lemon Jefferson was a family friend and Lonnie Johnson played nearby. By the age of 16, Walker was earning a living as a musician, playing local shows. In 1929, he won a talent contest to join Cab Calloway's band and made his first recordings. He also started a band with another local guitarist, Charlie Christian. He began touring a wider region and in 1934, moved to California, where he played and sang in various big bands.

Walker started playing amplified guitar in order to be heard, and his defining moment came in 1942 at a recording session with Freddie Slack's Big Band, when he got the chance to take the spotlight for a couple of blues songs. 'Mean Old World' was arguably the first electric blues record, and he followed it with 'Call It Stormy Monday', which became his signature tune and a blues classic. Before long, he was leading his own band and scoring blues hits with 'T-Bone Shuffle', 'Glamour Girl', 'The Hustle Is On' and 'Cold Cold Feeling'.

Walker's big-band background and the jazz musicians who played with him gave his blues a sophistication that was in marked contrast to the raw blues coming out of Chicago and the rock'n'roll coming out of Memphis. Ironically, this made him unfashionable for a while, although his reputation as a live performer never dipped. After a car accident in the early 1970s, his health deteriorated and he died of bronchial pneumonia following a stroke in 1975.

Playlists | Links
ebooks & more

FlameTreeRock.com

Muddy Waters
BRIDGING DELTA AND CHICAGO

Muddy Waters (1915–83) is the vital link between the pre-war Delta blues and the post-war Chicago blues. Born in Rolling Fork, Mississippi, he grew up on Stovall's Plantation near Clarksdale and became steeped in the slide-guitar blues of Son House and Robert Johnson. In 1941, he was recorded by archivist Alan Lomax, playing 'Country Blues' and 'I's Be Troubled'.

Two years later, Waters moved north to Chicago, following the general migration. While his voice still sounded as if it were coming from the cotton fields on his 1946 recordings, his amplified guitar (necessary if he were to be heard above his band) opened up a whole new dimension for his Delta licks. By 1948, when he had his first local hit with 'I Can't Be Satisfied' (an updated version of 'I's Be Troubled'), his guitar playing had developed a trademark style, bringing a more aggressive quality to his single-note Delta riffs and slide technique.

Waters put together a prime band of musicians he could rely on – guitarist Jimmy Rogers, bassist Willie Dixon, pianist Otis Spann and harmonica player Little Walter – and built a powerful reputation in Chicago's clubs and bars, helped by his own commanding presence. During the mid-1950s, Waters recorded a series of songs that would become anthems of Chicago blues: 'I Just Want To Make Love To You', 'Got My Mojo Working', 'I'm Ready' and '(I'm Your) Hoochie Coochie Man'. The last two used a variation on the call-and-response songs from the Delta plantations, with Waters filling in the spaces with moaning vocals or stinging guitar breaks.

By 1960, when he played the Newport Jazz Festival (released as *At Newport*, 1960), he was the leading Chicago bluesman. He took advantage of the British blues boom of the 1960s to broaden his audience, touring the UK and Europe and recording *The London Muddy Waters Sessions* (1971) with Rory Gallagher and

Georgie Fame. During the 1970s, he toured with the Rolling Stones and Eric Clapton and appeared in the Band's *The Last Waltz* concert and film. His record career was revived in the late 1970s with a trio of Johnny Winter-produced albums: *Hard Again* (1977), *I'm Ready* (1978) and *King Bee* (1981). He died in his sleep from a heart attack in 1983.

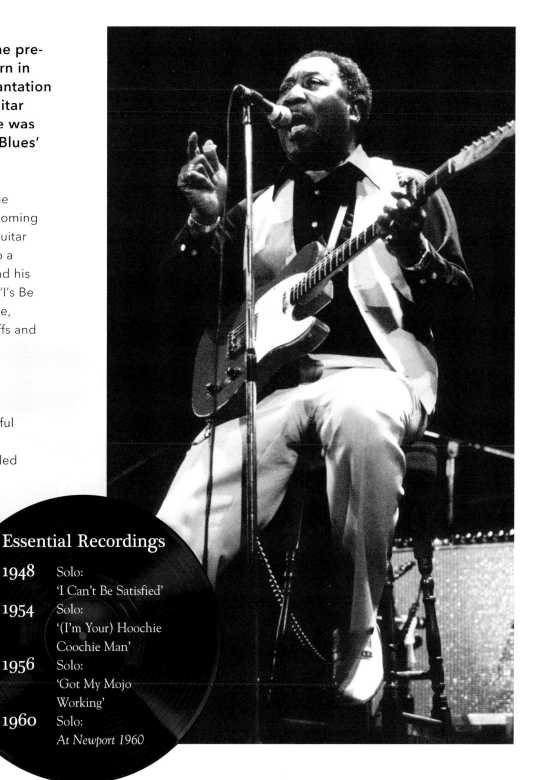

Essential Recordings

1948	Solo: 'I Can't Be Satisfied'
1954	Solo: '(I'm Your) Hoochie Coochie Man'
1956	Solo: 'Got My Mojo Working'
1960	Solo: *At Newport 1960*

Johnny 'Guitar' Watson
HERO OF ALL GENRES

Few guitarists have gone through as many career changes as Johnny 'Guitar' Watson (1935-96). Rock, blues, jazz, funk, disco – Watson excelled at all of them. He wasn't just a guitarist either. He could, and did, play anything except drums and horns on his records. But it is as a guitarist that he left the most admiration in his wake.

Essential Recordings

1967 with Larry Williams:
Two For The Price Of One

1976 Solo:
Ain't That A Bitch

1977 Solo:
A Real Mother For Ya

1994 Solo:
Bow Wow

Watson was a pianist when he arrived in Los Angeles at the age of 15. He had played guitar growing up in Houston, where he was born. He sometimes played with other budding blues maestros Albert Collins and Johnny Copeland. But it wasn't until he saw the flamboyant Guitar Slim perform that he made the guitar his main instrument. In 1954, Watson recorded the instrumental 'Space Guitar', a riot of reverb and feedback, producing sounds from his Stratocaster that no one else would emulate for at least a decade.

During the 1950s, Watson switched between blues and rock'n'roll, touring with Little Richard, Johnny Otis, Etta James and B.B. King. He had a rhythm and blues hit with 'These Lonely Lonely Nights' in 1955 and recorded the first of several versions of his theme tune, 'Gangster Of Love'. In the 1960s, he had another rhythm and blues hit with the ballad 'Cuttin' In' and recorded a jazz album, misleadingly titled *The Blues Soul Of Johnny Guitar Watson* (1964), before hooking up with rhythm and blues star Larry Williams for the live *Larry Williams Show With Johnny Guitar Watson* (1965) and the soulful *Two For The Price Of One* (1967).

In the early 1970s, he took his soul in a funkier direction with *Listen* (1973) and *I Don't Want To Be Alone, Stranger* (1975), before finding a flashy disco connection with the highly successful *Ain't That A Bitch* (1976), *A Real Mother For Ya* (1977), *Funk Beyond The Call Of Duty* (1977) and *Giant* (1978). He largely disappeared from view in the 1980s, returning with the funk/rap *Bow Wow* (1994). He was making a live-performance comeback when he suffered a fatal heart attack during a Japanese tour in 1996.

Neil Young
UNIVERSAL APPEAL

Canadian rock legend Neil Young (b. 1945) has become respected as much for his playing as for his composing and vocal work with his occasional partners Crosby, Stills & Nash. Born in Toronto, Canada, Young got a ukulele from his father for Christmas in 1958. In 1960, Young moved to Winnipeg with his mother. A poor student, he dropped out of high school to concentrate on the band he had formed, Neil Young & The Squires.

Young later played the Toronto coffee-house circuit, where he met a number of folk artists, including guitarists Richie Furay and Stephen Stills, with whom he formed Buffalo Springfield. They hit big with Stills' counterculture anthem 'For What It's Worth' and recorded three albums before splintering in 1968.

Young signed a solo deal with Reprise Records, and his second solo effort, *Everybody Knows This Is Nowhere*, with his new backing band Crazy Horse, became a major hit, going platinum on the strength of the songs 'Cinnamon Girl' and 'Down By The River'. Young joined David Crosby, Steven Stills and Graham Nash's supergroup in the summer of 1969. Young eventually recorded three albums as part of Crosby, Stills, Nash & Young, contributing the hits 'Helpless' and 'Ohio'. His solo career simultaneously blossomed, as *After The Gold Rush* (1970) and *Harvest* (1972) both became bestsellers. *Harvest* was the biggest-selling album of 1972, and the cut 'Heart Of Gold' remains Young's most successful single.

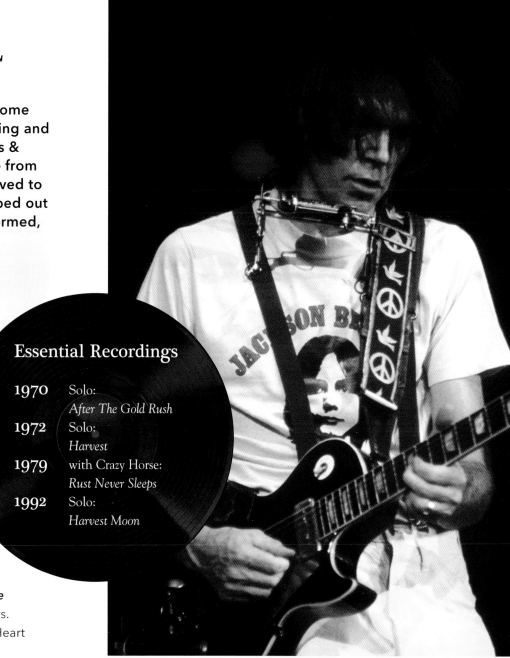

Essential Recordings

1970	Solo: *After The Gold Rush*
1972	Solo: *Harvest*
1979	with Crazy Horse: *Rust Never Sleeps*
1992	Solo: *Harvest Moon*

The iconoclastic Young was never comfortable with pop stardom, however, and in the ensuing years, created albums with themes that ranged from dispiriting ruminations on love, loss and injustice to affirmations of the simple life. He was hailed by punk rockers, grunge artists and country fans alike because of albums like *Rust Never Sleeps* (1979), *Freedom* (1989), *Broken Arrow* (1996) and *Harvest Moon* (1992). More recently, Young has reunited with Crazy Horse, touring and releasing *Americana* and *Psychedelic Pill* (both 2012), followed by the solo album *A Letter Home* (2014).

Young continues to maintain a busy schedule of new and archive releases.

Young collects guitars, but onstage and in the studio, he uses just a few instruments: a **1953 Gibson Les Paul Goldtop**; **Martin D-45** and **D-28** acoustics; **Gretsch 6120** and **White Falcon** electrics; and a **1927 Gibson Mastertone**, a six-string banjo, tuned like a guitar.

Playlists | Links
ebooks & more
FlameTree**Rock**.com

Acknowledgments

Author Biographies

Brian May (Foreword)

With a musical career spanning four decades, Queen founding member Brian May is a world-renowned guitarist and songwriter, with production and performance credits on recordings that have sold in excess of 100 million copies worldwide.

Rusty Cutchin (Consultant Editor and Author)

Rusty Cutchin has been a guitarist, recording engineer, producer and journalist for over 25 years. He has been technical editor of *Guitar One* magazine, as well as editor-in-chief of *Home Recording* magazine and an associate editor of *Electronic Musician* magazine. He has been a contributor and consultant editor to over 30 books on music, music history, guitar and recording. As a recording engineer, he worked on records by Richie Sambora, Mariah Carey, Yoko Ono and many others. His articles have appeared in *Billboard*, *Hits*, *Musician*, *Country Fever* and *Cash Box*.

Hugh Fielder (Author)

Hugh Fielder can remember the 1960s, even though he was there. He can remember the 1970s and 1980s because he was at *Sounds* magazine (RIP) and the 1990s because he was editor of Tower Records' *TOP* magazine. He has shared a spliff with Bob Marley, a glass of wine with David Gilmour, a pint with Robert Plant, a cup of tea with Keith Richards and a frosty stare with Axl Rose. He has watched Mike Oldfield strip naked in front of him and Bobby Womack fall asleep while he was interviewing him.

Mike Gent (Author)

Nurturing an obsession with pop music which dates back to first hearing Slade's 'Gudbuy T'Jane' in 1972, Mike Gent remains fixated, despite failing to master any musical instrument, with the possible exception of the recorder. A freelance writer since 2001, he has contributed to *Writers' Forum*, *Book and Magazine Collector*, *Record Buyer*, *When Saturday Comes*, *Inside David Bowie and the Spiders* (DVD), *The Kinks 1964–1978* (DVD), *The Beatles 1962–1970* (DVD), *Remember the Eighties*, *Where Were You When? – Music That Changed Our Lives*, *The Definitive Illustrated Encyclopedia of Rock* and *The Little Book of the World Cup*. His personal guitar hero is Johnny Marr.

Michael Mueller (Author)

Michael Mueller is a New York-based guitarist, author, editor and journalist. He is the former editor-in-chief of *Guitar One* magazine, where he interviewed such legendary guitarists as Angus Young, Joe Satriani, John Petrucci, Steve Vai, Zakk Wylde, Eric Johnson, Mark Tremonti and Frank Gambale, among many others. Currently, he is a contributor to *Guitar Edge* magazine and GuitarInstructor.com. He has also written for *Guitar World*, *Women Who Rock* and *Home Recording*.

As an author, Mueller has written several instructional books, including the *Hal Leonard Rock Guitar Method*, *Jazz for the Rock Guitarist* (Hal Leonard) and *Sight Reading for the Rock Guitarist* (Cherry Lane). Additionally, he has worked behind the scenes to produce several instructional guitar videos for the Hal Leonard Corporation, including the *Hal Leonard Guitar Method*, *Best of Lennon & McCartney* (for electric, acoustic and bass guitar) and *Guitar Soloing*.

Dave Simons (Author)

Dave Simons is a musician and journalist, and has covered the recording arts, past and present, for a variety of publications, including *Home Recording*, *Guitar One* and *Musician*. His recent books include *Studio Stories: How the Great New York Records Were Made* (Backbeat) and *Read the Beatles: Classic and New Writings on the Beatles, Their Legacy and Why They Still Matter* (Penguin).

Picture Credits

Jason Becker (www.jasonbeckerguitar.com): 92

Corbis: Joe Giron 96; Gene Ambo/Retna Ltd 106; Sayre Berman 119; Harvey L. Silver 145.

Getty Images: Ian Gavan 8; Mark Metcalfe/Stringer 60; Douglas Mason 86; Dave Etheridge-Barnes 115. **Redferns:** Petra Niemeier 4l, 26, 65; Peter Pakvis 4r 35, 51, 154; Michel Linssen 5l, 95, 149; David Redfern 5r 13l, 20, 48, 53, 54, 76, 77, 78, 79, 89, 133, 175, 177, 178; Lorne Resnick 7; Fin Costello 9, 18, 28, 29, 36, 43, 94, 104, 110, 120; Colin Fuller 10r; Mick Hutson 13r, 41, 55, 93, 98, 101, 108, 113, 116, 117, 118, 121, 148, 162; Ebet Roberts 11, 64, 105, 107, 126, 128, 136, 169; Gilles Petard Collection 12, 184; Richard E Aaron 16, 25, 37, 45, 49, 52, 69, 82, 84, 171, 180, 182, 187, 163; Andrew Putler 17; Ed Perlstein 19, 33, 59, 101; Jorgen Angel 21, 103; Carey Brandon 22, 44; Jon Super 23, 155; Fotex Agentur GMBH 24; Ron Howard 27; Ian Dickson 30, 130, 140, 152, 185; Rob Verhorst 31; RB 32; Neil Lupin 34; Robert Knight 38, 70, 102; Erica Echenberg 39, 68; Sandy Caspers 40, 189; Mick Hutson 41, 55, 93, 98, 101; Gary Wolstenholme 42; Paul Bergen 50, 135, 150; GEMS 56, 57, 61, 144; GAB Archives 58, 67, 168, 173; David Reed 63; Graham Lowe 74; Andrew Maclear 75; Clayton Call 88, 127; Peter Still 97; Hayley Madden 99, 157; Brend Muller 100; Mike Prior 109; Pete Cronin 114; Bob King 122; Gijsbert Hanekroot 129; Steve Morley 131; Simon Ritter 134; Tony Russell 137; Donna Santisi 138; Steve Thorne 139; Martin Philbey 142, 156, 159; Stuart Mostyn 151; Partick Ford 153, 164; Yani Yordanova 158; Gus Stewart 160; Suzie Gibbons 161; Tabatha Fireman 165; Keith Morris 176; Willaim Gottlieb 179, 181; Andrew Lepley 183; Virginia Turbett 186; Rico D'Rozario 188. **Hulton Archive:** Michael Putland 71, 85, 132; Tim Mosenfelder 72; Dave Hogan 83. **Michael Ochs Archives:** Stringer 62, 66, 73, 80, 87, 143, 172; Marc S Canter 112; Larry Hulst 123, 170. **WireImage:** Paul Natkin 111, 141. **Premium Archive:** Robert Johnson Estate 174.

© **Martin Pugh:** 81.

Index

Page numbers in **bold** indicate main entries, with illustrations. Page numbers in *italics* indicate illustrations outside of main entries.

Check out **FlameTreeRock.com** for loads more info, including further reading, recommended websites and lists of artists, links and free ebooks.

Playlists | Links ebooks & more

FlameTreeRock.com